Innovation in the University 4.0 System based on Smart Technologies

This text presents a comprehensive analysis of mathematical formulations for proving the effectiveness of artificial intelligence in education and investigates the possibilities for integrating advanced artificial intelligence algorithms. The book:

- presents an empirical analysis of the impact of information technology in the education system
- discusses student performance in University 4.0 using novel artificial intelligence algorithm with whale optimization
- elaborates the management of higher education based on information technology in the University 4.0 era
- explains the implementation of University 4.0 based on artificial intelligence
- focuses on the transformation of education system using artificial intelligence.

The text is primarily written for graduate students, postgraduate students, and academic researchers working in the fields of computer science and engineering, information technology and machine learning.

Innovation in the University 4.0 System based on Smart Technologies

Edited by
Shashi Kant Gupta and Joanna Rosak-Szyrocka

CRC Press
Taylor & Francis Group
Boca Raton London New York

CRC Press is an imprint of the
Taylor & Francis Group, an **informa** business

A CHAPMAN & HALL BOOK

Designed cover image: Canva

First edition published 2024

by CRC Press
2385 NW Executive Center Drive, Suite 320, Boca Raton FL 33431

and by CRC Press
4 Park Square, Milton Park, Abingdon, Oxon, OX14 4RN

CRC Press is an imprint of Taylor & Francis Group, LLC

ISBN: 978-1-032-54467-0 (hbk)
ISBN: 978-1-032-54619-3 (pbk)
ISBN: 978-1-003-42580-9 (ebk)

DOI: 10.1201/9781003425809

Typeset in Times
by Deanta Global Publishing Services, Chennai, India

Contents

Editors

Dr. Shashi Kant Gupta, Post-Doctoral Fellow and Researcher, Computer Science and Engineering, Eudoxia Research University, USA in collaboration with Eudoxia Research Centre, India. ORCID: 0000-0001-6587-5607. He has completed his Ph.D. in CSE from Integral University, LKO, UP, India, and Worked as AP, CSE Department, PSIT, Kanpur, U.P., India, Worked as Assoc. Prof., SOCA, BBD University, LKO, UP, India, Worked as AP, CSE Department, Ambalika Institute of Management and Technology, Lucknow, UP, India. Also worked as Sr. Lecturer, IT Dept., MCSCET, LKO, UP, India. He is currently working as Founder and CEO of CREP PVT. LTD., Lucknow, UP, India. He is a member of Spectrum IEEE & Magazine IEEE since 2019 and other international societies for research activities. He is an Editor-in-chief of *International Journal of Data Informatics and Intelligent Computing* (IJDIIC). He has published many research papers in reputed international journals with Scopus and SCI-indexed journals and published many papers in national and international conferences and as well as in seminars. He has organized various FDPs, seminars, workshops, and short-term courses at university level. He is currently working as a reviewer in various international journals like *BJIT* and many more. He is currently editor in many CRC & Taylor and Francis group Publication Books, Bentham Science Publishers, Routledge Publisher, Springer Nature Publisher, etc. He has published and granted many National and International Patents. He has 10 years of teaching experience, two years of Industrial Experience and 2.5 years as CEO and Founder of a firm.

Dr Joanna Rosak-Szyrocka, H-35 index Google Scholar, H-11 index Web of Science, H-12 index Scopus. Assistant Professor, Erasmus+ Coordinator at the Faculty of Management, Częstochowa University of Technology, Poland. She has specialized in the fields of digitalization, Industry 5.0, Quality 4.0, education, IoT, AI, and quality management. She has participated in in multiple Erasmus+ teacher mobility programs in Italy, the UK, Slovenia, Hungary, Czech Republic, Slovakia, and France. She also cooperates with many universities both within the country and abroad. She is on the Editorial Board of *Plos One Journal* and *PeerJ Journal*, and is on the Advisory Board of *Heliyon Journal*. She is Associate Editor for *Cogent Business and Management*, Taylor & Francis. She is Guest Editor of *Entertainment Computing Journal*, an Elsevier journal; *Resources MdPI, IJERPH MdPI, Energies MdPI, Sustainability MdPI, Springer Discover Sustainability Journal, Frontiers,*

and *Elsevier Measurement Journal.* She is Reviewer for a number of prestigious journals like *IEEE, Elsevier, MdPI, Frontiers, Sage, Springer,* and *Emerald.* She was a member of the Research Team at the Faculty of Management of the Częstochowa University of Technology 2022 and the interdisciplinary team 2022, and also a member of the team for surveying deans' offices and the course of studies in the field of occupational health and safety, and member of the technical team for evaluation at the Faculty of Management of the Częstochowa University of Technology. She was awarded a diploma of recognition from the Dean of the Faculty of Management of the Częstochowa University of Technology for her publishing activities, as well as a medal from the Dean of the Faculty of Management of the Częstochowa University of Technology in gratitude for long-term cooperation with the Faculty of Management (2017). In 2023, she was awarded the Medal of the President of the Republic of Poland for long-term service.

Contributors

Dr. Monika Agarwal
Jagan Institute of Management Studies
India

Dr. Suja A. Alex
St. Xavier's Catholic College of
    Engineering
India

Dr. Manar Alkhatib
The British University in Dubai
UAE

Dr. Bimal Anjum
DAV College
India

Suha Khalil Assayed
The British University in Dubai
UAE

Dr. Zeynep Aytaç
Aksaray University
Turkey

Dr. Ishfaq Hussain Bhat
Narsee Monjee Institute of Management
    Studies
India.

B. Gerald Briyolan
St. Xavier's Catholic College of
    Engineering
India

Luigi Pio Leonardo Cavaliere
Visiting – Università di Foggia
Italy

Megha Chhabra
Sharda University
India

Dr. Alessio Faccia
University of Birmingham
    Dubai
United Arab Emirates

Sourav Ghosh
SRM University-AP
India

Dr. Ashulekha Gupta
Graphic Era Deemed to be
    University
India

Dr. Shashi Kant Gupta
USA
Eudoxia Research
    University

Dr. Muhammad Abeer Irfan
University of Engineering and
    Technology
Pakistan

Yaseen Irshad
University of Engineering and
    Technology
Pakistan

Dr. Abid Iqbal
University of Engineering and
    Technology
Pakistan

Dr. Himanshu Kargeti
Graphic Era Hill University
India

Dr. Amaad Khalil
University of Engineering and
    Technology
Pakistan

Dr. Sheeba Khalid
Amity University
India

Miss Wahiza Khan
University of Engineering and
    Technology
Pakistan

Dr. Astadi Pangarso
Telkom University
Indonesia

P. Kanaga Priya
KPR Institute of Engineering and
    Technology
India

A. Reethika
Sri Ramakrishna Engineering College
India

Dr. Manjeet Ridon
De Montfort University
United Kingdom

Prof. Dr. Khaled Shaalan
The British University in Dubai
UAE

Bhagwati Sharan
SRM University-AP
India

Dr. Sushma Sharma
SRM University
India

Dr. Shitika
GGSIPU
India

R. Sivaranjani
Tamil Nadu College of Engineering
India

Dr. Joanna Rosak-Szyrocka
Czestochowa University of Technology
Poland

Dr. Rajesh Tiwari
Graphic Era Deemed to be University
India

1 Innovative Practices of Educational System based on Machine Learning Techniques and IT Proficiency Framework

Shashi Kant Gupta and Joanna Rosak-Szyrocka

1.1 INTRODUCTION

In today's world, which is moving quickly, the innovation of the educational system is a crucial undertaking. The study can design a more engaging, customized, and efficient educational system by fusing cutting-edge solutions with pedagogical techniques. Utilizing cutting-edge ML method is a significant field of innovation. Large volumes of data may be analyzed using ML, providing individualized learning experiences catered to specific students' requirements and tastes. With ML approaches, adaptive learning systems may provide personalized learning routes, real-time feedback, and suggestions to help students advance and become more proficient (Hilty et al., 2018). Intelligent teaching technologies may mimic one-on-one conversations and provide specialized help and direction. Furthermore, the incorporation of an information technology (IT) competency framework may provide students with the abilities they need to succeed in the IT era (Kumar et al., 2022). Students may acquire the abilities they need to function in a technologically advanced environment by integrating these competencies across various topics. Thanks to technology like virtual and augmented reality, innovative learning environments may take students outside of the classroom. Through interactive simulations, virtual field excursions, and hands-on experiments, these technologies encourage participation and in-depth comprehension (Chou, 2018). Students may interact with classmates worldwide via virtual collaborations and online learning platforms, widening their views and encouraging cultural exchange. By using data analytics and insights, the educational system is being made more innovative. By examining educational data, teachers may discover important information about student performance, spot learning gaps, and make data-driven choices to enhance curriculum development and teaching techniques (Anchal Pathak et al., 2023). Automated grading and feedback

DOI: 10.1201/9781003425809-1

systems driven by machine learning (ML) may expedite assessment procedures, giving students quick feedback and allowing professors to concentrate on delivering individualized coaching (Vega and Cañas, 2019). It is essential to approach the innovation of the educational system with an emphasis on ethics, inclusion, and equality. Prioritizing privacy and data security throughout technology integration will ensure that student data is handled responsibly. To ensure that all students, regardless of their socioeconomic circumstances, have equitable access to cutting-edge educational tools and resources, efforts must also be made to close the IT gap. Studies may continue to push the educational system's innovation via continual cooperation between educators, decision-makers, and technology. Research can establish an educational environment that equips students to flourish in the complex, interconnected world of the 21st century by embracing innovative technologies, applying IT proficiency frameworks, and encouraging a learner-centric approach (Iqbal et al., 2020). Innovative educational strategies that use ML methods and a framework for IT competency have the power to change how we teach and learn completely. Incorporating an IT competency framework and ML algorithms, instructors may design dynamic, individualized learning experiences that cater to the demands of today's students (Shashi Kant Gupta and Hayath, 2022). Massive volumes of educational data may be analyzed using ML algorithms, enabling the discovery of patterns, trends, and unique insights. Educators may better understand each student's requirements, preferences, and learning styles by using predictive analytics. The data may guide the creation of individualized learning paths and the dissemination of material, ensuring that students get the most relevant and interesting educational experiences possible (Garzón Artacho et al., 2020). A framework for IT proficiency integration also offers a disciplined method for acquiring crucial technological abilities. The information, competences, and skills necessary for students to survive and succeed in the IT sector are outlined in the framework. Teachers may make sure that students acquire the requisite IT literacy, information literacy, and critical thinking abilities by implementing the framework into curriculum design and instructional techniques. Innovative methods built on a foundation for ML and IT skills enable students to participate actively in their education. Students may obtain specialized help and advice that caters to their particular learning requirements using adaptive learning platforms, intelligent tutoring systems, and customized feedback mechanisms (Saif et al., 2021). The method encourages self-directed learning, encourages a growth attitude, and raises student motivation and engagement. ML algorithms may help teachers keep track of their students' development, identify areas for growth, and implement prompt interventions. Teachers may improve their teaching methods and curriculum design and solve learning gaps using data-driven insights (Çakır et al., 2021). The continuous feedback loop enabled by ML aids instructors in modifying their teaching strategies and enhancing learning results. The educational system may provide students with the skills and competences they need to thrive in the IT era by incorporating ML approaches and an IT competency framework (Ahmed Muayad Younus et al., 2022). These cutting-edge teaching methods promote the critical thinking, creativity, teamwork, and problem-solving abilities students need to succeed in a world that is changing quickly. The educational system can maximize each learner's potential and equip them ready for the challenges and possibilities of the future via individualized learning experiences, data-driven insights, and targeted assistance (Dillinger et al., 2022).

1.1.1 KEY CONTRIBUTIONS

Machine learning and the IT proficiency framework implemented with spider monkey swarm optimized gradient residual support vector machine (SMSO-GRSVM) may provide the following benefits to the educational system:

Using machine learning methods, such as SMSO-GRSVM, may improve the educational system by offering individualized learning opportunities catered to the requirements of specific pupils. As a result, learning outcomes and academic performance may increase.

Educational systems may design adaptive learning environments that dynamically modify the content, pacing, and degree of difficulty of teaching to each student's development and learning preferences. This individualized method may increase engagement and learning effectiveness.

The integration of cutting-edge ML methods, such as SMSO-GRSVM, and the framework for measuring IT competency in the educational system may change teaching and learning procedures, improve educational results, and make it possible to make decisions based on evidence for ongoing development.

The remainder of the paper is divided into the following sections: In section 2, the study's objectives or aims are reviewed together with the preliminary research, and any inconsistencies or gaps are identified. In Section 3, the research strategy and methods are covered. After going through the data and analysis in segment 4, we briefly and methodically summarize the results, assess the objectives or goals of the research, and provide interpretations. Section 5 of the Study provides a summary of the major parts.

1.2 RELATED WORKS

Research aimed to improve the e-learning process in the educational setting and anticipate pass or fail outcomes, an efficient and acceptable system for multiagent-based machine learning algorithms and feature selection techniques are provided. The primary characteristics from the database are chosen using the univariate and Extra Trees feature selection techniques. All features and a subset of features are subjected to five machine learning algorithms: decision tree (DT), logistic regression (LR), random forest (RF), naive bayes (NB), and K-nearest neighbors algorithm (KNN) (Hessen et al., 2022). The study developed ML algorithms that have been widely used in many scientific research and engineering fields to augment human information-gathering abilities. The fields include chemical production statistical process control, archeology text recognition, social and criminal investigation field fingerprint and image recognition, and genomic information research in biomedicine (Wang and Guo, 2022). Research aimed to analyze the structural variations among the dimensions to cluster dynamically. This research offers a tool that policymakers may use to track the construction and development process (Alnafrah and Zeno, 2019). The study developed the application's functionality is predicated on an MLA algorithm. It starts with gathering data from the user and then employs that data to streamline their workflow the next time they log in. Machine learning techniques are already being used by existing systems like support vector machine (SVM) and learning management systems to analyze and predict trends in higher education (Li, 2022). The research categorized education into five distinct categories (push, pull, coupling, integrated, and sustainable) according to the pedagogical approach, the scope of output, and the degree of interaction between students and educational institutions (Embarak, 2021). The study determined the educational model that can be maintained over time and optimizes the matrix of acquired information and skills for the targeted application. Taking stock of the requirements, researchers produced the European Framework for the Digital Competence of Educators. Teacher competency frameworks, in defining the needs of educators, may be useful in various contexts and settings. Microscopically, it may aid in the practice and Continuous Professional Development (CPD) of individual educators (Caena and Redecker, 2019). Research developed, the graduates will be equipped with the skills necessary to be lifelong students thanks to the competency-based, time-variable curriculum. While medicine has widely adopted the concept of competence as a guiding framework for educational institutions, formal educational programs continue to be structured and carried out under a time-based, competency-variable paradigm (Smadi et al., 2023).

1.3   EXPERIMENTAL PROCEDURE

This section provided a thorough explanation of the procedures involved in developing the suggested model in Figure 1.1 and its creation process and key components. This analysis is divided into four sections: Information gathering is the main goal of the first stage. Corpus auxiliary data preprocessing was a component of the second section. The most important information is found in the third section, which describes the effort made to develop the SMSO-GRSVM and acquire the necessary experiences. The fourth section shows the performance of each existing and new model and is assessed by comparing the pertinent parameters.

1.3.1   DATA COLLECTION

The competence map of Indonesian preservice teachers in their first through fifth study years (between the ages of 18 and 23), utilizing the framework and the Digital Competence Scale (DCS), with additional demographic data (Hidayat et al., 2023). The information was broken down into two categories: the determinant competencies, which include the dimensions of data and information literacy, communication and collaboration, digital content creation, safety, and problem-solving. Demographic information had gender, region, year of study, and department. As a method of mapping digital competence, 36 questions on a 5-point Likert scale were utilized to gauge respondents' knowledge levels. In total, 1400 preservice teachers

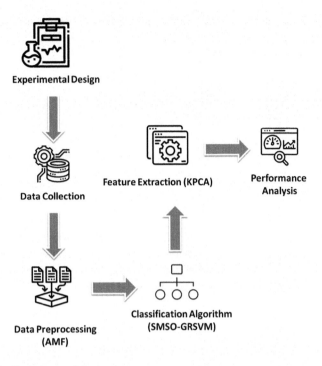

FIGURE 1.1   Experimental design.

from 14 provinces across 6 large Indonesian islands first participated in the research online using Google Forms.

1.3.2   DATA PREPROCESSING USING ADAPTIVE MEDIAN FILTER (AMF)

The AMF approach has improved the standard median filter. The use of spatial processing reduces impulse noise. The AMF recognizes each pixel in the skin image and its surrounding pixels to determine whether noise is present. It operates better than other filters since it safeguards fine visual details and reduces non-impulse noise. Additionally, it can adjust to abrupt loudness. The disorder of an image is the same for the median and mean channels. The median channel for two descriptions may vary, just as in Equation (1.1).

$$\text{med}\left(n_k\right)= \begin{cases} n_i + 1^a = 2i+1\left(\text{ODD}\right) \\ \dfrac{\left[n_i + n_{i+1}\right]}{2} a = 2i\left(\text{even}\right) \end{cases} \qquad (1.1)$$

Here n_i is the ith the biggest observed data, and n_1; n_2; n_3... n_i are the observed data. Consider a situation where there are seven samples overall in the data collection—2, 3.5, 1, 3, 1.5, 4 and the median filter yields an output of 2.5. The signal will be maintained if the pulse is n + 1 or longer; else, it will be dropped from the series. The median filter is distinct from other filters since it has the potential to reduce pulse noise while preserving local features. The signal produced by this approach is then sent to the feature extraction step.

1.3.3 FEATURE EXTRACTION BY USING KERNEL PRINCIPAL COMPONENT ANALYSIS (KPCA)

An approximate covariance matrix of the data in Equation (1.2) is diagonalized using a basis transformation known as kernel principal component analysis (KPCA).

$$D = \frac{1}{k} \sum_{i=1}^{k} v_1 v_i^S \tag{1.2}$$

The orthogonal projections onto the eigenvectors or the new coordinates in the tile eigenvector basis are principal components. In this work, this setting is further developed into a nonlinear setting of the following kind. If the data were initially nonlinearly mapped onto a feature space using Equation (1.3),

$$\Phi : Q^M \rightarrow E, v \rightarrow V \tag{1.3}$$

We'll show that, for certain values, even if it has arbitrarily large dimensionality, we can still do KPCA in E.

Let's assume that Equation (1.4) translates data into feature space. KPCA for the covariance matrix,

$$\bar{D} = \frac{1}{k} \sum_{i=1}^{k} \Phi(v_1) \Phi(v_1)^S \tag{1.4}$$

KPCA, a nonlinear variation, is often used in denoising and wavelet transform applications. When the manifold is linearly buried in the observation space, the standard PCA technique seeks to minimize the number of dimensions. To fulfill the demands of the PCA, the second component of KPCA, the manifold, is linearized using the kernel approach, one of the two components. KPCA uses feature mapping to automatically transform data into a pair-wise formula between the mapped data in the feature set. This pair-wise formula is computed by the kernel. Finding a suitable kernel that linearizes the surface in the feature space while taking the geometry of the input space into account is challenging. For a poor projection that does not meet these requirements, KPCA's nonlinear dimensionality reduction would be useless.

1.3.4 CLASSIFICATION BY USING SPIDER MONKEY SWARM OPTIMIZED GRADIENT RESIDUAL SUPPORT VECTOR MACHINE (SMSO-GRSVM)

The SMSO-GRSVM algorithm, which integrates machine learning methods with an IT proficiency framework, may be used in creative ways in the educational system.

By using the strength of optimization and gradient residuals inside the SVM algorithm, this strategy seeks to improve the learning experience. The educational system may adopt a framework for IT competency that specifies the fundamental technological abilities and competencies needed by pupils. This framework acts as a roadmap for teaching students problem-solving, computational thinking, digital communication, and IT literacy. The social interactions of spider monkeys serve as the basis for the meta-heuristic optimization technique known as SMSO. SMSO can effectively explore the solution space and identify ideal or nearly ideal solutions by imitating their search behaviors. The SVM algorithm's performance may be improved by using this optimization method. The variances between the actual target values and the SVM predictions are represented by the gradient residuals in GRSVM. GRSVM seeks to hone and enhance the initial predictions produced by the SVM algorithm by integrating gradient residuals. As a result, mistakes may be fixed, and complicated data patterns can be better adapted. The GRSVM model's hyperparameters and weights are optimized using the SMSO technique. The goal of this optimization procedure is to identify the optimal set of parameters that optimizes the effectiveness of the educational model while minimizing mistakes. Data-driven insights and ongoing improvement: SMSO-GRSVM's iterative optimization method enables ongoing improvement. Educators may acquire useful data-driven insights on the advantages and disadvantages of the educational system by studying the gradient residuals and keeping track of the model's performance. To improve the learning process, these insights may guide curriculum design, teaching choices, and targeted interventions.

The educational system may promote individualized learning, adaptive feedback, and data-driven decision-making by integrating the spider monkey swarm optimized gradient residual support vector machine (SMSO-GRSVM) algorithm with an IT proficiency framework. The power of optimization, machine learning, and IT know-how are combined in this ground-breaking method to provide a dynamic and effective learning environment that equips students for the challenges of the digital era. As a consequence, further details or accurate information about SMSO-GDTM are deemed necessary:

1.3.4.1 Spider Monkey Swarm Optimization

It uses a cluster of SMs whose activity is based on the foraging behavior of honey SMSs. SMSO is an algorithm based on the idea of swarm intelligence. Fission takes place, and the fusion time is determined when there are fewer monkeys in one group. There is a leader for each subgroup as well, although all answer to the overall leader. Spider monkeys have the following traits:

- Each ring has between 40 and 50 spider monkeys.
- The oldest female member of each group serves as the GL and controls the majority of the party's decisions.
- The local lady in charge of planning the foraging schedule leads each smaller group.

Here are more details about the main parts of Spider Monkey Optimization:

- **Setting up the population**

Each spider monkey's starting location in the population is represented by its initial parameters, TN_{or} (o=1, 2... N), an N-D vector where N specifies the number of issue variables to be improved. Each pinpoints an achievable goal that might fix the issue. It is defined as Equation (1.5). For each TN_{or}

$$TN_{or} = TN_{minq} + VQ(0,1) \times (TN_{maxq} - TN_{minq}) \tag{1.5}$$

Where TN_{maxq} and TN_{minq} are minimum and maximum values of TN_{or} in the direction and (0, 1).

- **Local leader phase**

At this step, the SMSO updates its actual role related to the decisions of its local group and local leader (LL), and it also determines the fitness values for the positions of any newly arrived monkeys. This is the stage when spider monkeys must increase their fitness by replacing their previous positions with new ones are shown in Equation (1.6). The equation for the $o^{th}er$ position is as follows,

$$TN_{newor} = TN_{or} + VQ(0,1) \times (KK_{kr} - TN_{or}) + VQ(-1,1) \times (TN_{qr} - TN_{or}) \tag{1.6}$$

In this case, the oth dimensions of the kth LL position correspond to the rth component of the kth. The dimensional TN_{qr} is the rthTN picked at random from the kth group where r is less than or equal to V in the rth dimensions.

- **Global leader phase (GLP)**

Members of both the GL and LL groups share their insights to aid in the spider monkeys' stance adjustment. The coordinates may be found in Equation (1.7),

$$TN_{newor} = TN_{or} + VQ(0,1) \times (HK_{kr} - TN_{or}) + VQ(-1,1) \times (TN_{qr} - TN_{or}) \tag{1.7}$$

where (r = 1, 2,) N is a randomly chosen index and the rth dimension of the GL location. At the GLP stage, spider monkeys (TN_{or}) have their positions updated according to the RI values of the probabilities that are taken into account for calculating their fitness. In this manner, the most qualified applicants may best present themselves. The following equation may be used to determine the probability of ri are shown in Equation (1.8):

$$ri = (fitness\,ix\,/\,fitness\,max) + 0.1 \tag{1.8}$$

where fitness max is the highest possible fitness level for the $o^{th}er$ group. In addition, the optimal location is selected by calculating a new fitness algorithm that relies on the created position and comparing it to the previous fitness parameter.

- **Global leader learning segment (GLLS)**

In the GLL segment, the pessimistic model is used to update and perform the feature extraction. The population is used to choose and create the fitness function value. The optimal value of the place determines the value of the world leader. Instead of updating, the value is increased by one and stored in the global limit count variable.

- **Local leader learning phase (LLLP)**

According to the fitness values of a community organization, the LLL is changed in the location, making it the best possible choice for the local community. It's worth whatever the current regional authority decides it's worth. As it increases by one with each new, no additional updates are supplied.

- **Local leader decision phase**

If the LLD doesn't update its location using initial randomization or the knowledge of the GL and LL, it does so using the perturbations rate which is represented in Equation (1.9),

$$TN_{newor} = TN_{or} + VQ(0,1) \times (HK_{kr} - TN_{or}) + VQ(0,1) \times (TN_{qr} - KK_{or}) \quad (1.9)$$

- **Global leader decision phase (GLDP)**

At this stage, the GL positioning is monitored for a certain amount of time. The GL then divides the population into subsets, always beginning with at least two and going as high as feasible. At the GLD stage, new groups are established, and LLL operations are initiated to choose the LL. The GL is unable to change its location. In addition, when the optimum number of distinct groups is reached, it takes its cue from the spider monkey's fusion-splitting social structure and merges all of the smaller groups into one supergroup.

Fitness is calculated by summing the relative relevance of each attribute. Each aspect of the input data is given a score based on the goal variables. When the likelihood of reaching the node drops before it is reached, the relevance of the feature is calculated based on the impurities of the junction with the values. We may get the node's probability by dividing the ratio of the observed numbers by the total number of specimens. For optimal feature selection, we utilize it to determine the fitness function shown in Equation (1.10).

$$fitness_{feature\ importance} = \frac{Number\ of\ specimens\ that\ reach\ the\ nodes}{Total\ number\ of\ samples} \quad (1.10)$$

Utilizing the low-level coevolutionary traits, the SMSO hybridized algorithm creates the hybrid mixed capability. There are merge and combine options available as part of the basic hybrid capability. Coevolutionary is used because variations are employed sequentially, in parallel. The two types are combined, and both contribute to the creation of answers to the challenges. With this adjustment, the hierarchical SMSO generates variations using the strength of SMSO. The velocity is revised using the combined SMSO variations, as suggested in Equation (1.11-1.12),

$$u_j^{l+1} = x * (u_j^l + d_1 q_1 (w_{1-} w_j^l) + d_2 q_2 (w_{2-} w_j^l) + d_3 q_3 (w_{3-} w_j^{l+1})) \qquad (1.11)$$

$$w_j^{l+1} = w_j^l + u_j^{l+1} \qquad (1.12)$$

The most optimal value is chosen by maximizing the fitness value. The proposed method employs the Rosen Brock function, often called the optimization problem. With the in-built localized without a framework to guide and a proper coordinate system, the Rosen Brock product is effectively maximized which is represented in Equation (1.13),

$$e(w) = \sum_{j=1}^{m} d_j Y_j \left[100(y_{j+1} - y_j^2)^2 + (1 - y_j)^2 \right] \qquad (1.13)$$

Each variable's goal function is added together to get the best possible outcome. Equation (1.14) gives the generic form of the optimal solution,

$$Minimize \, or \, Y \, or \, hbest = \sum_{j=1}^{m} d_j Y_j \qquad (1.14)$$

where Y the ith control is input, and $\sum_{j=1}^{m} d_j Y_j$ is the optimization problem factor for

the ith parameter. Hence, a function is used to choose the optimal set of characteristics from the subgroup, and data augmentation is calculated if there is any ambiguity among the features.

1.3.4.2   Gradient Residual Support Vector Machine (GRSVM)

A modification of the standard support vector machine method that takes gradient residuals into account is called the GRSVM. GRSVM is a well-liked machine learning technique that is utilized for both regression and classification problems. In a conventional SVM, the algorithm looks for the hyper-plane that best maximizes the separation of classes, or it attempts to fit the data to a regression line. GRSVM, on the other hand, goes beyond SVM by taking into account the gradient residuals, which describe the discrepancies between the actual target values and the SVMs predictions. During the training phase of GRSVM, the gradient residuals are computed by comparing the predicted values of the SVM with the actual target values. The inaccuracies or disparities between the expected and actual values are represented by these residuals. The goal of GRSVM is to increase performance by refining the initial predictions generated by the GRSVM and introducing the gradient

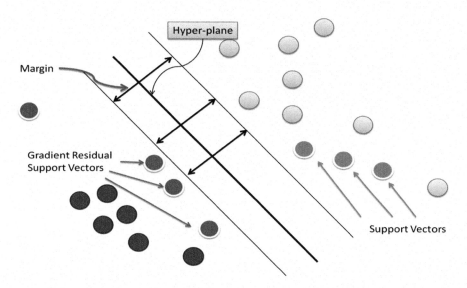

FIGURE 1.2   Architecture of GRSVM.

residuals into the training process. The GRSVM predictions are modified according to the gradient residuals as part of the iterative optimization procedure used by the GRSVM method (Pathak et al., 2021) as shown in Figure 1.2. Iteratively reducing the residuals and altering the model's parameters are how the method updates the GRSVM model. Until convergence or predetermined ending criteria are satisfied, this iterative process keeps going. GRSVM can more effectively adapt to complicated patterns and increase the Precision and robustness of the SVM predictions by taking into account the gradient residuals. Gradient residuals provide the model the ability to capture the details and disparities in the data, resulting in predictions that are more honed and precise. The GRSVM technique may be used for a range of tasks, such as classification tasks, where the purpose is to categorize data points, and regression tasks, where the goal is to forecast continuous values. By taking into account the gradient residuals during the training phase, the GRSVM expands the capabilities of the conventional SVM method. By doing this, it hopes to better the accuracy and performance of classification and regression tasks by enhancing the initial predictions produced by the GRSVM.

1.3.4.3   Mathematical Equations of GRSVM

As a result of the description above, the ideal separation surface may be defined as the following restricted optimization problem, which is represented in Figure 1.3, and aims to minimize the function shown in Equation (1.15) is coefficients.

$$\phi(u) = \frac{1}{2}u^2 = \frac{1}{2}(u.u) \tag{1.15}$$

Equation (1.16-1.18) allows us to define the Lagrange function as follows:

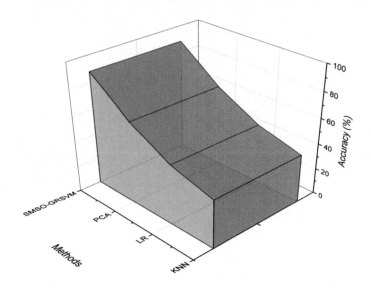

FIGURE 1.3   Comparison of accuracy.

$$K\left(u,a,\alpha\right)=\frac{1}{2}\left(u.u\right)-\sum_{j=1}^{m}\alpha_{j}\left\{\left[\left(u.v_{j}\right)+a\right]-1\right\} \tag{1.16}$$

$$\sum_{j=1}^{m}z_{j}\alpha_{j}=0 \tag{1.17}$$

$$\alpha\_j\geq0,j=1,2,\ldots,m \tag{1.18}$$

where $\alpha\_j>0$ is the coefficient of language. The problem is finding the Lagrange function's minimum of α. u and α seek partial differential and make them equal to zero;

$$R\left(\alpha\right)=\sum_{j=1}^{m}\alpha_{j}-\frac{1}{2}\sum_{j,i=1}^{m}\alpha_{j}\alpha_{i}z_{j}z_{i}\left(v_{j}.v_{i}\right) \tag{1.19}$$

$$u^{*}=\sum_{j=1}^{m}\alpha_{j}^{*}z_{j}v_{j} \tag{1.20}$$

$$\alpha_{j}\left(z_{j}\left(u.v_{j}+a\right)-1\right)=0, j=1,2,\ldots,m \tag{1.21}$$

$$e(v) = sgn\left\{\left(u^*.v\right) + a^*\right\} = sgm\left\{\sum_{j=1}^{m} \alpha_j^* z_j\left(v_j.v\right) + a^*\right\} \tag{1.22}$$

The original issue may be reduced to the dual issue below, which is straightforward: the restrictions that Equation represents (1.19-1.22):

1.3.4.4 Algorithm for GRSVM

The GRSVM approach, as illustrated in approach (1), requires incrementally changing the weights and biases of the SVM model depending on the gradient residuals computed from the discrepancy between the actual labels and the SVM predictions. Up to convergence or the maximum number of iterations, this procedure is iterative.

```
Algorithm 1: GRSVM

function GRSVM(train_set, test_instance, max_iterations,
learning_rate):
    initialize_weights()
    for iteration in range(max_iterations):
        residuals = calculate_residuals(train_set)
    update_weights(residuals, learning_rate)
      if convergence_criteria_met(residuals):
            break
    prediction = predict(test_instance)
     return prediction
 function calculate_residuals(train_set):
     residuals = []
   for instance, in train_set:
        predicted_value = predict(instance)

    actual_value = instance.target_value
        residual = actual_value - predicted_value
        residuals.append(residual)
    return residuals
function update_weights(residuals, learning_rate):
        for i, instance in enumerate(train_set):
            for j, feature in
 enumerate(instance.features):
        instance_weight = instance.weights[j]
        residual = residuals[i]
        updated_weight = instance_weight + learning_rate *
residual * feature
        instance.weights[j] = updated_weight
function predict(instance):
        prediction = 0
        for i, feature in enumerate(instance.features):
          instance_weight = instance.weights[i]
```

```
        prediction += instance_weight * feature
        return prediction
 function convergence_criteria_met(residuals):
        # Check if convergence criteria are met, e.g., small
change in residuals function initialize_weights():
        # Initialize weights for each feature in the training
instances
# Main code
train_set = load_training_data()


 test_instance = load_test_instance()
 max_iterations = determine_max_iterations()
 learning_rate = determine_learning_rate()
predicted_value = GRSVM(train_set, test_instance, max_
iterations, learning_rate)
 print("Predicted value:", predicted_value)
```

The approach tries to increase the model's performance in binary classification problems by improving the original SVM predictions.

1.4   RESULTS AND DISCUSSION

The results section presents the factual findings of a study, while the discussion section provides an interpretation and analysis of those findings, placing them in the broader context of existing knowledge and theories.

1.4.1   RESULTS

The results section presents the findings of a study or experiment. It is typically presented in a factual and concise manner, providing a clear description of the data or outcomes obtained. This section often includes tables, graphs, or figures to visually represent the data.

1.4.1.1   Accuracy

The term accuracy refers to a performance metric that assesses the accuracy of predictions made by the SMSO-GRSVM model in the context of cutting-edge practices of the educational system based on machine learning techniques and the IT proficiency framework using the SMSO-GRSVM as shown in Equation (1.23). In other words, the ratio of right predictions (all true positives and all true negatives) to the total number of predictions (all true positives and all true negatives, all false positives and all false negatives) is the definition of accuracy. It displays how accurate the model's predictions were all around.

$$\text{Accuracy} = \frac{TP + TN}{TP + TN + FP + FN} \qquad (1.23)$$

TABLE 1.1

Numerical Outcomes of Accuracy

Methods	Accuracy (%)
KNN	38
LR	47
PCA	64
SMSO-GRSVM	88

The proposed technique performs better than the currently used KNN (38%), LR (47%), and PCA (64%), with SMSO-GRSVM having a high accuracy performance of 88%. Table 1.1 displays the SMSO-GRSVM recommendation, which outperformed other in-use methods in terms of data categorization accuracy.

1.4.1.2 Precision

Precision is a performance metric that assesses the model's capacity to generate reliable positive predictions in the context of cutting-edge practices of the educational system based on machine learning techniques and the IT proficiency framework using the SMSO-GRSVM. The ratio of true positives (TP) to the total of true positives plus false positives (FP) is the definition of precision. It focuses on the percentage of events that were accurately predicted as positive out of all instances that were projected to be positive, as shown in Equation (1.24).

$$precision = \frac{TP}{TP + FP} \tag{1.24}$$

With a high accuracy performance of SMSO-GRSVM of 54%, the recommended technique outperforms the already in-use KNN (22%), LR (32%), and PCA (43%). Table 1.2 displays the SMSO-GRSVM recommendation, which outperformed other in-use methods in terms of data categorization accuracy.

1.4.1.3 Recall

Recall is a performance metric that measures the model's accuracy in correctly identifying positive instances in the context of cutting-edge practices of the educational

TABLE1.2

Numerical Outcomes of Precision

Methods	Precision (%)
KNN	22
LR	32
PCA	43
SMSO-GRSVM	54

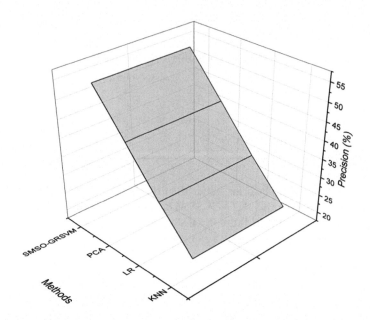

FIGURE 1.4 Comparison of precision. Source is Author

system based on machine learning techniques and the IT proficiency framework using the SMSO-GRSVM. The ratio of true positives (TP) to the total of true positives and false negatives (FN) is known as recall, sometimes referred to as sensitivity or true positive rate as shown in Equation (1.25). It focuses on the percentage of all really positive events that were accurately recognized.

$$Recall = \frac{FN}{FN + TP} \qquad (1.25)$$

The proposed technique outperforms currently used KNN (28%), LR (37%), and PCA (52%), with SMSO-GRSVM having a high recall performance of 62%. Table 1.3 displays the SMSO-GRSVM recommendation, which outperformed other in-use methods in terms of data classification recall.

TABLE 1.3
Numerical Outcomes of Recall

Methods	Recall (%)
KNN	28
LR	37
PCA	52
SMSO-GRSVM	62

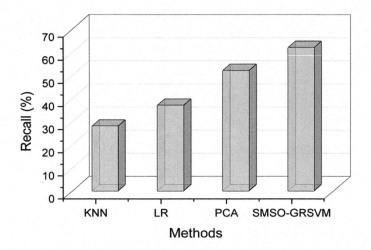

FIGURE 1.5 Comparison of recall. Source is Author

1.4.1.4 Mean Square Error Rate (MSE)

Mean square error (MSE) is a frequently employed performance metric to assess a machine learning model's accuracy and predictive capability, including in the context of novel educational practices based on the SMSO-GRSVM and the IT proficiency framework. The average squared difference between the predicted values and the actual values is what the MSE calculates while doing regression jobs when the objective is to predict continuous values, as shown in Equation (1.26). The average squared error between the model's anticipated outcomes and the actual results is quantified.

$$MSE = \frac{1}{m}\sum_{j=1}^{m}\left(\hat{\phi}_j - \phi_j\right)^2 \qquad (1.26)$$

The suggested approach surpasses the presently utilized KNN (44%), LR (32%), and PCA (20%), with a low MSE performance of SMSO-GRSVM of 10%. The recommended approach SMSO-GRSVM, which performed better than other methods already in use in terms of data classification MSE, is shown in Table 1.4.

TABLE 1.4
Numerical Outcomes of MSE

Methods	MSE (%)
KNN	44
LR	32
PCA	20
AMSO-GRSVM	10

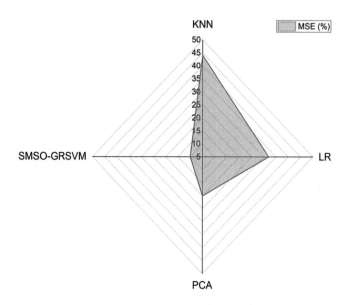

FIGURE 1.6   Comparison of MSE. Source is Author

1.4.1.5   F1-Score

The SMSO-GRSVM is one example of a machine learning model, and the F1 score is a performance metric that combines Precision and recall into a single value to evaluate the overall effectiveness of a machine learning model in the context of innovative practices in the educational system based on the IT proficiency framework. Given that it takes into account both false positives and false negatives, the F1 score is especially helpful when there is an imbalance between the dataset's positive and negative classifications. It strikes a compromise between Precision and recall by accounting for both the model's capacity for making precise predictions of positive outcomes (precision) and for properly identifying positive examples (recall), as shown in Equation (1.27).

$$F1-score = \frac{(\text{precision}) \times (\text{recall}) \times 2}{\text{precision} + \text{recall}} \tag{1.27}$$

With a high recall performance of SMSO-GRSVM of 74%, the proposed technique outperforms the currently used KNN (33%), LR (43%), and PCA (59%). Table 1.5 displays the SMSO-GRSVM recommendation, which outperformed other in-use methods in terms of data categorization recall.

1.4.2   DISCUSSION

Research determined the educational system has to be modernized and innovative, with the inclusion of digital resources, to accommodate students with impairments in the

TABLE 1.5

Numerical Outcomes of F1-Score

Methods	F1-Score (%)
KNN	33
LR	43
PCA	59
AMSO-GRSVM	74

teaching and learning processes. The teaching staff's medium-low level was shown using logistic regression (LR), particularly at the higher education level. Additionally, elements that affect the growth of a teacher's knowledge include gender, motivation, attitude, and the presence of pupils with special needs (Cabero-Almenara et al., 2022). The study evaluated the education sector includes a number of assessment phases, including those that are organization-, staff-, and student-related. Because of their own protocols and systems, colleges and universities often have a monopoly on KNN (Saravanakumar et al., 2021). The research examines the principal components analysis using principal component analysis (PCA) was used to verify the constructs with 320 high school English instructors. Following the removal of seven variables from the questionnaire, a 53-variable scale was created, which demonstrated that the constructs had substantial factor loadings (Aghajanzadeh Kiasi, 2022). By comparing the current system, the combination of recommended technique SMSO-GRSVM and IT proficiency frameworks may empower educators and students by offering individualized learning experiences, targeted interventions, and data-driven insights. It might increase the efficacy and efficiency of the educational system, which would eventually result in better learning results for students.

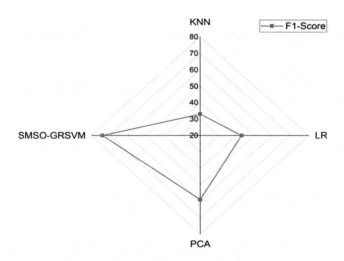

FIGURE 1.7   Comparison of F1-score. Source is Author

1.5 CONCLUSION

The SMSO-GRSVM integration into the educational system introduces novel approaches that make use of machine learning methodologies and frameworks for IT competency. The SMSO-GRSVM technique, which combines gradient residual support vector machine with Spider Monkey Optimization, has special advantages for increasing educational experience. Personalized learning is one cutting-edge technique. As students go through their curriculum, these technologies give quick feedback and direction, fostering interactive and adaptable learning experiences. The SMSO-GRSVM algorithm may help identify pupils who are at risk of experiencing academic difficulties early on. The system can identify students who may need further help or intervention by examining multiple criteria, including performance patterns, attendance records, and engagement levels. Using the DCS dataset, the competence map of Indonesian preservice teachers from the first to fifth study years (between ages 18 and 23) was studied. The AMF filter removes erratic data from samples of raw data. The properties are separated from the segmented data using an analytical process called a KPCA. According to the effectiveness of the study, some of the evaluation criteria for classification tasks include accuracy, Precision, recall, F1 score, and mean square error rate. SMSO-GRSVM is evolving to be more effective, efficient, and in line with contemporary demands by using the power of technology and data. We come to the conclusion that the SMSO-GRSVM algorithm's integration into the educational system provides cutting-edge methods that make use of frameworks for machine learning and IT expertise. Some of the main advantages are personalized learning, clever tutoring systems, early detection of at-risk pupils, and reduced administrative procedures. Despite its difficulties, SMSO-GRSVM adoption has the power to transform the educational system by enhancing learning opportunities and promoting student achievement.

REFERENCES

Alnafrah, I. and Zeno, B., 2019, "A New Comparative Model for National Innovation Systems Based on Machine Learning Classification Techniques," *Innovation and Development*. https://doi.org/10.1080/2157930X.2018.1564124.

Aghajanzadeh Kiasi, G., 2022, "Realization and Development of the English Language Teachers' Pedagogical Competence: A Principal Component Analysis," *International Journal of Research in English Education*, 7(2), pp.22–49. http://ijreeonline.com/article-1-640-en.html.

Cabero-Almenara, J., Guillén-Gámez, F.D., Ruiz-Palmero, J. and Palacios-Rodríguez, A., 2022, "Teachers' Digital Competence to Assist Students with Functional Diversity: Identification of Factors through Logistic Regression Methods," *British Journal of Educational Technology*, 53(1), pp.41–57. https://doi.org/10.1111/bjet.13151.

Caena, F. and Redecker, C., 2019, "Aligning Teacher Competence Frameworks to 21st Century Challenges: The Case for the European Digital Competence Framework for Educators (Digcompedu)," *European Journal of Education*, 54(3), pp.356–369. https://doi.org/10.1111/ejed.12345.

Çakır, R., Korkmaz, Ö., İdil, Ö. and Erdoğmuş, F.U., 2021, "The Effect of Robotic Coding Education on Preschoolers' Problem Solving and Creative Thinking Skills," *Thinking Skills and Creativity*, 40, p.100812. https://doi.org/10.1016/j.tsc.2021.100812.

Chou, P.N., 2018, "Skill Development and Knowledge Acquisition Cultivated by Maker Education: Evidence from Arduino-Based Educational Robotics," *EURASIA Journal of Mathematics, Science and Technology Education*, 14(10), p.em1600. https://doi.org /10.29333/ejmste/93483.

Dillinger, F., Bernhard, O. and Reinhart, G., 2022, "Competence Requirements in Manufacturing Companies in the Context of Lean 4.0," *Procedia Cirp*, 106, pp.58–63. https://doi.org/10.1016/j.procir.2022.02.155.

Embarak, O., 2021, "A New Paradigm through Machine Learning: A Learning Maximization Approach for Sustainable Education," *Procedia Computer Science*, 191, pp.445–450. https://doi.org/10.1016/j.procs.2021.07.055.

Garzón Artacho, E., Martínez, T.S., Ortega Martin, J.L., Marin Marin, J.A. and Gomez Garcia, G., 2020, "Teacher Training in Lifelong Learning—The Importance of Digital Competence in the Encouragement of Teaching Innovation," *Sustainability*, 12(7), p.2852. https://doi.org/10.3390/su12072852.

Gupta, S. K., Dr. and T M., H., 2022, "Lack of it Infrastructure for ICT Based Education as an Emerging Issue in Online Education, TTAICTE," July; 1(3), pp.19–24. Published online 2022 July. https://doi.org/10.36647/TTAICTE/01.03.A004.

Hessen, S.H., Abdul-Kader, H.M., Khedr, A.E. and Salem, R.K., 2022, "Developing Multiagent E-learning System-Based Machine Learning and Feature Selection Techniques," *Computational Intelligence and Neuroscience*, 2022, 2941840.

Hidayat, M.L., Astuti, D.S., Sumintono, B., Meccawy, M. and Khanzada, T.J., 2023, "Digital Competency Mapping Dataset of Pre-service Teachers in Indonesia," *Data in Brief*, 49, p.109310. https://doi.org/10.1016/j.dib.2023.109310.

Hilty, D.M., Zalpuri, I., Stubbe, D., Snowdy, C.E., Shoemaker, E.Z., Myint, M.T., Joshi, S.V. and Liu, H.Y., 2018, "Social Media/Networking and Psychiatric Education: Competencies, Teaching Methods, and Implications," *Journal of Technology in Behavioral Science*, 3, pp.268–293. https://doi.org/10.1007/s41347-018-0061-7.

Iqbal, H.M., Parra-Saldivar, R., Zavala-Yoe, R. and Ramirez-Mendoza, R.A., 2020, "Smart Educational Tools and Learning Management Systems: Supportive Framework," *International Journal on Interactive Design and Manufacturing (IJIDeM)*, 14, pp.1179–1193. https://doi.org/10.1007/s12008-020-00695-4.

Kumar, V.S., Alemran, A., Gupta, S.K., Hazela, B., Dixit, C.K. and Haralayya, B., 2022, "Extraction of SIFT Features for Identifying Disaster Hit Areas using Machine Learning Techniques," 2022 International Conference on Knowledge Engineering and Communication Systems (ICKES), Chickballapur, 2022, pp.1–5. https://doi.org/10 .1109/ICKECS56523.2022.10060037.

Li, Y., 2022, "Similar Classification Algorithm for Educational and Teaching Knowledge Based on Machine Learning," *Wireless Communications and Mobile Computing*, 2022. https://doi.org/10.1155/2022/7222236.

Pathak, A., Dixit, C.K., Somani, P. and Gupta, S.K., 2023, *Prediction of Employee's Performance Using Machine Learning (ML) Techniques* (1st Ed.), CRC Press. https:// doi.org/10.1201/9781003357070.

Pathak, D.K., Kalita, S.K. and Bhattacharya, D.K., 2021, "Hyperspectral Image Classification using Support Vector Machine: A Spectral, Spatial Feature-Based Approach," *Evolutionary Intelligence*, pp.1–15. https://doi.org/10.1007/s12065-021-00591-0.

Saif, A.S., Mahayuddin, Z.R. and Shapi'i, A., 2021, "Augmented Reality Based Adaptive and Collaborative Learning Methods for Improved Primary Education towards Fourth Industrial Revolution (IR 4.0)," *International Journal of Advanced Computer Science and Applications*, 12(6) pp. 614–623.

Saravanakumar, C., Geetha, M., Govindaraj, V., Mohan, P. and Vijayakumar, K., 2021, January, "An Efficient Generic Review Framework for Assessment of Learners Ability using KNN Algorithm," In *Proceedings of the First International Conference on Advanced Scientific Innovation in Science*, Engineering and Technology, ICASISET 2020, 16–17 May 2020, Chennai. http://dx.doi.org/10.4108/eai.16-5-2020.2304199.

Smadi, A., Al-Qerem, A., Nabot, A., Jebreen, I., Aldweesh, A., Alauthman, M., Abaker, A.M., Al Zuobi, O.R. and Alzghoul, M.B., 2023, "Unlocking the Potential of Competency Exam Data with Machine Learning: Improving Higher Education Evaluation," *Sustainability*, 15(6), p.5267. https://doi.org/10.3390/su15065267.

Vega, J. and Cañas, J.M., 2019, "PyBoKids: An Innovative Python-Based Educational Framework using Real and Simulated Arduino Robots," *Electronics*, 8(8), p.899. https://doi.org/10.3390/electronics8080899.

Wang, D. and Guo, X., 2022, "Research on Evaluation Model of Music Education Informatization System Based on Machine Learning," *Scientific Programming*, 2022, pp.1–12. https://doi.org/10.1155/2022/9658735.

Younus, A.M., Abumandil, M.S.S., Gangwar, V.P. and Gupta, S.K., 2022, "AI-Based Smart Education System for a Smart City Using an Improved Self-Adaptive Leap-Frogging Algorithm," CRC Press. https://doi.org/10.1201/9781003252542-14.

2 Impact of IT in the Education System on Students in the University 4.0 System

P. Kanaga Priya, R. Sivaranjani and A. Reethika

2.1 INTRODUCTION

The 21st century is frequently referred to as the technological age. Technology is important to our daily lives and is seen as a key factor in the expansion of an economy. In the current environment, an economy is unlikely to prosper without technical innovation. This is because technology streamlines and expedites our work, increasing its efficiency. Technology has an impact on several industries, including education. The quality of teaching and learning outcomes has increased dramatically over the past ten years as a result of technology integration in the classroom. Teachers now routinely include computers and related apps in their lectures to the point where it is seen as a typical component of the learning environment. Technology can improve learning, strengthen the bonds between teachers and students, and increase access and equity. It can also make it possible for learning experiences that support cooperation and cater to the requirements of all students. Educators must successfully employ technology in their work to reap its full benefits. Additionally, stakeholders in education must work together to leverage technology to improve education. Leaders, educators, researchers, policymakers, funders, technology developers, members of the community, students, and their families are some of these stakeholders.

The University 4.0 perspective is at the forefront of this revolution, which has been largely driven by the impact of IT on the educational system. Technology is incorporated into every facet of the educational system according to the University 4.0 approach, giving students access to a more individualized and flexible learning environment. Students can access course materials from anywhere and at any time; learn at their own pace; and get tailored feedback thanks to the utilization of e-learning platforms, multimedia content, and adaptive learning technology. Technology integration has also made it easier for teachers to collaborate and communicate more effectively, raising the standard of instruction.

DOI: 10.1201/9781003425809-2

2.2 LITERATURE REVIEW

Robots are an innovative tool that supports students in developing collaborative skills, critical thinking, logical thinking, and problem-solving skills (Chevalier et al., 2020). Educational robots are a powerful educational tool that helps students to learn concepts (Lin et al., 2022). It also improves student's programming and computational thinking abilities. AI plays an important role in education which helps students in the learning process. Robots play the role of teachers (Yang and Zhang, 2019). It is essential to create robots for educational purposes that utilize gaming elements to foster student engagement in learning.

Gamification employs the principles of game design to motivate individuals to engage in particular actions or behaviors (Kapp, 2012). Various educational applications have incorporated gamification techniques, as evidenced by recent research (de-Marcos et al., 2016). Higher education institutions have utilized game elements such as leaderboards, levels, points, feedback, badges, and imagery, resulting in noticeable improvements in student's attitudes, engagement, and academic performance (Subhash and Cudney, 2018). It has been found that gamification enhances the logical reasoning skills of school students and increases their eagerness to engage in competitive activities. But there are some drawbacks to gamification which include an insufficient theoretical explanation (Hsu and Wang, 2018). Then (Huang and Hew, 2018) proposed a theory-based gamification model that overcomes the above gamification drawbacks. Huang et al. (2019) explored the impact of gamification on students and the result showed positive feedback. Previous research has demonstrated the utilization of theories like self-determination theory and flow theory in the implementation of gamification (Kalogiannakis et al., 2021). Thus, the gamification design model used the above theories the support feasibility (Huang and Hew, 2018).

2.3 REVOLUTION OF UNIVERSITY 4.0

In University 4.0, version 1.0 emerged in medieval times. It evolved into a liberal arts education where the mode of learning is limited to a privileged few. Version 2.0 emerged in postindustrial societies. It became the focal point for research advancement, and it mainly focuses on economic development. It is characterized by access to knowledge of democratic education. Version 3.0 could be described as an entrepreneurial university that serves many diverse functions and communities. It represents the integration of digital services such as learning and teaching tools. Version 4.0 is described as an ecological university or university for others. It mainly serves the need of students and integrates automation, adaptation, and the learning process. The main aim of University 4.0 is to apply Industry 4.0 in universities for education. By considering the requirements of Industry 4.0, University 4.0 provides automated learning based on physical and digital world integration. The common features between the industrial and educational revolutions are represented in Figure 2.1.

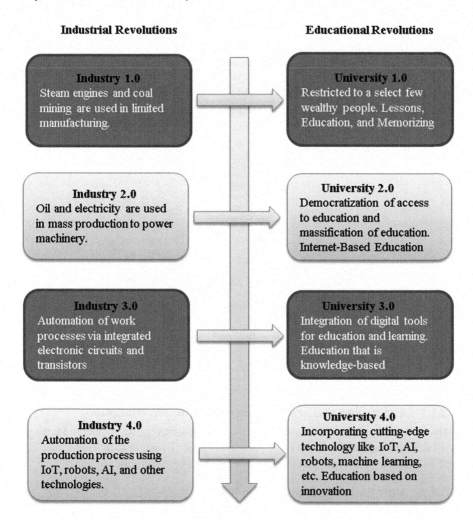

Industrial Revolutions   **Educational Revolutions**

Industry 1.0
Steam engines and coal mining are used in limited manufacturing.

University 1.0
Restricted to a select few wealthy people. Lessons, Education, and Memorizing

Industry 2.0
Oil and electricity are used in mass production to power machinery.

University 2.0
Democratization of access to education and massification of education. Internet-Based Education

Industry 3.0
Automation of work processes via integrated electronic circuits and transistors

University 3.0
Integration of digital tools for education and learning. Education that is knowledge-based

Industry 4.0
Automation of the production process using IoT, robots, AI, and other technologies.

University 4.0
Incorporating cutting-edge technology like IoT, AI, robots, machine learning, etc. Education based on innovation

FIGURE 2.1   The industrial and educational revolution.

2.3.1 MAJOR TRENDS OF UNIVERSITY 4.0

With the revolution of Industry 4.0 in mind, University 4.0 aims to change education in the future by utilizing cutting-edge technology and automation. University 4.0 is built on creativity. The need of preparing pupils to face obstacles head-on is emphasized. One needs to take a futuristic look at the existing educational paradigms to keep up with progress. The abilities required by the rapidly evolving technology should be mastered by students, who should be guided rather than instructed and given access to information rather than being spoon-fed it. Some of the major trends of University 4.0 are shown in Figure 2.2.

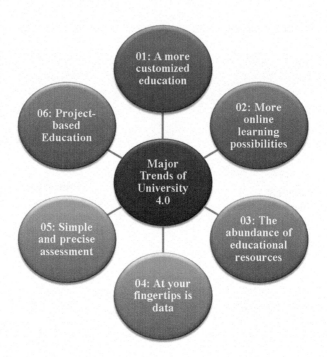

FIGURE 2.2   The major trends of University 4.0.

2.3.1.1   A More Personalized Learning or Customized Education

University 4.0 appreciates the student's individuality. Having personalized learning will create an impact on students to achieve their goals. Faculties identify the strength and weaknesses of students and feedback will also be given to the students.

2.3.1.2   More Online Learning Possibilities

University 4.0 allows students to learn from anywhere at any time with the help of e-learning tools, for example, active blended learning (ABL). It allows the students for both practical and experimental learning.

2.3.1.3   The Abundance of Educational Resources

University 4.0 allows students to choose the tools and techniques for which they want to gain knowledge, for example flipped learning and blended learning.

2.3.1.4   At your Fingertips Is Data

University 4.0 allows staff to learn about the students by analyzing the statistical data of student's journeys and guiding them appropriately.

2.3.1.5   Simple and Precise Assessment

University 4.0 offers offline and online assessments to students. Students are assessed based on projects, assignment scores, and fieldwork.

2.3.1.6 Project-Based Education

The project-based approach is followed by the students to learn time management skills, collaborative skills, and organizational skills.

2.4 COMPREHENDING EDUCATION 4.0: THE FUTURE OF LEARNING DRIVEN BY ARTIFICIAL INTELLIGENCE (AI)

The widespread use of digital technology and virtual learning environments in education provides stimulating and potentially vast challenges for both individuals and societies. Similar to how they have been in other industries, machine learning and artificial intelligence are anticipated to be significant drivers of growth and innovation in the educational sector. AI-enabled smart and intelligent learning tools and resources can support people in developing more comprehensive expertise, knowledge, and skills as well as unlocking their creative potential. Although there have been AI-powered solutions in the EdTech space for a while, the market has been slow to adopt them.

However, the epidemic has fundamentally altered the environment, compelling educators to use technology for online learning. AI can enhance teaching and learning, assisting in the evolution of the education sector for the benefit of both teachers and students. To develop education and prepare students for careers using enterprise AI, educational institutions might take a cue from enterprises and mega-corporations. To discover and disseminate organizational knowledge, data, and information in a way that closely matches how people search for and analyze information, enterprise AI refers to the use of sophisticated machine learning and cognitive abilities.

The fourth industrial revolution's "Education 4.0" learning paradigm seeks to reinvent education by utilizing cutting-edge technology and automation. Smart technology, artificial intelligence, and robots are all a part of this industrial revolution and have an impact on our daily life. To ensure the production of successful graduates, universities must equip their students with the skills necessary to navigate a world where cyberphysical systems are ubiquitous in all industries. This entails leveraging technology to enhance the university experience, completely revolutionize the learning process, and integrate it into the curriculum as shown in Figure 2.3.

2.4.1 THE ADOPTION OF ENTERPRISE AI

Applications for enterprise AI offers a wide range of applications and can address previously intractable problems. Corporate AI solutions are currently being implemented by businesses in practically every sector to address a variety of use cases, from the predictive maintenance of industrial assets to machine learning for diverse jobs. Every industry is changing as a result of the advancement of technology, making it essential to modify the educational system by changing needs to the new development requirements of society. Only acquired knowledge can assist in advancing Industry 4.0 safely under these new conditions.

FIGURE 2.3   The future of learning driven by machine learning.

Workers in various organizations and industries are impacted by the introduction of new technology. Depending on the industrial sector, specialized skills and human activities for Industry 4.0 may vary. Human capital will be very important in the workplace, and jobs and learning will be redirected as a result of numerous alterations in terms of skills and tasks.

2.4.2   What Advantages Does Artificial Intelligence Have for Education?

2.4.2.1   Educating Students for Changing Markets

Getting students ready for changing industries and the skills required of employees will surely evolve as more organizations combine cyberphysical systems. In 60% of all professions, at least a third of the duties might be automated as a consequence of the fourth industrial revolution. Education 4.0 is all about adapting to change, and for institutions of higher learning, that involves determining what their prospective graduates will require.

2.4.2.2   Automated Basic Administrative Tasks

Teachers spend a lot of time on administrative chores; thus, it makes sense to automate the most fundamental ones. By automating activity grading and assessment, artificial intelligence and machine learning in education can enable teachers to spend more time with pupils and enhance learning.

2.4.2.3 Personalized Education Delivery

Instead of replacing teachers, the purpose of AI and machine learning in education is to assist teachers in understanding the potential and limitations of each student.

2.4.2.4 Constructive Feedback

Teachers can employ artificial intelligence (AI) in the classroom to improve the guidance they give their pupils and make learning more fascinating and engaging. Students gain from immediate feedback since it helps them identify their weaknesses and figure out how to fix them.

2.4.2.5 Providing Access for All Students

By integrating AI and machine learning into the classroom, it is possible to remove physical barriers to learning and make education available to all students, wherever they may be. To give incoming students the skills they need for the workforce, universities must embrace technological innovations and incorporate them into their curriculum and daily operations. A contemporary learning strategy called Education 4.0, aligned with the principles of the fourth industrial revolution, takes into account the usage of AI in business and corporate settings, changing the type of candidate that companies are looking for. Every job opportunity will require specific competencies as a result of the inclusion of machine learning in universities.

Students may keep up with industry trends by using AI and machine learning in the classroom, which also emphasizes the value of problem-solving abilities. Traditional educational paradigms need to be reevaluated from a futuristic angle to stay current. In addition to being steered rather than instructed and having knowledge made available to them rather than spoon-fed, students must learn the abilities necessary by the quickly growing technology. The goal of general education and vocational training should be to prepare students for employment success.

2.5 IMPACT OF IT IN THE EDUCATION SYSTEM IN THE UNIVERSITY 4.0 PERSPECTIVE

The University 4.0 with the use of technology in education, however, also given rise to new difficulties, such as the requirement to bridge the digital divide to guarantee equal access to technology in the classroom. Through discussion of the advantages, difficulties, and potential future directions of technology integration in education, this chapter intends to investigate the influence of IT on the educational system from a University 4.0 perspective.

2.5.1 Understanding University 4.0

Technology integration into the educational system is described by the ground-breaking idea known as "University 4.0." It represents a fundamental shift in how we think about education and is quickly altering the conventional classroom setting. The idea that technology can dramatically improve learning for students, professors, and administrators is at the heart of University 4.0. Universities may offer a more individualized and adaptive learning experience that better matches the needs of individual students by utilizing the most recent technological breakthroughs. This manner of teaching is distinct from the conventional "one-size-fits-all" model, in which all students regardless of their learning preferences or aptitudes are taught using the same techniques and resources.

The focus on communication and collaboration within University 4.0 is an additional important component. Students and teachers can now work together and interact with one another more effectively than ever thanks to technology. Students today find it simpler to engage with one another and with their teacher's thanks to social media platforms, video conferencing, and other communication tools, which encourage the exchange of knowledge and ideas. The teaching methodologies have also undergone a considerable transformation as a result of University 4.0. With the advent of new teaching methodologies like gamification, project-based learning, and flipped classrooms, students now have access to more interesting and interactive learning opportunities. With the aid of technology, these techniques produce a more engaging and interactive learning environment that better equips students with the difficulties of the contemporary world.

In conclusion, University 4.0 is a game-changing idea that is transforming the educational sector. Universities can offer a more individualized, adaptable, and interesting learning experience that better matches the needs of individual students by incorporating technology into education as shown in Figure 2.4. A more participatory and immersive learning environment that better prepares students for the difficulties of the modern world has been established thanks to the emphasis on collaboration, communication, and novel teaching approaches.

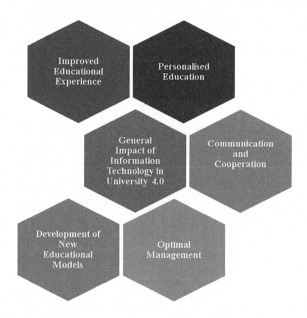

FIGURE 2.4   The impact of IT in University 4.0.

2.5.1.1   Improved Educational Experience

Students learning experiences have been considerably improved by the incorporation of information technology. The ability to access course materials and resources from any location at any time is now possible for students thanks to e-learning platforms and adaptive learning technology. Student's overall learning experiences have improved as a result of being capable of learning at their pace and using their preferred learning style. Teachers are now better able to communicate difficult ideas to students clearly and concisely thanks to the usage of multimedia content including simulations, films, and interactive graphics. For instance, a student who is having trouble understanding a certain subject can watch a video that explains it as many times as necessary until they do.

2.5.1.2   Personalized Education

Students can now receive personalized instruction thanks to adaptive learning technologies. These tools examine how students learn and offer tailored criticism and suggestions to help them comprehend the material better. This ensures that students have the flexibility to learn at their preferred speed and use their preferred learning method. which produces superior results. The achievement gap is a problem that can be helped by personalized learning as children from underprivileged backgrounds may have different learning needs than their counterparts.

2.5.1.3   Communication and Cooperation

Students now find it simpler than ever to work together and interact with their professors and peers thanks to information technology. Students can now communicate with their friends and teachers through collaboration tools like chat rooms, discussion forums, and video conferencing platforms, which fosters a feeling of community and enhances learning results. These platforms can be utilized for collaborative assignments as well, allowing students to collaborate regardless of where they are in the world. As an illustration, two students from different parts of the world can work together to finish an assignment.

2.5.1.4   Optimal Management

Administrative chores are now more effectively performed thanks to information technology. Systems for managing university operations can take care of chores like scheduling, registration, and grade keeping, saving time and lightening the workload of academic and support personnel. Additionally, routine work can be automated with artificial intelligence, leaving teachers to concentrate on more crucial responsibilities like student engagement and individualized education. For instance, lessons can be automatically scheduled using a university administration system based on the availability of lecturers and students.

2.5.1.5   Development of New Educational Models

The introduction of new teaching methodologies like flipped classrooms and blended learning is a result of the integration of information technologies. Flipped classrooms allow teachers to concentrate on problem-solving and critical thinking because students study course material through online resources like videos and interactive materials before attending class. By combining traditional classroom instruction with online resources, blended learning allows students to customize their learning experience by providing the flexibility to learn at their own pace and in their preferred manner. These instructional strategies provide students greater freedom to choose how they want to study and give them more flexibility.

2.6   PROPOSED WORK

2.6.1   AI-Based Gamified Robotic Model Architecture (AIBGRM)

A gamified robotic model is developed based on artificial intelligence which helps students to learn effectively in their curriculum. This model consists of three main modules. They are the database module, teacher's module, and student's module. The database module consists of different databases such as image recognition databases, databases for speech recognition, educational material, and gaming content. On the other hand, a teacher's module can have four different submodules. The architecture of the AI-based gamified robotic model (AIBGRM) is represented in Figure 2.5.

First, there will be a learning content module that has learning content for students to acquire knowledge about the game. Second, the learning material display module consists of videos, text, voice, and drawings for a better understanding of students. Third, the interactive practice module provides certain tasks for students

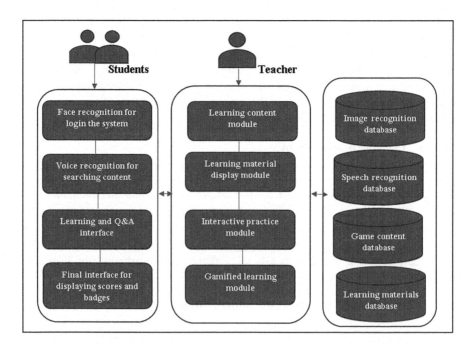

FIGURE 2.5   The architecture of the AI-based gamified robotic model (AIBGRM).

regarding particular concepts and assessments will also be given. Finally, gamified learning module calculates the scores based on assessment and awards students with necessary badges. These data are stored in a database for increasing the model's performance.

2.6.2 Working of AIBGRM

This robotic model has the functions such as face recognition, voice recognition, and interaction. Students can log in to the system using their faces and they can ask for any learning content. This model quickly recognizes the student's language and searches the particular content from the database and displays it to the student. If the content is not available, the model automatically searches for the content online and displays it to the student. Once the student completed their learning process, they can attend an assessment in the question and answer interface. The questions are asked in two categories such as theoretically oriented and application-oriented questions. Theoretical-oriented has 15 questions followed by 25 questions application-oriented. Application-oriented questions will be in fuzzy phrases. Once the assessment is completed, the model calculates the scores. The different types of badges are awarded based on the below scores represented in Table 2.1. Then scores, login and logout time, and content searched are stored in the database to improve the performance.

2.6.3 Fundamental Components of AIBGRM

With the help of motivation theory (Huang and Hew, 2018), AIBGRM can be mapped to five fundamental components: goals, challenge, access, collaboration, and feedback. The goal component is represented as scores and badges. The method helps students create both short-term and long-term goals, with badge earning serving as a short-term goal and finishing the course as a long-term objective. The access component also acts as a motivational element by enabling the subsequent level, enhancing student spirit. The model contains a variety of lecture videos, learning resources, and quizzes. The initial level has zero points, when the students complete

TABLE 2.1
The Badges Awarded Based on Scores

Scores	Badges
35–40	Elite + Diamond
30–34	Elite + Gold
25–29	Elite + Silver
20–24	Elite
15–19	Completed
<15	Fail

Source: Own study

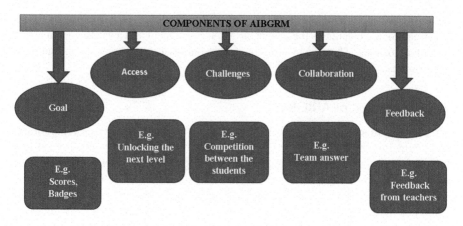

FIGURE 2.6   The components of AIBGRM

the particular level, they can unlock the next level. The challenge component can be competition between the students based on scores. The collaboration component can be mapped as a team answer. It allows students to communicate and discuss with each other. And finally, the feedback can be given based on the student's right and wrong answers. For the right answer, the student will get a cheering sound, and for the wrong answer, the student will be notified of the right answer with a detailed explanation. The five fundamental components are illustrated in Figure 2.6.

2.7   EXPERIMENTAL PROCESS

A class of 60 students is split into 2 groups, each containing 30 students. Group A used AIBGRM as a learning tool and group B used presentations and other traditional learning materials and concepts for learning a particular topic. Both groups A and B spent 60 minutes to fulfilling the learning objectives. Then all the students were asked to attend a test for 20 minutes. The questions were asked in both theoretical-oriented and application-oriented formats. Then 10 students were selected from each group for an interview to ask about the feedback of both learning sessions. The experimental process is illustrated in Figure 2.7.

A sample gamified quiz in the learning module is shown in Figure 2.8.

2.7.1   IMPACT OF GAMIFICATION AND ITS ANALYSIS

From the above experiment, it is found that students of group B face a lot of problems while studying and the workload for teaching faculty is also high. They also scored low marks when compared to the group A students. This gamified application not only increases student motivation but also decreases the faculty load. The descriptive data of both group scores are represented in Table 2.2 and Figure 2.9. Then selected students from each group are called for an interview to ask about the feedback. The feedback responses are illustrated in Figure 2.10.

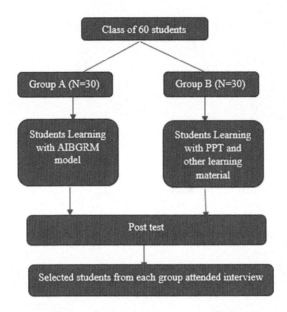

FIGURE 2.7 The experimental process of AIBGRM.

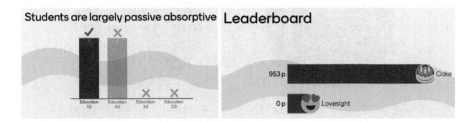

FIGURE 2.8 The sample gamified quiz and its score.

TABLE 2.2
The Scores Gained by Groups A and B

Group	No.	No. of the students obtained scores between 30 and 40	No. of the students obtained scores between 20 and 29	No. of the students obtained scores between 10 and 19
A	30	23	7	-
B	30	8	15	7

Source: Own study

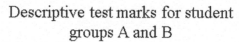

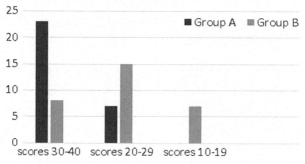

FIGURE 2.9   The distribution of scores gained by groups A and B.

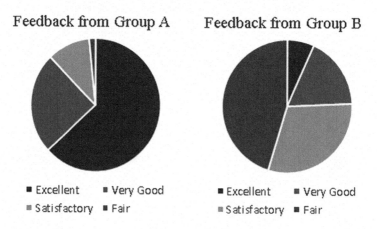

FIGURE 2.10   The feedback responses by groups A and B.

2.8   UNIVERSITY 4.0 CHALLENGES WITH TECHNOLOGY INTEGRATION IN EDUCATION

The University 4.0 paradigm emphasizes the importance of integrating technology into education, although doing so presents several difficulties. First, maintaining and developing IT infrastructure may be expensive, especially for organizations with tight budgets. Second, for instructors to effectively incorporate technology into their teaching, professional development is also necessary. Third, because of the digital divide, there are differences in connectivity and access to technology, necessitating the need to guarantee fair access to technology. Fourth, safeguarding student data and ensuring moral and responsible use of technology need the implementation of privacy and security safeguards. Finally, incorporating technology necessitates a cultural shift toward a fresh approach to education that promotes creativity and experimentation. To meet these difficulties, institutions, decision makers, and educators must work together and commit to promoting a culture of innovation and experimentation that embraces new technologies and pedagogical approaches.

2.8.1 IDENTIFYING AND ADDRESSING BARRIERS TO EQUITABLE ACCESS TO TECHNOLOGY IN HIGHER EDUCATION

Access to technology has emerged as a crucial component of contemporary education, but it can be difficult to guarantee equal access for all students, especially those from disadvantaged and marginalized groups. It is possible to successfully address this issue by establishing collaborations between educational institutions, nonprofit organizations, and the private sector, deploying mobile learning solutions, adopting open educational resources, and investing in digital infrastructure in underserved communities. These strategies can lower the cost of instructional materials, alleviate the digital divide, and give kids the connectivity and technology they need to learn and prosper. To address this issue and ensure that all students in the University 4.0 paradigm have equitable access to technology in education, the public, corporate, and academic sectors must work together.

2.8.2 UNIVERSITY 4.0 FUTURE DIRECTIONS OF TECHNOLOGY INTEGRATION IN EDUCATION

Technology integration in education has been the driving force behind the University 4.0 paradigm, and as technology develops further, it is necessary to consider potential future directions for this integration. AI and machine learning for personalized learning, virtual and augmented reality for immersive learning, Internet of Things for monitoring student progress and developing more effective learning environments, blockchain for secure and transparent storage of educational records, gamification for more engaging and interactive learning experiences, wearable technology for monitoring student health are some potential future directions for technology integration in education. For educational institutions to adequately educate students about the challenges of the future, they must be proactive in implementing new technologies.

2.9 CONCLUSION

This chapter summarizes the impact of IT in the education system has been immense, revolutionizing traditional teaching and learning methods and empowering students and teachers with new tools and techniques. A system called AIBGRM is developed for learning and an experiment has been done to check the impact of gamification among students. In conclusion, feedback obtained from students shows that the AIBGRM improved the student's achievement, provides motivation to complete the next level of study when compared to traditional learning methods, and also reduces the faculty load. While there are certainly challenges and concerns associated with the use of IT in education, the benefits are clear, and the future of education is likely to be shaped by continued advances in technology. Thus, the usage of University 4.0 concepts to a given model with the help of IT revealed that the students will have a greater impact on the education system. Finally, the future directions of IT have also made administrative tasks more efficient for educators to focus more time and energy on teaching and interacting with students.

REFERENCES

Chevalier, M., Giang, C., Piatti, A., and Mondada, F. (2020), "Fostering computational thinking through educational robotics: A model for creative computational problem solving", *International Journal of STEM Education*, 7(1). https://doi.org/10.1186/s40594-020-00238-z

de-Marcos, L., GarciaLopez, E., and GarciaCabot, A. (2016), "On the effectiveness of gamelike and social approaches in learning: Comparing educational gaming, gamification & social networking", *Computers and Education*, 95, 99–113. https://doi.org/10.1016/j.compedu.2015.12.008

Hsu, C.-C., and Wang, T.-I. (2018), "Applying game mechanics and studentgenerated questions to an online puzzlebased game learning system to promote algorithmic thinking skills", *Computers and Education*, 121, 73–88. https://doi.org/10.1016/j.compedu.2018.02.002

Huang, B., and Hew, K. F. (2018), "Implementing a theory-driven gamification model in higher education flipped courses: Effects on out-of-class activity completion and quality of artifacts", *Computers and Education*, 125, 254–272. https://doi.org/10.1016/j.compedu.2018.06.018

Kalogiannakis, M., Papadakis, S., and Zourmpakis, A. (2021), "Gamification in science education. A systematic review of the literature", *Education Sciences*, 11(1), 22. https://doi.org/10.3390/educsci11010022

Huang, B., Hwang, G.-J., Hew, K. F., and Warning, P. (2019), "Effects of gamification on students' online interactive patterns and peer-feedback", *Distance Education*, 40(3), 350–379. https://doi.org/10.1080/01587919.2019.1632168

Kapp, K. M. (2012), "The gamification of learning and instruction: Game-based methods and strategies for training and education", *International Journal of Gaming and Computer-Mediated Simulations*, 4(4), 81–83.

Lin, V., Yeh, H.-C., and Chen, N.-S. (2022), "A systematic review on oral interactions in robotassisted language learning". https://doi.org/10.3390/electronics11020290

Subhash, S., and Cudney, E. A. (2018), "Gamified learning in higher education: A systematic review of the literature", *Computers in Human Behavior*, 87, 192–206. https://doi.org/10.1016/j.chb.2018.05.028

Yang, J., and Zhang, B. (2019), "Artificial intelligence in intelligent tutoring robots: A systematic review and design guidelines". https://doi.org/10.3390/app9102078

3 The Impact of Video-Based Learning on Student Engagement and Motivation

Ishfaq Hussain Bhat

3.1 INTRODUCTION

In recent years, video-based learning has become an increasingly popular instructional approach in both traditional and online classrooms. Videos can provide engaging and dynamic content that can help students to understand complex concepts, visualize abstract ideas, and retain information more effectively (Xu et al., 2023). Furthermore, videos can be accessed anytime and anywhere, making them a flexible and convenient tool for both students and teachers (Xu et al., 2022). The use of video-based learning in education has been shown to have a positive impact on student engagement and motivation. When used effectively, videos can capture students' attention and spark their curiosity, encouraging them to take an active role in their own learning (Zhao & Wagner, 2022). Video-based learning can also help students to connect with the material on a deeper level, leading to improved comprehension and retention.

Despite the potential benefits of video-based learning, there are also challenges to its effective implementation. For example, poorly designed videos or those that are too long or too short may fail to engage students or may distract them from the learning objectives. In addition, videos may not be accessible to all students, particularly those with disabilities or those who do not have access to reliable technology. Education has always been a crucial component of society, providing individuals with the necessary knowledge and skills to navigate the world around them. However, traditional methods of education have been criticized for their limitations in promoting student engagement and motivation (Jin et al., 2021). In recent years, there has been a growing interest in the use of video-based learning as an effective tool for enhancing student engagement and motivation.

Video-based learning provides a unique opportunity to deliver educational content in an interactive and engaging manner (Xu et al., 2022; Pal & Patra, 2021). Unlike traditional classroom activities, video-based learning allows students to learn

DOI: 10.1201/9781003425809-3

at their own pace, pause, and rewind content and engage with material in a more dynamic way (Pal & Patra, 2021). In addition, video-based learning has been shown to have a positive impact on student motivation as it allows for more personalized and self-directed learning experiences (Zhou & Zhang, 2022).

The potential benefits of video-based learning are particularly relevant for high school education, where students are faced with a range of academic and personal challenges (Pal & Patra, 2021). High school students are often required to learn complex subject matter, while also managing the pressures of social and emotional development. Therefore, it is important to investigate the impact of video-based learning on student engagement and motivation in this context (Xu et al., 2023; Zhao & Wagner, 2022).

Therefore, the purpose of this chapter is to explore the impact of video-based learning on student engagement and motivation, with a focus on identifying effective strategies for using videos in the classroom. Through a review of the relevant literature and analysis of empirical studies, this chapter will examine the benefits and drawbacks of video-based learning, as well as the best practices for designing and implementing effective video-based learning experiences. By doing so, this chapter aims to contribute to a better understanding of how video-based learning can be used to enhance student learning and achievement.

This study aims to contribute to the literature by exploring the impact of video-based learning on student engagement and motivation in a high school setting. Specifically, we aim to investigate the effectiveness of video-based learning in promoting engagement and motivation, as well as identify any factors that may impact the effectiveness of this approach. The findings of this study have the potential to inform educational policy and practice, providing educators with evidence-based strategies to enhance student engagement and motivation in high school education.

3.2   REVIEW OF LITERATURE

In recent years, video-based learning has emerged as a popular approach to education, particularly in the online learning environment. The use of video content in education offers a number of potential benefits, including increased accessibility, flexibility, and engagement (Zhao & Wagner, 2022; Xu et al., 2020). However, there is a need for further research to explore the impact of video-based learning on student engagement and motivation and to identify key factors that influence its effectiveness (Zhang, Basham, & Yang, 2020). This literature review aims to provide a comprehensive overview of the literature on video-based learning and its impact on student engagement and motivation and to identify gaps and limitations in the existing research.

3.2.1   THEORETICAL FRAMEWORK

The theoretical framework for this study draws on several related concepts, including self-determination theory, social cognitive theory, and multimedia learning theory. Self-determination theory proposes that students are more likely to be engaged and motivated when they have a sense of autonomy, competence, and relatedness in their learning environment (Ryan & Deci, 2017). Social cognitive theory suggests that students learn through observation and modeling and that the use of video content can provide opportunities for vicarious learning (Schunk & DiBenedetto, 2020). Multimedia learning theory highlights the importance of matching the presentation format of instructional materials with the cognitive processing demands of the task (McTigue, 2009).

3.2.1.1 Self-Determination Theory

Self-determination theory (SDT) is a framework for understanding human motivation and behavior that emphasizes the importance of three basic psychological needs: autonomy, competence, and relatedness (Ryan & Deci, 2017). According to SDT, these needs are essential for individuals to develop a sense of well-being, and they play a crucial role in fostering engagement and motivation in various contexts, including education (Ryan & Deci, 2017). Autonomy refers to the sense of control and agency that individuals experience in their lives (Niemiec, Ryan, & Deci, 2010). In the context of education, autonomy means that students have the freedom to make choices and take ownership of their learning (Fernández-Gutiérrez et al., 2020). This includes having a say in the topics they study, the methods they use to learn, and the pace at which they progress. When students have a sense of autonomy, they are more likely to be engaged and motivated because they feel a sense of control over their learning and a sense of responsibility for their progress (Fernández-Gutiérrez et al., 2020).

Competence refers to the sense of mastery and effectiveness that individuals experience in their activities. In the context of education, competence means that students feel capable of understanding and mastering the content they are studying (Ryan & Deci, 2017). This includes having access to appropriate resources and support, receiving feedback on their progress, and having opportunities to demonstrate their learning. When students feel competent, they are more likely to be engaged and motivated because they feel that they are making progress and achieving their goals (Fernández-Gutiérrez et al., 2020).

Relatedness refers to the sense of connection and belonging that individuals experience in their relationships with others (Korpershoek et al., 2020). In the context of education, relatedness means that students feel connected to their peers and their teachers and that they feel supported and valued by their learning community (Korpershoek et al., 2020). This includes having opportunities for collaboration and social interaction, receiving positive feedback and encouragement, and feeling that their contributions are valued. When students feel relatedness, they are more likely to be engaged and motivated because they feel that they are part of a community and that their efforts are appreciated (Ryan & Deci, 2017).

Self-determination theory proposes that students are more likely to be engaged and motivated when they have a sense of autonomy, competence, and relatedness in their learning environment (Ryan & Deci, 2017). Educators can promote these needs by providing opportunities for choice and ownership, creating a supportive and collaborative learning community, and providing appropriate resources and feedback to support student learning and progress.

3.2.1.2 Social Cognitive Theory

Social cognitive theory (SCT) is a learning theory that emphasizes the role of observation, modeling, and self-reflection in the learning process (Schunk & DiBenedetto, 2020). According to SCT, individuals learn through a combination of their own experiences, feedback from their environment, and observations of others' behavior. The theory proposes that individuals can acquire new behaviors and knowledge by observing others and that this process of observation and modeling can be facilitated by the use of video content (Schunk & DiBenedetto, 2020).

Video content provides opportunities for vicarious learning, which is the process of learning by observing others' behavior and the consequences of that behavior (Xu et al., 2022). Through video content, students can observe a wide range of behaviors and actions and see how those behaviors lead to different outcomes (Zhao & Wagner, 2022). The students can watch a video of a scientist conducting an experiment and see how the scientist makes decisions and carries out the experiment. Through this observation, students can learn about the process of scientific inquiry and develop a better understanding of scientific concepts.

In addition to providing opportunities for observation and modeling, video content can be used to enhance self-reflection and metacognition (Chan et al., 2022). Through video self-reflection, students can watch recordings of their own behavior and reflect on their performance. This can help them identify areas where they need to improve and develop strategies for self-improvement (Giannakos, Sampson, & Kidziński, 2016). A student can watch a recording of a presentation they gave and identify areas where they need to work on their public speaking skills (Chan et al., 2022). Social cognitive theory suggests that students learn through observation and modeling and that the use of video content can provide opportunities for vicarious learning. By providing students with opportunities to observe and reflect on their own behavior, educators can facilitate the learning process and help students develop new skills and knowledge.

3.2.1.3 Multimedia Learning Theory

Multimedia learning theory is a framework for designing instructional materials that integrate different forms of media, such as text, images, audio, and video (McTigue, 2009). This theory highlights the importance of matching the presentation format of instructional materials with the cognitive processing demands of the task (McTigue, 2009). According to the theory, individuals have limited working memory capacity, and cognitive overload can occur when the presentation format of instructional materials exceeds their processing capacity (McTigue, 2009). To avoid cognitive overload, instructional designers should consider the cognitive processing demands of the task when selecting the presentation format of instructional materials. The complex tasks may require the use of visual aids to help learners visualize abstract concepts, while simple tasks may not require as much visual support (Sablić, Mirosavljević, & Škugor, 2021).

The theory also emphasizes the importance of coherence, or the organization and integration of information, in promoting learning. Instructional materials should be organized in a way that makes sense to learners and promotes meaningful connections between different pieces of information (Giannakos et al., 2014). According to Bhat and Gupta (2019), all the related information should be grouped together, and transitions between different topics should be clear and concise.

The theory also highlights the importance of using multiple modes of representation, such as text and images, to enhance learning (Xu et al., 2023). Different modes of representation can provide complementary information and help learners build a more comprehensive understanding of the material. Multimedia learning theory emphasizes the importance of designing instructional materials that match the cognitive processing demands of the task and promote coherence and multiple modes of representation. By doing so, instructional designers can help learners avoid cognitive overload and facilitate the learning process (McTigue, 2009).

3.2.2 Effects of Video-Based Learning on Engagement and Motivation

Numerous studies have explored the impact of video-based learning on student engagement and motivation, with generally positive findings. According to Xu et al. (2023), students who watched video lectures in an online course reported higher levels of engagement and motivation compared to those who read text-based materials. Similarly, Zhao and Wagner (2022) found that students who watched video-based tutorials in a statistics course reported higher levels of self-efficacy and motivation compared to those who used traditional textbook materials. Moreover, research conducted by Svinicki and McKeachie (2014) found that the use of videos to supplement traditional classroom instruction can increase student engagement and motivation, particularly for students who have different learning styles. In addition, a study by Jin et al. (2021) found that the use of video-based case studies in a business course increased students' motivation and engagement, as well as their ability to apply course concepts to real-world situations.

3.2.3 Factors Affecting the Effectiveness of Video-Based Learning

While video-based learning has been shown to have a positive impact on engagement and motivation, there are several factors that may influence its effectiveness. These include the length and format of the videos, the level of interactivity and feedback provided, and the perceived relevance and authenticity of the content (Pal & Patra, 2021). A study by Chan et al. (2022) found that shorter, more concise video segments were more effective for learning compared to longer, more complex segments. Similarly, a study by Brame and Biel (2015) found that providing interactive elements, such as quizzes and discussions, improved engagement and motivation in video-based courses. Moreover, Zhou and Zhang (2022) found that the use of high-quality video content, such as professionally produced videos, was associated with higher levels of engagement and motivation compared to low-quality content. Zhang et al. (2020) found that students were more likely to be engaged and motivated by videos that were perceived as relevant and authentic to their learning goals. The past literature suggests that video-based learning can have a positive impact on student engagement and motivation, particularly when it is designed to align with key theoretical principles and incorporates interactive elements (Xu et al., 2023). However, further research is needed to identify optimal design features and to explore the potential limitations

3.3 METHODOLOGY

3.3.1 PARTICIPANTS

The participants in this study were 100 high school students, aged between 14 and 18 years, from two public high schools in India. Participants were selected based on their enrollment in a math course, as video-based learning was implemented in this subject area. Informed consent was obtained from all participants and their parents/ guardians prior to the start of the study.

3.3.2 MATERIALS

The video-based learning content for this study was created by the research team, in collaboration with high school math teachers. The content was designed to align with the curriculum of the math course being studied and was presented in a series of short, engaging videos. The videos were accessible to students via an online platform, which was also used to track student progress and engagement with the content.

3.3.3 PROCEDURE

This study employed a pre- and posttest design, with participants completing a survey to assess their engagement and motivation at the beginning and end of the study. The survey includes items from established measures, the Student Engagement Scale was adopted from Bhat and Gupta's (2019) the Academic Motivation Scale (Berestova et al., 2022). Following the pretest survey, participants were engaged in video-based learning for a period of 6 weeks, during which time they had access to the online platform and were encouraged to engage with the content at their own pace. Teachers were also integrating the video content into their classroom instruction. After 6 weeks, participants had complete the posttest survey, and a subsample of participants ($n=20$) were selected for semi-structured interviews to gain further insight into their experiences with video-based learning. Interviews was also conducted with participating teachers to gain their perspective on the effectiveness of the approach.

3.4 DATA ANALYSIS

Quantitative data from the surveys was analyzed using descriptive statistics and paired-samples t-tests to determine if there are significant changes in student engagement and motivation from pre- to posttest. Qualitative data from the interviews was transcribed and analyzed using thematic analysis to identify common themes and patterns in participant responses. The findings of this study provide insight into the impact of video-based learning on student engagement and motivation. The present study conducted a thematic analysis of the qualitative data collected through student interviews. Once the initial codes have been generated, the researcher searches for themes, which are patterns or recurring ideas in the data. The themes are then reviewed and refined by comparing and contrasting them with other themes and codes in the data and by checking whether each theme is internally coherent and externally relevant. The researcher defines and names the themes, by summarizing the content and meaning of each theme in a concise and descriptive manner.

The initial coding process identified several interesting features related to student engagement and motivation, such as the use of interactive videos, the relevance of the video content to the course material, and the perceived effectiveness of video-based learning. The study searched for themes based on these initial codes and identified several themes related to student engagement and motivation, such as the importance of interactivity in video-based learning, the role of video content in reinforcing course material, and the impact of video-based learning on student motivation and engagement.

Further, the data was reviewed and refined these themes, comparing and contrasting them with other themes and codes in the data, and checking their internal coherence and external relevance. We then defined and named the themes, providing a concise and descriptive summary of each theme based on the content and meaning of the data. Thematic analysis allowed us to identify and analyze patterns and themes in the qualitative data, providing valuable insights into the impact of video-based learning on student engagement and motivation. This approach allowed us to explore the experiences and perspectives of students in depth, highlighting the importance of interactivity and relevance in video-based learning, and the potential of video-based learning to enhance student motivation and engagement. The data collected from the survey responses and interviews revealed four key themes in Figure 3.1.

3.4.1 THEMATIC ANALYSIS

Theme 1: Improved Engagement
One of the most significant findings of this study is that video-based learning has a positive impact on student engagement. A majority of respondents reported that they felt more engaged with the course material when it was presented through videos as compared to traditional lectures. Students reported that videos helped them to better understand the concepts and stay focused during class.

Theme 2: Increased Motivation
The second theme that emerged from the data was that video-based learning also increased student motivation. Students reported feeling more motivated to learn when the course material was presented in an engaging and interactive format, such as through videos. This was particularly true for students who may have struggled with the course material in the past.

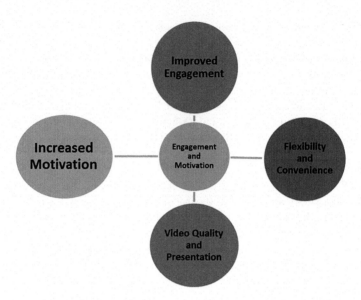

FIGURE 3.1   Thematic analysis results.

Theme 3: Flexibility and Convenience
Another theme that emerged from the data was the flexibility and convenience offered by video-based learning. Many students reported that they appreciated being able to access the videos at their own pace and on their own time. This flexibility allowed students to fit their coursework into their busy schedules, which may have otherwise been difficult with traditional lecture-based courses.

Theme 4: Video Quality and Presentation
The final theme that emerged from the data was the importance of video quality and presentation. Students reported that they were more likely to engage with and be motivated by high-quality videos that were well-presented and visually appealing. In contrast, low-quality videos or videos that were difficult to understand or follow negatively impacted their engagement and motivation.

The findings of this study provide evidence that video-based learning has a positive impact on student engagement and motivation. Students reported feeling more engaged, motivated, and satisfied with the course material when it was presented through videos (Xu et al., 2023; Rashid et al., 2021). Moreover, the flexibility and convenience offered by video-based learning was appreciated by many students. However, the quality and presentation of the videos was found to be an important factor in determining their effectiveness.

3.4.2   ANALYSIS OF QUANTITATE DATA

Table 3.1 summarizes the descriptive statistics for the variables included in this study. The sample consisted of 200 participants, with a mean age of 23.4 years (SD =

TABLE 3.1
Descriptive Statistics

Variable	Mean	SD	Range
Age	23.4	2.1	18–30
Gender (female = 1, male = 0)	0.6	0.49	0–1
Education level (undergraduate = 1, graduate = 0)	0.7	0.46	0-1
Video-based learning	3.6	1.5	1–5
Student engagement	4.8	1.2	1–7

Source: Own work

2.1). The majority of participants were female (60%) and enrolled in undergraduate programs (70%). The average score for the dependent variable, student engagement, was 4.8 (SD = 1.2), while the average score for the independent variable, video-based learning, was 3.6 (SD = 1.5).

3.4.3 REGRESSION ANALYSIS

A multiple regression analysis was conducted to examine the effect of video-based learning on student engagement, while controlling for age, gender, and education level. The results of the regression analysis are presented in Table 3.2. The independent variable, video-based learning, was found to have a significant positive effect on student engagement ($\beta = 0.58$, p<0.01). The model accounted for 38% of the variance in student engagement ($R^2 = 0.38$, $F(4,195) = 28.5$, p<0.01).

3.4.4 EXPERIMENT RESULTS

Descriptive statistics were calculated for the pre- and postsurveys for both the experimental and control groups. Table 3.3 shows the means and standard deviations for the presurvey scores.

TABLE 3.2
Multiple Regression Analysis

Variable	B	SE	β	t	p
(Constant)	1.46	0.87	—	1.67	0.09
Age	0.02	0.06	0.03	0.34	0.74
Gender	−0.08	0.12	−0.05	−0.70	0.49
Education level	−0.06	0.10	−0.04	−0.57	0.57
Video-based learning	0.54	0.09	0.58	6.10	<0.01

Source: Own work
Note: $R^2 = 0.38$, $F(4,195) = 28.5$, p<0.01

TABLE 3.3

Presurvey Means and Standard Deviations

Group	N	Mean	SD
Experimental	30	3.75	0.76
Control	30	3.68	0.72

Source: Own work

TABLE 3.4

Postsurvey Means and Standard Deviations

Group	N	Mean	SD
Experimental	30	4.15	0.72
Control	30	3.75	0.68

Source: Own work

As shown in Table 3.3, the mean presurvey score for the experimental group was 3.75 (SD = 0.76), while the mean presurvey score for the control group was 3.68 (SD = 0.72). As shown in Table 3.4, the mean postsurvey score for the experimental group was 4.15 (SD = 0.72), while the mean postsurvey score for the control group was 3.75 (SD = 0.68).

3.4.5   Statistical Analysis

To test for significant differences between the experimental and control groups, a paired-samples t-test was conducted. The results of the t-test are presented in Table 3.5.

The results of the t-test showed that there was no significant difference between the pretest scores of the experimental and control groups (t (58) =1.15, p = 0.254).

TABLE 3.5

Paired-Samples T-Test Results

Measure	t	df	p	95% CI
Pretest	1.15	58	0.254	−0.22 to 0.06
Posttest	3.68	58	0.001	0.16 to 0.54

Source: Own work
This table presents the comparison between the control group and the experimental group.

However, there was a significant difference between the posttest scores of the experimental and control groups (t (58) =3.68, p = 0.001). The 95% confidence interval for the difference in posttest means ranged from 0.16 to 0.54.

3.5 DISCUSSION

The chapter aimed to investigate the impact of video-based learning on student engagement and motivation. The findings of the study suggest that video-based learning has a positive impact on both student engagement and motivation. The results of our quantitative analysis indicate that there is a significant relationship between video-based learning and student engagement and motivation (Kuo, Tsai, & Wang, 2021; Rashid et al., 2021). Our findings reveal that students who were exposed to video-based learning had higher levels of engagement and motivation compared to those who were taught using traditional methods. This finding is consistent with the previous research which suggests that video-based learning is an effective way to engage students and motivate them to learn (Xu et al., 2023; Jin et al., 2021; Zhao & Wagner, 2022). The use of videos in education has become increasingly popular over the years, and our study provides further evidence of its effectiveness.

Moreover, our study also found that the level of engagement and motivation was higher among students who had access to interactive videos compared to those who had access to noninteractive videos. This suggests that interactivity plays a crucial role in the effectiveness of video-based learning. Our findings align with the previous research which highlights the importance of interactivity in video-based learning (Bhat & Gupta, 2019; Pal & Patra, 2021). The study provides valuable insights into the effectiveness of video-based learning in improving student engagement and motivation. Our findings suggest that educators should consider incorporating videos, especially interactive videos, into their teaching practices to enhance student learning outcomes.

The students reported that the use of videos in the classroom helped to make the learning experience more interesting and engaging (Bhat et al., 2022; Xu et al., 2023). They felt that videos provided a visual and in learning method that helped to capture their attention and maintain their interest. The students also repo using videos allowed them to learn at their own pace and in their own time, which helped to increase their motivation toward learning (Bhat, Bhat, & Sobiya, 2022). They also felt that the videos provided them with an opportunity to revisit difficult concepts and to reinforce their understanding of the subject. The students felt that the role of the teacher was crucial in providing guidance, support, and feedback to help them to understand the content and to stay motivated (Rashid et al., 2021).

The pretest and posttest results provide valuable insights into the impact of video-based learning on student engagement and motivation. The findings of the study reveal that video-based learning has a positive impact on student engagement and motivation. Before the implementation of video-based learning, the pretest results showed that the students had a low level of engagement and motivation toward the subject (Kuo et al., 2021). However, after the implementation of video-based learning, the posttest results showed a significant improvement in the level of engagement and motivation among the students. The results suggest that video-based learning can be an effective tool for enhancing student engagement and motivation toward learning. The use of videos in the classroom can provide students with a visual and interactive way of learning, which can help to increase their interest and engagement in the subject (Giannakos et al., 2014; Sablić et al., 2021; Giannakos et al., 2016). Moreover, the posttest results also showed a significant improvement in the academic performance of the students. This suggests that video-based learning can not only improve student engagement and motivation but can also have a positive impact on their academic performance (Bhat & Gupta, 2019). The pretest and posttest results provide strong evidence in support of the use of video-based learning as an effective tool for enhancing student engagement, motivation, and academic performance.

3.6   THEORETICAL IMPLICATIONS

The theoretical implications of the study are significant. The findings of the study align with the previous research that suggested that video-based learning can enhance student engagement and motivation. The study provides empirical evidence to support the positive relationship between video-based learning and student engagement, which is consistent with the self-determination theory (SDT). SDT posits that autonomy, competence, and relatedness are critical for intrinsic motivation and engagement. Video-based learning provides students with autonomy, as they can control the pace of their learning, and it enhances their competence by providing them with access to high-quality content. The interactive features of video-based learning also promote relatedness by fostering a sense of community among learners.

The study also extends the literature by showing the indirect effect of video-based learning on motivation through student engagement. The study's findings suggest that video-based learning positively affects student engagement, which, in turn, has a positive impact on motivation. This result is consistent with the literature that suggests that student engagement is a crucial determinant of academic achievement.

3.7   PRACTICAL IMPLICATIONS

The practical implications of the study are also noteworthy. The findings of the study suggest that video-based learning can be an effective instructional tool to enhance student engagement and motivation. Educational institutions can incorporate video-based learning into their curriculum to supplement traditional classroom instruction. Teachers can use video-based learning to provide students with additional learning opportunities, to reinforce content taught in class, or to provide remedial instruction.

The study also highlights the importance of student engagement in enhancing motivation. Teachers can promote engagement by using interactive features in video-based learning, such as quizzes, polls, and discussion forums. Teachers can also provide feedback to students to reinforce their engagement and enhance their motivation.

3.8 LIMITATIONS AND FUTURE DIRECTIONS

Despite the significant findings of the study, it is not without limitations. One limitation of the study is that it was conducted in a specific context, and the generalizability of the findings to other settings may be limited. Additionally, the study relied on self-reported measures of engagement and motivation, which may be subject to response biases.

Future studies should address these limitations by conducting studies in different contexts and using more objective measures of engagement and motivation, such as behavioral observations or physiological measures. Future research should also investigate the optimal duration and frequency of video-based learning to maximize its impact on student engagement and motivation.

3.9 CONCLUSION

In conclusion, the present study provides empirical evidence to support the positive impact of video-based learning on student engagement and motivation. The findings of the study have significant theoretical and practical implications for educators and policymakers. Educational institutions should consider incorporating video-based learning into their curriculum to supplement traditional classroom instruction and enhance student engagement and motivation. Future research should address the limitations of the present study and investigate the optimal use of video-based learning to maximize its impact on student engagement and motivation.

REFERENCES

Berestova, A., Kolosov, S., Tsvetkova, M., & Grib, E. (2022). Academic motivation as a predictor of the development of critical thinking in students. *Journal of Applied Research in Higher Education*, *14*(3), 1041–1054. https://doi.org/10.1108/JARHE-02-2021-0081

Bhat, G. M., Bhat, I. H., & Sobiya, S. (2022). Self-directed learning and undergraduate medical curriculum. *Interdisciplinary Journal of Virtual Learning in Medical Sciences*, *13*(4), 299–305. https://doi.org/10.30476/ijvlms.2022.97036.1191

Bhat, G. M., Bhat, I. H., Shahdad, S., Rashid, S., Khan, M. A., & Patloo, A. A. (2022). Analysis of feasibility and acceptability of an e-learning module in anatomy. *Anatomical Sciences Education*, *15*(2), 376–391. https://doi.org/10.1002/ase.2096

Bhat, I. H., & Gupta, S. (2019). Mediating effect of student engagement on social network sites and academic performance of medical students. *International Journal of Sociology and Social Policy*, *39*(9/10), 899–910. https://doi.org/10.1108/IJSSP-05-2019-0093

Brame, C. J., & Biel, R. (2015). Test-enhanced learning: The potential for testing to promote greater learning in undergraduate science courses. *CBE: Life Sciences Education*, *14*(2), es4. PMID: 25999314; PMCID: PMC4477741. https://doi.org/10.1187/cbe.14-11 -0208

Chan, A. H., Kok, E. Y., Razali, M. A. M., Lawrie, G. A., & Wang, J. T. (2022). Student perceptions and engagement in video-based learning for microbiology education. *International Journal of Innovation in Science and Mathematics Education*, *30*(3). https://doi.org/10.30722/IJISME.30.03.001

Fernández-Gutiérrez, M., Gimenez, G., & Calero, J. (2020). Is the use of ICT in education leading to higher student outcomes? Analysis from the Spanish Autonomous Communities. *Computers & Education*, *157*, 103969. https://doi.org/10.1016/j.compedu.2020.103969

Giannakos, M. N., Sampson, D. G., & Kidziński, Ł. (2016). Introduction to smart learning analytics: Foundations and developments in video-based learning. *Smart Learning Environments*, *3*(1), 1–9. https://doi.org/10.1186/s40561-016-0034-2

Giannakos, M., Chorianopoulos, K., Ronchetti, M., Szegedi, P., & Teasley, S. (2014). Video-based learning and open online courses. *International Journal of Emerging Technologies in Learning (Online)*, *9*(1), 4. https://doi.org/10.3991/ijet.v9i1.3354

Jin, Y. Q., Lin, C. L., Zhao, Q., Yu, S. W., & Su, Y. S. (2021). A study on traditional teaching method transferring to E-learning under the COVID-19 pandemic: From Chinese students' perspectives. *Frontiers in Psychology*, *12*, 632787. https://doi.org/10.3389/fpsyg.2021.632787

Korpershoek, H., Canrinus, E. T., Fokkens-Bruinsma, M. & de Boer, H. (2020). The relationships between school belonging and students' motivational, social-emotional, behavioural, and academic outcomes in secondary education: A meta-analytic review. *Research Papers in Education*, *35*(6), 641–680. https://doi.org/10.1080/02671522.2019.1615116

Kuo, T. M., Tsai, C. C., & Wang, J. C. (2021). Linking web-based learning self-efficacy and learning engagement in MOOCs: The role of online academic hardiness. *The Internet and Higher Education*, *51*, 100819. https://doi.org/10.1016/j.iheduc.2021.100819

McTigue, E. M. (2009). Does multimedia learning theory extend to middle-school students? *Contemporary Educational Psychology*, *34*(2), 143–153. https://doi.org/10.1016/j.cedpsych.2008.12.003

Niemiec, C. P., Ryan, R. M., & Deci, E. L. (2010). Self-determination theory and the relation of autonomy to self-regulatory processes and personality development. *Handbook of Personality and Self-Regulation*, 169–191. https://doi.org/10.1002/9781444318111.ch8

Pal, D., & Patra, S. (2021). University students' perception of video-based learning in times of COVID-19: A TAM/TTF perspective. *International Journal of Human–Computer Interaction*, *37*(10), 903–921. https://doi.org/10.1080/10447318.2020.1848164

Rashid, S., Hassan, A. U., Bhat, I. H., & Bhat, G. M. (2021). Analyzing the attitude of medical students toward class absenteeism. *National Journal of Clinical Anatomy*, *10*(4), 226. https://doi.org/10.4103/NJCA.NJCA_52_20

Ryan, R. M., & Deci, E. L. (2017). *Self-determination theory. Basic psychological needs in motivation, development, and wellness*. https://doi.org/10.1521/978.14625/28806

Sablić, M., Mirosavljević, A., & Škugor, A. (2021). Video-based learning (VBL)—past, present and future: An overview of the research published from 2008 to 2019. *Technology, Knowledge and Learning*, *26*(4), 1061–1077. https://doi.org/10.1007/s10758-020-09455-5

Schunk, D. H., & DiBenedetto, M. K. (2020). Motivation and social cognitive theory. *Contemporary Educational Psychology*, *60*, 101832. https://doi.org/10.1016/j.cedpsych.2019.101832

Svinicki, M. D., & McKeachie, W. J. (2014). *McKeachie's teaching tips: Strategies, research, and theory for college and university teachers* (14th ed.). Belmont, CA; Wadsworth: Cengage Learning.

Xu, Z., Ritzhaupt, A. D., Umapathy, K., Ning, Y., & Tsai, C.-C. (2020). Exploring college students' conceptions of learning computer science: A draw-a-picture technique study. *Computer Science Education*, 1–23.

Xu, Z., Zhao, Y., Liew, J., Zhou, X., & Kogut, A. (2023). Synthesizing research evidence on self-regulated learning and academic achievement in online and blended learning environments: A scoping review. *Educational Research Review*, 100510. https://doi.org/10.1016/j.edurev.2023.100510

Xu, Z., Zhao, Y., Zhang, B., Liew, J., & Kogut, A. (2022). A meta-analysis of the efficacy of self-regulated learning interventions on academic achievement in online and blended environments in K-12 and higher education. *Behaviour & Information Technology*, 1–21. https://doi.org/10.1080/0144929X.2022.2151935

Zhang, L., Basham, J. D., & Yang, S. (2020). Understanding the implementation of personalized learning: A research synthesis. *Educational Research Review, 31*, 100339. https://doi.org/10.1016/j.edurev.2020.100339

Zhao, H., & Wagner, C. (2022). How TikTok leads users to flow experience: Investigating the effects of technology affordances with user experience level and video length as moderators. *Internet Research* (ahead-of-print). https://doi.org/10.1108/INTR-08-2021-0595

Zhou, T., & Zhang, W. (2022). Effectiveness study on online or blended language learning based on student achievement: A systematic review of empirical studies. *Sustainability, 14*(12), 7303. https://doi.org/10.3390/su14127303

4 Artificial Intelligence-Enabled Tools to Enhance Education

Suja A. Alex and B. Gerald Briyolan

4.1 INTRODUCTION

Artificial intelligence (AI) secures a lightning reply in the human ecosystem. In our day-to-day life, various changes are occurring in technologies and these changes are being adopted by the various field sectors like education, medicine, communication, traffic, transportation, etc. The researchers and the AI scientists are putting their remarkable efforts to make a comfortable and technologically improvised human ecosystem within the upcoming revolutions in AI. New challenges occur due to the optimal changes in the current trend technologies. There are radical changes in the teaching and learning in schools and the institutes of education and still extend educational settings for teaching beyond the traditional way of classroom teaching. In the account of performance in computing and making up a decision, AI is comparatively one step ahead of humans. Sneaking into the past in a scenario of evaluating a bunch of students' exam papers and assigning a mark list for the whole class. It requires a lot of effort in evaluating and assigning the grade without the help of technology, there might be a possibility of certain human errors while evaluating or grading. In this scenario, the operation of AI is totally different since it is automatically programmed by humans it works according to the rules or the instructions which are provided. Due to this, the process of evaluation is totally error and provides an accurate result. Humans need to work hard and stress themselves to produce the result it is a time-consuming process and a waste of resources and money, but the concept of AI totally varies since it is preprogrammed by humans whenever work is provided to it, the AI provides an accurate and genuine result without any flaws. This procedure is a time-saving process, and it can save a lot of resources. Even though it varies from scenario to scenario, the AI provided better results in all the cases since the performance of the processors is higher and higher compared to the human brain. AI had reached a point that protects a number of resources and a lot of precious time in the life of humans. There are certain tools that can be used to accomplish various trends in the educational sector to seek a lot of learners, which provides an opportunity to learn anything in any situation and place. This motivates the learners to train themselves and to accomplish their dreams due to the tools that

DOI: 10.1201/9781003425809-4

are present in the online platform. The trends in artificial intelligence have gradually uplifted the technology-based application which is mainly focused on the increase of production and also its execution, the tools of AI are a forced combination of human intelligence with machine intelligence (Ikedinachi, 2019).

4.2 AI TRENDS AND CHALLENGES

The research on the trends of AI was from general purpose to intelligence transfer. Compared with the performance of humans in computing and decision-making, AI performs quietly better and higher (Banerjee et al., 2018). Machine intelligence is also named artificial intelligence, in which the machine or else computer is programmed to complete a task in an effortless manner (Solanki et al., 2021). Complex functionalities can be easily emulated with the technologies of AI rather than human computation on tasks such as sensing, analyzing, predicting, etc. (Russell et al., 2015). The research which is held in 1956 determined that AI has acknowledged the academic discipline of humans thus the initial programization begins in this stage to develop the machine to work for humans. In the field of education, AI is a recent trend that educators and researchers are highly interested in, due to the terms that it seems to contribute more significantly to the platform of education thereby personalizing the learning experience of the learners.

To enhance the learning and development of young learners, the tools of AI are being utilized to increase early childhood education (ECE) at the very early stages of the learners (Lin et al., 2020; Nan, 2020). However, there are some discussions about early childhood education. Even though there are several proof of concepts, the researchers have demonstrated that AI tools effectively improvised learning and teaching. Yet, there is a lack of knowledge about the studies and how these are conducted, and how these AI is being utilized across these aspects. AI research is now focused on perception and the audiovisuals of human literacy, the ability to see, hear, wrote, and read. There the main focus has to be cultivating students in reasonable thinking in addition to their computational thinking. The significant data inferences help us what we don't know and subsequently employ all the reasoning for insight and which makes it more difficult to reveal what we don't know. In this case, the AI is used to identify many hidden features and unknown values. There is a shift from size fits precision approach and precision education which refers to the utilization of machine learning and learning analytics of artificial intelligence to improvise the quality of teaching and produce effects in the learning process by means of addressing the risk to students and enabling interventions timely. The usage of artificial intelligence and the technologies which are related to the learning conditions could allow interference in real-time to enhance the learning of students to provide an outstanding outcome. In the enhancement of artificial intelligence, the productivity of human productivity through technology. The design of artificial intelligence which is considered in the human conditions has an approach human-oriented when trying to attempt to augment human intelligence with the approach of machine intelligence.

The shift in AI research has been the main reason for the innovations in more and more applications which is more dominant in the sector of education, the adoption of new deep learning algorithms, and the generation of transfer intelligence bidirectional encoder representations from transformers (BERT) and generative pretraining 2 (GPT-2) (Klein and Nabi, 2019) for a fine-tune a pretrained knowledge is being utilized, the results which are produced by it are more effective compared to the previous generations models of deep learning and traditional machine learning algorithms. The algorithm of new models can achieve a performance, which is nearly close to the human performance that's miserable a success. In addition to it, precision education is committed to applying the AI concept to their research in intelligent tutoring for precise adaptation and personalization and also to precise profiling, diagnosis, prediction, treatment, and prevention for smart assessment and evaluation. Potential ethical issues are involved as the AI requires a huge amount of learner data, and sometimes there might be sensitive information for the training model (Chen et al., 2020).

4.2.1 AI IN EDUCATION

There are many studies have been published on the subject which has increased in lockstep with the growing usage of the technology of AI in education (Chen et al., 2020). AI literacy is termed as the capacity which is to comprehend the essential process and the opinion that are underpinning Artificial intelligence in various products and services (Kandlhofer et al., 2016). Ng et al. have proposed a framework of four dimensions of AI literacy, covering the knowledge and understanding of AI, using and applying AI, evaluating and creating AI, and the ethics of AI. For instance, Chen et al. identified that there are innumerable applications of AI in the sector of education such as intelligent tutoring systems for special education, processing of natural language to language education, educational robots for AI education, educational data mining for the performance for prediction, discourse analysis in the computer supported collaborative learning, neural networks for teaching ad evaluation activities, affective computing for the learner emotion detection, and personalization for recommended systems. In addition to it, there are some other crucial facts that are unpacked in Chen et al.'s review paper on AI in education.

In the beginning, there was a growing interest in and an impact of research on education in AI. Second, there is insufficient effort had been made to integrate deep learning technologies into the settings of education. Third, traditional AI methodologies such as the process of natural language are widely been utilized in educational contexts, whereas the more advanced techniques are utilized very rarely. At the last, there was a scarcity of studies that employed AI technologies while simultaneously delving extensively into the theories of education.

4.2.2 TEACHER KNOWLEDGE FOR AI INSTRUCTIONS

As per the opportunities which are available the dramatic evolution of AI has a large implementation on industrial tutoring (Luckin et al., 2019). For the educational contributions of AI-based tools which are available to exploit the opportunities for teachers about artificial intelligence in education or tutoring (Xu, 2020). When there is sufficient knowledge for the tutors on how to utilize these AI tools for their respective concerns then that's the development that can be achieved in an effective way of teaching (Cavalcanti et al., 2021). In the occurrence, AI-based tools that are more recognized by the teachers become an energetic motivation for the foster learners which becomes an inspiration to them for more and more endeavors (Wang et al., 2021). For their appropriate purpose of teaching, the teachers to select the appropriate AI tools to provide a better understanding to the learners (Edwards et al., 2018). For personalized learning, the teacher's knowledge of AI enables them to use particular AI tools for better analysis and proper feedback (Popenici & Kerr, 2017). Consequently, it is very important to recognize the knowledge of integrating Artificial Intelligence tools in the field of education. The fact that the part of technological and pedagogical knowledge is vital for the fortunate educational integration of any technology.

In the future, it is not assumed that AI won't replace teachers (Hrastinski et al., 2019). This is due to the particular circumstances which come with the interactions between the teachers and the students are irreplaceable, it is an essential part of the learning process and which is mainly helpful for individual development (Tsai & Gasevic 2017). Moreover, the environment of teaching and learning is surrounded by artificial intelligence and its subfields due to their rapid advancement (Ng et al., 2021; Xu, 2020). It shows that AI will transform the professional knowledge of teachers for AI-based instruction (Seufert et al., 2021). In this aspect of the point, the knowledge of the technologies and pedagogically is being utilized the AI technologies are crucial for the profession of teaching. The technological, pedagogical, and content knowledge (TPACK) of the framework could explain the necessary knowledge for teachers to integrate AI-based tools in education. TPACK refers to the teachers' professional knowledge of which the use of technology for the purpose of industry. TPACK has been regarded as flexible in the framework for a variety of pedagogical approaches and technological tools (Vickers, 2017). Assume that the TPAK framework, when it is aligned with the technologies and the pedagogical contributions of AI, will provide a robust framework for a better understanding of knowledge for AI-based instructions.

In spite of the opportunities of artificial intelligence-based technologies for better teaching and learning, there are the rises of some ethical issues which has to be faced. Systematic and repeatable errors can be detected and the tools of AI can make a decision (Sao Pedro et al., 2013; Shin, 2020). Errors might cause discrimination among students from various cultures and races, which causes violation inclusiveness of education (DE Cremer & De Schutter, 2021; Dietvorst et al., 2018). Some of the specifications in AI-based applications for language learning can malfunction to recognize the difference in the voices of gender (Akgun & Greenhow, 2021). There is a possibility of the output of an automated scoring system may emerge concerns in terms of fairness (Almusharraf & Alotaibi, 2022). There is a possibility that it challenges educators to identify or to understand the justifications which are under the decision of AI-based tools. This is due to the black-box nature of the decisions of

AI (Dorr & Hollnbunchner, 2017). Due to the ethical contents of the AI-based tools, there is a possibility in the arise of uncertainty for developers of the relevant AI software (Shin, 2020). Therefore, it is a controversial issue when teachers of the students are provided with less amount of information or data on the responsible organization for the technology which is AI-based.

Assessing the decisions that are based on AI for ethical issues requires all the stakeholders in the education system. The comments are about those who need to gain more knowledge about recent technologies and how to utilize them properly and also to justify and evaluate the results that have been provided by AI-based tools. Knowledge about genuine assessments is so critically necessary for tutors to develop an inclusive generation for the future (Luckin et al., 2019). In addition to it, tutors must have a good touch with the technological and pedagogical bits of knowledge, which their ethical assessments will play a major role in the effective development of AI integration.

4.2.3 AI IN THE ATMOSPHERE OF CHILDREN

During the time teaching in preschools, the quality of the teaching must in high standards which improves the teaching atmosphere of the teacher and it's a basic need in the form of teaching. To improvise the learning interest of the children, the teacher must be able to create a good and well-known teaching atmosphere which is a primary one; next, the teaching quality and the teacher's effect play a vital role. In the traditional way of teaching, the teaching is used to conduct some small activities to interact with the children; these interactions are used to change the atmosphere of the children in order to seek attraction. Even though the teachers put forward a lot of activities to seek attention, it's all about the children's interest in it, and that's the main reason the activities are limited. There must be a vary in the activity to change the atmosphere since the same activity will cause boredom to the children and will lead to lose the interest. Teachers who are really skilled in the technology of AI can utilize these techniques to provide a good atmosphere for the children.

In certain cases, the effective use of artificial intelligence technologies by the teachers will effectively activate the vocals of the classroom in the children's teaching. In some preschools, voice robots of artificial intelligence are being used for better understanding and it is also a new innovative method for the children to teach them different technologies. The voice robot of artificial intelligence can play rhymes, music, fairy tales, etc.; according to the voice of the teachers, this way of communicating with the children is more effective and they will learn more about things very easily. To the enhancement of the atmosphere, the teacher will permit the children to communicate with the voice robot which helps to learn and know more information about the music or the rhymes. For another case, in the process of teaching how to draw a picture, the teachers can seek the help of artificial intelligence robots in the system of the computer, and this will help the students to follow the guidance of the robot, the commands that include how to use pens or fingers to draw the images in the AI-based tools such as tablets. This leads to the strengthening of artificial intelligence, and it also creates interest among the students to enhance more about modern technologies. In order to improvise the effects on the teaching standards of preschool education classrooms, kindergarten teachers must be in fully flourish in their teaching. If the teachers have a fully comprehensive understanding of AI, the application of the technologies will be better in the day-to-day life.

4.2.4 CURRENT EDUCATION SYSTEM

The development in artificial intelligence genuinely reminds the supercomputers. These computers with the capability of immense processing, including flexible behavior, which includes the sensors, and other capabilities, which also enable one to obtain a human-like cognition that acts as functional abilities. In fact, the interactions of the supercomputer with human beings are improved. Indeed the abilities of AI have been showcased in various motion pictures, which include smart buildings, which have the capability to manage the air quality of the building, humidity, or also the playing music depending upon the mood of the occupant in the sector of education there is a lot of useful application for the learners which is purely based on the artificial intelligence, which have been going over and above the conventional understandings of a supercomputer as AI which also includes the embedded systems of computer.

The best example is the embedded robots, AI, or computers and the equipment which are supporting the creation of the robots that are used to improvise the experience of learning as a student, which is the most basic form of education and in the early years of education as a childhood. In fact, the Timms posited that the Cobots or which is the application for the robots. These Cobots work along with the teachers or as colleague robots which are being applied to teach the routine of the children's tasks, which includes the teaching of spelling, the pronunciation of the words and also by adjusting the student's ability to complete the work which has been assigned to the students (Timms, 2016; Snyder, 2019; Fang, 2019). Just the same, web-based teaching is done on the online platform and enumerates the various studies, which has the simple availing material on one as a transitioned one or the web page for the students just to simply download and study by themselves also the assignments just to pass, which includes the intelligent and as an adaptive system based web, these web wed-based systems usually learn from the instruction and learner behavior to maintain a balance in a process of learning, which basically enrich the learning experience of the education (Kahraman, 2010; Peredo, 2011). Artificial intelligence in the sector of education has been incorporated into the administration, instruction, or teaching and of learning. These areas have been identified as the framework for better analyzing and understanding AI in the field of education.

4.3 ARTIFICIAL INTELLIGENCE AND E-LEARNING

In the past and the present years, artificial intelligence has enhanced with huge development and has also attained huge success which provided us with a set of generic technologies for problem-solving in the world to obtain a permanent solution (Stone and Hirsh, 2005). One of the most useful things of AI is that it enhances E-learning. With more personalization and with mot more improved learning outcomes, AI will play a major role (Laanpere et al., 2012; Luckin et al., 2019); these researchers have contributed their ideas and their understandings in the field of AI which can be a main source for the enhancing the learning of the students and also includes the management. There is another field known as computer-assisted learning (CAL) which is also used to help students to learn efficiently using technologies and AI (Schittek et al., 2001). There are some studies that show that the process of learning can be improvised by the utilization of AI in a proper way (Luckin et al., 2019). Kim et al. (2018) recommended the introduction of smart classrooms with these three components will increment the high-quality computation which included data acquisition, preprocessing system, and computing component. Uskov et al. (2015) have suggested that a smart classroom of ontology will provide a unique maturity level of smartness which self-learning enhances. The devices include mobile phones, desktop computers, and laptops which contain sensors to detect the activities of the user when they are reading any test or watching any clips. All the information can be collected and can be monitored which includes motion detectors, eye trackers, clickstream records, keystroke counts, and the enlargement of large files which can be achieved by "Ambient intelligent Classroom".

Customized learning looks into the learner's incremental progress due to the focus on AI-enabled assessment. The assessments are AI-enabled in the tutoring of intelligence systems (Nye, 2015; VanLehn, 2011). By using the logfiles and the clickstream analyses for success in learning, the games, and the simulation for the enlargement in the contiguous states, mining of text resources for the recognition and the understanding of text speech, and for the peer assessment for the computer.

It seems that artificial intelligence plays a significant and a major role in facilitating e-learning through the information which is provided for the learner using a personal learning profile (PLP), and it also links with the right network of people with personal learning network (PLA) and provides them with personal learning environment (PLE). These cases can be unsegregated with e-learning.

4.3.1 Personal Learning Network (PLN)

The outcome of the role of e-learning also depends upon the environmental factors which provide satisfaction in the outcome. Arbaugh (2000) says that the learner's levels of satisfaction in e-learning can be improvised by providing more interactions and being well-connected in the network. Personal learning networks furnish the learner will is needed with all the input sources and output devices for ideal communication and also to access wirelessly connected technologies which is an advantage. The point of Leone (2013) is requisite, and the consequences are supported by the system and the web pages which are available for the learners which is also another platform to attain knowledge in social networks too.

For a successful scattering of bits of knowledge, there must be a dramatical contribution from the learners, there are many tools and technologies being utilized the facilitate academic connections that are widely used effectively. Websites are the learning objectives for the new learners which assist them to co-operate and also to contribute to their augment that already have a massive online base knowledge. Gurzick and White (2013) have fortunately shown that the technologies provide certain knowledge to the learners and increase the chance of workers to communicate the information within the supportive networks. This shows that the PLN will enhance the perceived effectiveness.

4.3.2 PERSONAL LEARNING PROFILE (PLA)

The essential predictor of learner satisfaction is emphasized by the learner's attitude toward the computer which has been said by many researchers. The profile for the learners is the most important feature which plays an important role and is used to refer to the digital or the electronic versions of the learner's profile encapsulates is known as personal learning profile (PLP). The PLP acts as a digital profile for the learners. The portfolios for personal learning can become superior to the employees within the online environment which permits the user to the right resources to match the same portfolio that makes the user more comfortable and efficient.

In the academicians, a learning portfolio is very useful and is defined as the student's academic record that will accurately enrapture the work, which has been undertaken by the user and the achievements attained over the years (Gooren-Sieber et al., 2012). The definition is just one of out of the categories of six of PLPs functionalities. It is employed to determine the specific academic content that satisfies the tailored needs of learners. Daunert and Price (2014) suggested that the PLPs which are the practical tools that encourage self-directed learning that will reflect the learners with the achievements in the academic domain. Some of the researchers attribute that the usage of the portfolios will raise enthusiasm as the learners initiate and also participate in new learning processes, especially when they are connected in the network.

Vargas-Vera and Lytras (2008) has been utilized the environment of e-learning to capture each learner's trend of learning and the future of the educational experiences of the same learner to enlarge their learning process. Hence, the PLP is being utilized to influence the learner's perceived ease of the user of e-learning and perceived effectiveness and usefulness if it suits their individual needs and interest. The attitude and satisfaction toward e-learning will surely improvise.

4.3.3 PERSONAL LEARNING ENVIRONMENT (PLE)

The environment of personal learning or PLE is not just a concept of the previous one, but it also ties up with PLN and PLP but also encapsulates the spirit of the customized way of education. The fusion of the personal network and the portfolio acts as an essential and also establishes a healthy and fruitful environment for learning. The learners will be able to create a close and personal academic atmosphere. In numerous ways, the notion of employing a PLE has been explored by various researchers. The personal assembly of the learners will support and also will contribute not as a normal way of the learning process, but it includes encouraging new and different ways of learning methods.

The researcher points out that the PLE is learner-centered even, especially its usage and the application which rather has an educator dictate which resources have used and under which type of format, and the order in which academic materials are presented. The goals that have determined the framework of the PLE which hosts this learner-educator way of approach to impulse education and inspire the learners with the motivation for self-regulating support the transformation of the cycle of creating PLE is required (Dabbagh and Kitsantas, 2012). The PLE will develop a pleasing way of learning and also influence the ease of utilization and the effectiveness of learners and their usefulness. This will generate a better attitude toward learning and also increases the satisfaction level in e-learning.

4.4 TECHNICAL ASPECTS OF AI

Artificial intelligence assists in education which includes intelligence in education, creativity in virtual learning, and data analysis and prediction. The major scenarios of the AI in education and its key feature of the technologies which are supporting are listed in Table 4.1. It is noted that AI enables education which is playing a vital role in the learning requirements and also promotes (Rus et al., 2013). The educational intelligent system provides timely and personalized feedback and instructions for both the instructors and also for the learners, which is also designed to improvise the value of learning and the efficient multiple

TABLE 4.1

Techniques for Scenarios of AI Education

Scenarios of AI education	AI-related techniques
Assessment of students and schools	Adaptive learning method and personalized learning approach, academic analytics
Grading and evaluation of papers and exams	Image recognition, computer vision, a prediction system
Personalized intelligent teaching	Data mining or Bayesian knowledge interference, intelligent teaching systems, learning analytics
Smart school	Face recognition, virtual labs, A/R, V/R, hearing and sensing technologies
Online and mobile remote education	Edge computing, virtual personalized assistants, real-time analysis

Source: Kahraman et al., 2010

computing technologies (Kahraman et al., 2010) and is closely related to the statistical model and a theory of cognitive learning.

Here, the techniques for scenarios of AI education is shown in Table 4.1.

There are various techniques that are incorporated into the systems of AI for the analysis of learning, recommendation, understanding the knowledge, and acquirement which is based on machine learning, data mining, and the model of knowledge. AI in the education system generally consists of the contents of teaching, data, and the intelligence algorithm, which can be split up into two different parts, one is the system model which includes the model for the learners, models for teaching, and knowledge, the second is the intelligent technologies (Kim et al., 2018). As shown in Figure 4.1, the model helps to build a data map that is crucial for the improvement of learning, which establishes structures and association rules for collecting the data for education. As a core for the AI system, it works in the model, with technologies providing power for the system.

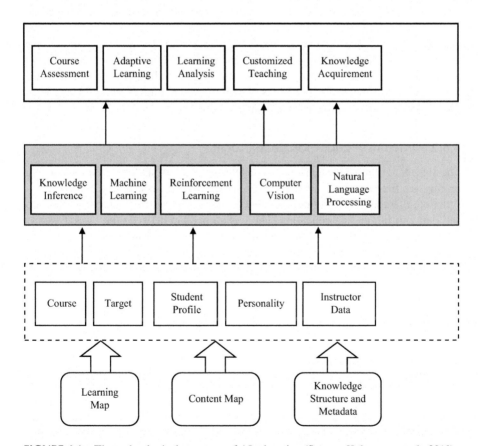

FIGURE 4.1 The technological structure of AI education (Source: Kahraman et al., 2010)

4.4.1   AI EDUCATION MODEL

In the systems of learning AI, the learner model, there is an improvement in the learning independent capabilities. This has been established and is totally based on the behavior data of the learners who are generated from the learning process. The learning ability that has been determined by the thinking and capability of the individual learner has been analyzed. To obtain the knowledge mastery of the learner, the knowledge analysis is being mapped. The learner model establishes the interactions between the results of learning and which includes various factors that include material for learning, resources, and the behaviors of teaching. The establishment of the knowledge models enhances the structure map with learning contents in detail, which usually includes the knowledge of the experts and the mistakes made by learners which is a common flaw and misunderstanding (Kahraman et al., 2010). The combination of the model of the knowledge field and the model for the learner, the teaching model which is used to determine the instructions for the accession of the knowledge field. Which totally enables the instructors to tailor the teaching strategies and actions. As the evaluation of the education, the learner's behavior is positive, to take action or to seek help. The tutoring modes have been developed on the basis of teaching theories in which the AI system can always be prepared to offer aid. The user interface will explain the performance of the learners through multiple input media services such as voice, typing, and clicking. The output will be produced as text, figures, cartoons, and agencies. The advance of the human-machine interface will provide AI-related functionalities, which include natural learning interactions, speech recognition, and the learner's emotion detection.

4.4.2   INTELLIGENT EDUCATION TECHNOLOGIES

The algorithm of machine learning uses a learning analytic and the technique of data mining are the two closely related technologies used for education. In the present situation, there are two communities that have evolved based on learning analytics and data mining in data education. There is an overlap between the objectives and the techniques and its benefit from a variety of disciplines, which includes machine learning, data mining, psychometrics of statistics, and the modeling of data (Estevez et al., 2019). The learning analytics field is mainly focused on the management of learning content and the results of large-scale tests. Data mining originates from the community of the intelligent system of tutoring, which works on a very small-scale cognition.

4.4.3   MACHINE LEARNING

The knowledge discovery at the core of machine learning, the training data is defined as the process of parsing the samples which are based on data samples, which is used to generate a pattern that is meaningful and knowledge that is structured. Machine learning plays a vital role in many applications like smart healthcare applications (Alex et al., 2022). Similarly, in education, machine learning is used to create recommendations for the learners as they can select the classes accordingly and are even applicable for selecting the universities. The achievement data, aspirations, and preferences of the students are leveraged to make a match with the institutions in which they are interested and where there can see and develop their best version. This type of technology can be used to get aid from the instructors to gain an understanding of the student's understanding of the concepts. This is a method that the instructor can adjust and develop the possible method of teaching work which is purely based on the student's cumulative records, which may help the students to grasp the course materials better. Particularly for a student in an assessment, the recognition of the image and the machine learning prediction can be utilized to grade the assignments of the students and the examinations; these technologies will provide faster and more genuine results compared to human beings. The concept of deep learning shall be noted that in the subfield of machine learning which attracts more and more attention. The decision tree algorithm is a widely used technique that is a logical inductive programming, clustering, reinforcement learning, and the networks of Bayesian. The perspective of deep learning emphasizes representations increasingly from the successive learning layers. The neural networks are a via the model of the layered features structured in the literal layers stacked on top of each other.

4.4.4 LEARNING ANALYTICS

The analytics of the learning is mainly focused on the data which the characteristics of the students and the objectives of the knowledge for the model for the learners and the field model of knowledge. New technologies are being introduced from the concept of learning analytics, which includes machine learning, which is being used in the world of nontechnical education. The main purpose of the tailored method of education is for the individual learners and the need and the ability, which has the intervening with the students at risk by providing feedback and as instructional content. The techniques are related to machine learning, visualization of data, the sciences of learning, and semantics. For any instances, competency learning which is based on AI is used to generate critical data from the students, which can effectively find the insights of the students and also predict the critical competencies which they can pursue, for active productivity this will help the institutions. Competency-based learning is an additional part that enables learning analytics to exploit the capability, which is versatile of an AI to learn. With respect to the issues of dropout, for the classification of incoming students, various parameters are considered by the AI such as the dropping out generates an early warning system and actionable data for the institution. Move out of the comfort zone toward a broader scope which includes the skills which are interpersonal, arts, literature, or among the raise to a whole new level of complexity in terms of measurement and the assessment of the competencies or the outcome of learning is the next main challenge for the learning analytics. In the specified learning contexts, learning analytics is applied which is a challenge; meanwhile, the need to be general enough to be used across the different courses and institutions. Learning analytics would be increased which are used to integrate advanced techniques used to support the learning for the students, instructors, administrators, and institutions.

4.4.5 DATA MINING

For educational purposes, data mining tries to generate systematic and automated responses to the learners. Data mining is based on AI education and mainly aims for the inherent association's rules that are developing, and the knowledge offers the objectives to the students to meet up their personal needs. For any instances, the demography of the students of the characteristic data and the data grading can be analyzed from a small number of assignments that are written, which can be achieved by machine learning and the method of regression which can also be used to predict the future performance of the students. In addition to it, the mining of data is becoming a powerful tool to improvise the process of learning and the mastery of learning, which leads to a better understanding of the settings of education and the learners. In other says, data mining can also be seen as a discovery of patterns and a model for prediction which is applied to the hidden extract of knowledge to improve the curriculum development in the educational system which allows the instructors to make adjustments. One of the most important applications is that data mining-based AI can be achieved by personalized learning from the field data of knowledge, in which the students perform their own learning and their own pace and decide their own way of learning methods which are aided by AI. Flawlessly, the use of personalized learning, the students choose what they are interested in, and the instructors adjust the courses for teaching according to the interest of students. With the mining of the data, the building of AI and its intelligence is more accurate and the outcome which is produced is more reliable.

4.5 THE ROLE OF AI IN EDUCATION

The researcher Timms delivered his observation which is more interesting; according to him, artificial intelligence is more powerful and has the potential to permeate heavily and cause changes in the various sectors of society, in the sector of education which is the one that is likely to be impacted majorly in AI. In the review of the various articles, it is noted and evident that AI has been adopted and which is applied in the sector of education, and the promotion of improvements is applicable in the different sectors of areas which is more specifically, the context within the narrative and the proposed framework by the researchers which forms the scope of this study, is evidenced that artificial intelligent has applied in the sector of education, which is more particularly in teaching and administration, and a subsequently, influencing or an impact in students learning.

The study, which included the analysis and inclusion of scholarly sources, demonstrated that it has in fact applied to the educational institution in a variety of ways. These ways include the automation of administrative procedures and services, curriculum and content development, student instruction, and the learning process of the students. Artificial intelligence has enhanced the efficiency of the performance of administrative tasks, which includes the content of reviewing the work of students, grading, and the feedback which are provided along with the assignments through automation using a web-based platform or the programs of the computer. Comparing to other sectors in which AI has been applied in various sectors of education which included the curriculum and the development of the content, and the leveraging technologies of the instructions such as virtual reality, a web-based platform, robotics, conferencing the video, files of audiovisuals, and the 3-dimension (3-D) technology, which has made it possible of the students to learn better. The teachers are more effective and more efficient and the students have a personalized experience in learning.

There are various studies which are discussed and demonstrated AI applications in education. The research by Chassignol et al. provided the overview and the transitions that strongly defined the application can be well defined and can be well established in the sector of education. According to the researcher, he observed the adoption of AI in the form of computers and the technologies that are related to computers, for example, the internet and World Wide Web (WWW) (Chassignol et al., 2018). There exist records of progressive technological advancements in a macro-operating environment, ranging from the widespread use of computers to online and web-based technologies and AI systems. The transition from simple computers to embedded systems in education is possible and attained due to AI. The development of robots or robots for a colleague (Cobots) that work along with the instructors or the educators or even not dependent upon anyone who can perform the functionalities of the teachers (Chassignol et al., 2018). Timms concluded that artificial intelligence in education (AIED) has been undertaken in different forms but is evidence of dissociation computers of AI or the main focus on the apprehension of utilizing the AI systems as only computers, which is used to include in the embedded systems of the computers as smart classes and as Cobots (Timms, 2016). AI not only included computers or desktops but also the applications as conventionally understood. This has been already demonstrated in other studies that are related to AI in education.

The functions of AI in the scenarios of education are shown in Table 4.2.

4.6 RESULTS

Depending upon the various research and studies, there are certain shreds of evidence that the innovations of technologies and advancements, computers, and the related technologies of the computer have encouraged the evolution of artificial intelligence, which paves the way for various sectors of the society, with a major potential impact in the various industries in which these certain criteria are applied. The major impact has been displayed in one sector which is the sector of education, which has a lot of AI applications. As a strong foundation and basis for understanding AI impacts in education, a definition and descriptions of AI have essentially been deemed. There are tenets that are different and characteristics and the gleaned nature of AI from the various definitions that are derived and evaluated from various studies. There are

TABLE 4.2

The Functions of AI in the Scenarios of Education

	Role of AI in education
Administration	• Perform administration tasks faster than consume much instruction time, such as grading exams and providing feedback. • Identify the learning style and the preferences of each of their students, helping them to build personalized learning plans. • Assist instructors in decision support and data-driven work. • Give feedback and work with students timely and direct.
Instruction	• Anticipate how well a student exceeds expectations in projects and exercises and the odds of dropping out of school. • Analyze the syllabus and course material to propose customized content. • Allow instruction beyond the classroom and into higher-level education, supporting collaboration. • Tailor teaching methods for each student based on their data. • Help instructors create Personalized learning plans for each student.
Learning	• Uncover the learning shortcomings of students and address them easily in education. • Customize the university course selection for students. • Predict the career path for each student by gathering studying paths. • Detect the learning state and apply the intelligent adaptive intervention to students.

Source: Pokrivcakova, 2019

certain key characteristics and tenets of AI, which as the name intimates, are that there are some levels is intelligence and characteristics that have been preserved by human beings until the AI onsets (Chassignol et al., 2018; Crowe, 2017; Rowe et al., 2011). AI provides the intelligence, the extensions of the computers, and the systems which are embedded, which includes the robots and the facilities, with the ability of humans, cognition, learning, adaptability, the and functions of decision-making (Peredo et al., 2011). The developments and innovations, culminate in the development using AI, which is accorded in the sector of education, specifically in the institutions of academics, with an opportunity to hold and use AI.

It is cited that the different sources that are reviewed and analyzed are the steps to uptake and the utilization of AI in the various forms of education. AI education started off with computers and related technologies, which were used to carry out a variety of administrative and instructional chores as well as to motivate students to learn. There are many different applications for AI, and they can be found in a wide range of fields. (Chassignol et al., 2018; Mikropoulos, 2011; Peredo et al., 2011). The transitions of AI technologies alone, embedded systems and platforms, including web-based technologies, are indicators of the development and use of AI-developed tools in web-based and other online platforms, and robotics, which is demonstrated by the creation and application of humanoid robots like chatbots and Cobots that can function autonomously or respond to human commands, as well as the responsibilities of educators, which include distributing educational materials to students at different educational levels. In addition to it, the analysis and the descriptions of various platforms provide various evaluated articles and observed that the application in different forms of education has assented the learners a richer with more rewarding learning experience (Peredo et al., 2011; Murphy, 2019; Jones et al., 2018; Rowe et al., 2011).

In the current trends, AI learning is considered as the assistant in education in the early stages as AI enables role in education plays a major role in the changes in the learning requirement. It is provided that the courses of various difficulties are based on simple rule judgments and haven't reached the best intelligence level in education. There are various education studies which are for the systems of AI which include the map of knowledge and the model of probability. There are frequently increasing interactions in the process of education, and the system of AI will provide more and more amount of data that are used to process a clear-cut picture in the process of learning and also in teaching, which has established and enables more accurate recommendations of information. The learner analytics which is aided by machine learning and also data mining, the system of AI will furnish high-quality content to the teachers and the students, to hold up both the teaching and learning which makes the whole process a measurable one. During these stages, the users would have access to the multiple approaches for the answer which is correct for any question. Shortly, the total desirable of the system of AI would shape the imagination and creativity of the students which analyzes their learning style and the conditions which are emotional conditions and initiative which is to improve the capabilities of learning and the development of creativity in the stimulative subjective initiative. The systems of AI are used to be more widely, which is expected to thrive on the aspects of all students, that is the personal skills, knowledge mastery, the ability of learning, and the development in career, instead of just assisting the students in understanding of the specific knowledge.

4.7 CONCLUSION

There are certain objectives or there are certain purposes in this research study that provides the assessment to understand the impacts on education due to AI. There are some qualitative research studies in which the literature review is the design of research and the methods which are being utilized. Development in the utilization of computers and computers are related to the technologies the research of harbingered which are innovated which have led to a part of development in the utilization of AI in the various sectors. More particularly in the overall improvement of the personal computers, and the developments which are done later which have improved the processing and the capabilities of the computing, the abilities which integrate or the technologies which are embedded in the computer in the different machines, equipment, the various platforms, which have encouraged in the development of AI, which provides a major impact in the permeates of the sectors. AI has totally stuck on with the educational sector which provides more output compared to the other sectors is particularly focused in this study. The analysis is mainly focused on the evaluation of the impact of the administration in AI, also in the learning aspect of education, which concentrated on assessing how AI has been utilized and the effects which have been produced.

The education which depends on and is developed by AI has taken from the computers and the systems which are related to the computers, and later than the forms of web-based and the platforms which are online based. The embedded systems have done the possibilities of using AI in the usage of robots in the forms of Cobots or the robots of humanoid as colleagues of teachers or the functions of instructors. The usage of these platforms and the tools which are enabled to improve efficiency and effectiveness which results in the improvement of the instruction quality. Correspondingly, the improvement of AI in the learning experiences is because of the enabled customization and the personalization of the materials of learning which are needed in the capabilities of students or learners. The overall conclusion of AI has a huge impact on education, administration, instruction, and a lot more sectors within the context of individual learning institutions.

REFERENCES

Akgun, S., Greenhow, C. (2021). "Artificial intelligence in education: Addressing ethical challenges in K-12 settings", *AI and Ethics*, 1–10, https://doi.org/10.1007/s43681-021-00096-7

Alex, S. A., Ponkamali, S., Andrew, T. R., Jhanjhi, N. Z., Tayyab, M. (2022). "Machine learning-based wearable devices for smart healthcare application with risk factor monitoring", In *Empowering Sustainable Industrial 4.0 Systems With Machine Intelligence*, pp. 174–185, IGI Global, ISBN: 9781799892014, https://doi.org/10.4018/978-1-7998-9201-4.ch009

Almusharraf, N., Alotaibi, H. (2022). "An error-analysis study from an EFL writing context: Human and Automated Essay Scoring Approaches", *Technology, Knowledge and Learning*, 1–17, https://doi.org/10.1007/s10758-022-09592-z

Arbaugh, J. B. (2000). "Virtual classroom characteristics and student satisfaction with internet-based MBA courses", *Journal of Management Education*, 24(1), 32–54, https://doi.org/10.1177/105256290002400104

Banerjee, S., Singh, P. K., Bajpai, J. (2018). "A comparative study on decision-making capability between human and artificial intelligence", In *Nature Inspired Computing: Proceedings of CSI 2015*, pp. 203–210, Springer Singapore, https://doi.org/10.1007/978-981-10-6747-1_23

Burgsteiner, H., Kandlhofer, M., Steinbauer, G. (2016, March). "Irobot: Teaching the basics of Artificial Intelligence in high schools", In *Proceedings of the AAAI Conference on Artificial Intelligence*, Vol. 30, No. 1, https://doi.org/10.1609/aaai.v30i1.9864

Cavalcanti, A. P., Barbosa, A., Carvalho, R., Freitas, F., Tsai, Y. S., Gašević, D., Mello, R. F. (2021). "Automatic feedback in online learning environments: A systematic literature review", *Computers and Education: Artificial Intelligence*, 2, 100027, https://doi.org/10.1016/j.caeai.2021.100027

Chassignol, M., Khoroshavin, A., Klimova, A., Bilyatdinova, A. (2018). "Artificial Intelligence trends in education: A narrative overview", *Procedia Computer Science*, 136, 16–24, https://doi.org/10.1016/j.procs.2018.08.233

Chen, X., Xie, H., Zou, D., Hwang, G. J. (2020). "Application and theory gaps during the rise of artificial intelligence in education", *Computers and Education: Artificial Intelligence*, 1, 100002, https://doi.org/10.1016/j.caeai.2020.100002

Crowe, D., LaPierre, M., Kebritchi, M. (2017). "Knowledge based artificial augmentation intelligence technology: Next step in academic instructional tools for distance learnin", *TechTrends*, 61(5), 494–506, https://doi.org/10.1007/s11528-017-0210-4

Dabbagh, N., Kitsantas, A. (2012). "Personal Learning Environments, social media, and self-regulated learning: A natural formula for connecting formal and informal learning", *The Internet and Higher Education*, 15(1), 3–8, https://doi.org/10.1016/j.iheduc.2011.06.002

Daunert, A. L., Price, L. (2014). "E-portfolio: A practical tool for self-directed, reflective, and collaborative professional learning", *Discourses on Professional Learning: On the Boundary Between Learning and Working*, 231–251, https://doi.org/10.1007/978-94-007-7012-6_13

De Cremer, D., De Schutter, L. (2021). "How to use algorithmic decision-making to promote inclusiveness in organizations", *AI and Ethics*, 1(4), 563–567, https://doi.org/10.1007/s43681-021-00073-0

Dietvorst, B. J., Simmons, J. P., Massey, C. (2018). "Overcoming algorithm aversion: People will use imperfect algorithms if they can (even slightly) modify them", *Management Science*, 64(3), 1155–1170, https://doi.org/10.1287/mnsc.2016.2643

Dörr, K. N., Hollnbuchner, K. (2017). "Ethical challenges of algorithmic journalism", *Digital Journalism*, 5(4), 404–419, https://doi.org/10.1080/21670811.2016.1167612

Edwards, C., Edwards, A., Spence, P. R., Lin, X. (2018). "I, teacher: Using artificial intelligence (AI) and social robots in communication and instruction", *Communication Education*, 67(4), 473–480, https://doi.org/10.1080/03634523.2018.1502459

Estevez, J., Garate, G., Graña, M. (2019). "Gentle introduction to artificial intelligence for high-school students using scratch", *IEEE Access*, 7, 179027–179036, https://doi.org/10.1109/ACCESS.2019.2956136

Fang, Y., Chen, P., Cai, G., Lau, F. C., Liew, S. C., Han, G. (2019). "Outage-limit-approaching channel coding for future wireless communications: Root-protograph low-density parity-check codes", *IEEE Vehicular Technology Magazine*, 14(2), 85–93, https://doi.org/10.1109/MVT.2019.2903343

Gooren-Sieber, S., Henrich, A. (2012). "Systems for personalised learning: Personal learning environment vs. e-portfolio?", In *Hybrid Learning: 5th International Conference, ICHL 2012*, Guangzhou, August 13–15, 2012, pp. 294–305, Springer, Berlin, https://doi.org/10.1007/978-3-642-32018-7_28

Gurzick, D., White, K. F. (2013). "Online personal networks of knowledge workers in computer-supported collaborative learning", *Computer-Supported Collaborative Learning at the Workplace: CSCL@ Work*, 225–239, https://doi.org/10.1007/978-1-4614-1740-8_1

Hrastinski, S., Olofsson, A. D., Arkenback, C., Ekström, S., Ericsson, E., Fransson, G., Utterberg, M. (2019). "Critical imaginaries and reflections on artificial intelligence and robots in postdigital K-12 education", *Postdigital Science and Education*, 1, 427–445, https://doi.org/10.1007/s42438-019-00046-x

Ikedinachi, A. P., Misra, S., Assibong, P. A., Olu-Owolabi, E. F., Maskeliūnas, R., Damasevicius, R. (2019). "Artificial intelligence, smart classrooms and online education in the 21st century: Implications for human development", *Journal of Cases on Information Technology (JCIT)*, 21(3), 66–79, https://doi.org/10.4018/JCIT.2019070105

Jones, A., Bull, S., Castellano, G. (2018). "I know that now, i'm going to learn this next promoting self-regulated learning with a robotic tutor", *International Journal of Social Robotics*, 10, 439–454, https://doi.org/10.1007/s12369-017-0430-y

Kahraman, H. T., Sagiroglu, S., Colak, I. (2010, October). "Development of adaptive and intelligent web-based educational systems", In *2010 4th International Conference on Application of Information and Communication Technologies*, pp. 1–5, IEEE, https://doi.org/10.1109/ICAICT.2010.5612054

Kim, Y., Soyata, T., Behnagh, R. F. (2018). "Towards emotionally aware AI smart classroom: Current issues and directions for engineering and education", *IEEE Access*, 6, 5308–5331, https://doi.org/10.1109/ACCESS.2018.2791861

Klein, T., Nabi, M. (2019). "Learning to answer by learning to ask: Getting the best of gpt-2 and bert worlds", *arXiv preprint arXiv:1911.02365*, https://doi.org/10.48550/arXiv.1911.02365

Laanpere, M., Pata, K., Normak, P., Põldoja, H. (2012). "Pedagogy-Driven design of digital learning ecosystems: The case study of dippler", In *Advances in Web-Based Learning-ICWL 2012: 11th International Conference*, Sinaia, September 2–4, 2012, Proceedings 11, pp. 307–317, Springer, Berlin, https://doi.org/10.1007/978-3-642-33642-3_33

Leone, S. (2013). *Characterisation of a Personal Learning Environment as a Lifelong Learning Tool*, New York: Springer, https://doi.org/10.1007/978-1-4614-6274-3

Lin, P., Van Brummelen, J., Lukin, G., Williams, R., Breazeal, C. (2020, April). "Zhorai: Designing a conversational agent for children to explore machine learning concepts", In *Proceedings of the AAAI Conference on Artificial Intelligence*, Vol. 34, No. 09, pp. 13381–13388, https://doi.org/10.1609/aaai.v34i09.7061

Luckin, R., Cukurova, M. (2019). "Designing educational technologies in the age of AI: A learning sciences-driven approach", *British Journal of Educational Technology*, 50(6), 2824–2838, https://doi.org/10.1111/bjet.12861

Mikropoulos, T. A., Natsis, A. (2011). "Educational virtual environments: A ten-year review of empirical research (1999–2009)", *Computers & Education*, 56(3), 769–780, https://doi.org/10.1016/j.compedu.2010.10.020

Murphy, R. F. (2019). "Artificial Intelligence applications to support K-12 teachers and teaching: A review of promising applications, opportunities, and challenges perspective", RAND Corporation, https://doi.org/10.7249/PE315

Nan, J. (2020, August). "Research of application of artificial intelligence in preschool education", *Journal of Physics: Conference Series*, 1607(1), 012119, IOP Publishing, https://doi.org/10.1088/1742-6596/1607/1/012119

Ng, D. T. K., Leung, J. K. L., Chu, S. K. W., Qiao, M. S. (2021). "Conceptualizing AI literacy: An exploratory review", *Computers and Education: Artificial Intelligence*, 2, 100041, https://doi.org/10.1016/j.caeai.2021.100041

Nye, B. D. (2015). "Intelligent tutoring systems by and for the developing world: A review of trends and approaches for educational technology in a global context", *International Journal of Artificial Intelligence in Education*, 25, 177–203, https://doi.org/10.1007/s40593-014-0028-6

Peredo, R., Canales, A., Menchaca, A., Peredo, I. (2011). "Intelligent Web-based education system for adaptive learning", *Expert Systems with Applications*, 38(12), 14690–14702, https://doi.org/10.1016/j.eswa.2011.05.013

Popenici, S. A. D., Kerr, S. (2017). "Exploring the impact of artificial intelligence on teaching and learning in higher education", *Research and Practice in Technology Enhanced Learning*, 12(1), 22, https://doi.org/10.1186/s41039-017-0062-8

Rowe, J. P., Shores, L. R., Mott, B. W., Lester, J. C. (2011). "Integrating learning, problem solving, and engagement in narrative-centered learning environments", *International Journal of Artificial Intelligence in Education*, 21(1–2), 115–133, https://doi.org/10.3233/JAI-2011-019

Rus, V., D'Mello, S., Hu, X., Graesser, A. (2013). "Recent advances in conversational intelligent tutoring systems", *AI Magazine*, 34(3), 42–54, https://doi.org/10.1609/aimag.v34i3.2485

Russell, S., Dewey, D., Tegmark, M. (2015). "Research priorities for robust and beneficial artificial intelligence", *Ai Magazine*, 36(4), 105–114, https://doi.org/10.1609/aimag.v36i4.2577

Sao Pedro, M. A., Baker, R. S., Gobert, J. D. (2013, April). "What different kinds of stratification can reveal about the generalizability of data-mined skill assessment models", In *Proceedings of the Third International Conference on Learning Analytics and Knowledge*, pp. 190–194, https://doi.org/10.1145/2460296.2460334

Schittek, M., Mattheos, N., Lyon, H. C., Attström, R. (2001). "Computer assisted learning. A review", *European Journal of Dental Education: Review Article*, 5(3), 93–100, https://doi.org/10.1034/j.1600-0579.2001.050301.x

Seufert, S., Guggemos, J., Sailer, M. (2021). "Technology-related knowledge, skills, and attitudes of pre-and in-service teachers: The current situation and emerging trends", *Computers in Human Behavior*, 115, 106552, https://doi.org/10.1016/j.chb.2020.106552

Shin, D. (2020). "How do users interact with algorithm recommender systems? The interaction of users, algorithms, and performance", *Computers in Human Behavior*, 109, 106344, https://doi.org/10.1016/j.chb.2020.106344

Snyder, H. (2019). "Literature review as a research methodology: An overview and guidelines", *Journal of Business Research*, 104, 333–339, https://doi.org/10.1016/j.jbusres.2019.07.039

Solanki, S. L., Pandrowala, S., Nayak, A., Bhandare, M., Ambulkar, R. P., Shrikhande, S. V. (2021). "Artificial intelligence in perioperative management of major gastrointestinal surgeries", *World Journal of Gastroenterology*, 27(21), 2758, https://doi.org/10.3748/wjg.v27.i21.2758

Stone, M., Hirsh, H. (2005). "Artificial intelligence: The next twenty-five years", *AI Magazine*, 26(4), 85–85, https://doi.org/10.1609/aimag.v26i4.1852

Timms, M. J. (2016). "Letting artificial intelligence in education out of the box: Educational cobots and smart classrooms", *International Journal of Artificial Intelligence in Education*, 26, 701–712, https://doi.org/10.1007/s40593-016-0095-y

Tsai, Y. S., Gasevic, D. (2017, March). "Learning analytics in higher education-Challenges and policies: A review of eight learning analytics policies", In *Proceedings of the Seventh International Learning Analytics & Knowledge Conference*, pp. 233–242, https://doi.org/10.1145/3027385.3027400

Uskov, V. L., Bakken, J. P., Pandey, A. (2015). "The ontology of next generation smart classrooms", In *Smart Education and Smart E-Learning*, pp. 3–14, Springer International Publishing, https://doi.org/10.1007/978-3-319-19875-0_1

Valtonen, T., Sointu, E., Kukkonen, J., Kontkanen, S., Lambert, M. C., Mäkitalo-Siegl, K. (2017). "TPACK updated to measure pre-service teachers' twenty-first century skills", *Australasian Journal of Educational Technology*, 33(3), https://doi.org/10.14742/ajet.3518

VanLehn, K. (2011). "The relative effectiveness of human tutoring", In *Intelligent Tutoring Systems*, https://doi.org/10.1080/00461520.2011.611369

Vargas-Vera, M., Lytras, M. D. (2008). "Exploiting semantic web and ontologies for personalised learning services: Towards semantic web-enabled learning portals for real learning experiences", *International Journal of Knowledge and Learning*, 4(1), 1–17, https://doi.org/10.1504/IJKL.2008.019734

Vickers, N. J. (2017). "Animal communication: When i'm calling you, will you answer too?", *Current Biology*, 27(14), R713–R715, https://doi.org/10.1016/j.cub.2017.05.064

Xu, L. (2020, December). "The Dilemma and countermeasures of AI in educational application", In *2020 4th International Conference on Computer Science and Artificial Intelligence*, pp. 289–294, https://doi.org/10.1145/3445815.3445863

5 The Key Challenges in Educational Advising Chatbot Dialogue System

*Suha Khalil Assayed, Manar Alkhatib
and Khaled Shaalan*

5.1 INTRODUCTION

Over the last decade or so, the rapid growth of the internet and communication technology around the world has utilized numerous smart applications by applying state-of-the-art algorithms and models. As a result, in this era of time, technology is growing at an alarming rate and thus is becoming a part of everyday life. That is why schools and colleges should deploy the latest technologies in order to empower students to benefit from it. According to Haristiani (2019), a chatbot is considered one of the advanced technologies that has been used within various academic and educational platforms. It is basically a computer application that uses various functions and algorithms from the natural language processing (NLP) and artificial intelligence (AI) models. Interestingly, students enjoy using different digital communication channels during their education as it can increase their learning experiences. However, the conversational chatbot and dialogue system have varying level of complexities, which depends on the architecture, as well as, the size of the training corpus (Sun et al., 2022).

5.1.1 Dialogue System (Chatbot) Architecture

The chatbot taxonomy is classified by researchers from different perspectives, where Vishwakarma and Pandey (2021) have classified the chatbot based on goal, knowledge, service, and response-based systems. On the other hand, Agarwal and Wadhwa (2020) categorized the chatbot into rule-based and neural network-based categories only. In general, the classification depends on the complexities of the task and the response-based approach, as well as, the type of the domain. If the task is limited to basic and simple scenarios, then a rule-based chatbot can be an option; however, if the task needs to speak using a particular human language, then natural language processing (NLP) and deep learning approaches are essential to be applied into the chatbot. Indeed, the NLP and national language understanding (NLU) are responsible in comprehending the language and the text. Moreover, the dialog manager

DOI: 10.1201/9781003425809-5

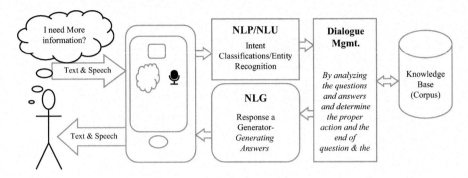

FIGURE 5.1 The main framework of the chatbot.

with Natural language generation (NLG) takes care of generating the appropriate answers with the priority-based responses (Vishwakarma & Pandey, 2021). Figure 5.1 illustrates the main architecture of the chatbot or the dialogue system.

5.1.1.1 Rule-Based Chatbot

The rule-based chatbot depends on specific, predefined rules, where the input pattern should match with the predefined rule in order to answer the question properly (Thorat & Jadhav, 2020). Hence, these type of chatbots can give reliable and correct answers as long as the question and the answer are defined in the knowledge base (Prasannan et al., 2020). Figure 5.2 explains the process of the rule-based chatbot, as it searches for particular keywords from the user's input, after which the keyword is matched with the appropriate intent, and then eventually, the response is executed based on the right intent.

5.1.1.2 Artificial Intelligence-Based Chatbot

AI chatbot, also known as machine learning chatbot, deals with more complex problems, which are not possibly solved with a rule-based chatbot. The most important components that compose a successful AI chatbot are the natural language processing (NLP) and machine learning (ML) (Khan & Rabbani, 2021; Bird et al., 2021; Satheesh et al., 2020; Ranavare & Kamath, 2020; Lalwani et al., 2018). The NLP enables the machine to understand and interpret the user's request either as it's spoken or written. Consequently, the users' interpretation can be boosted by using the

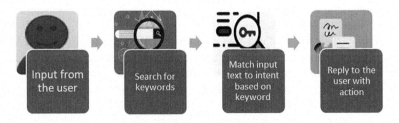

FIGURE 5.2 The process of rule-based dialogue system (chatbot).

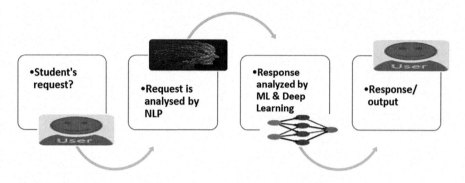

FIGURE 5.3   The process of AI-based dialogue system (chatbot).

machine learning algorithms as a chatbot can learn continuously as long as it is answering more questions from users. Interestingly, AI chatbots can generate a new dialogue to the user's question based on the training data by using the sequence to sequence (seq2seq) model and recurrent neural networks (RNN). Figure 5.3 depicts the processes of AI chatbots.

5.1.2   EDUCATIONAL ADVISING CHATBOT

Due to the growth of the state-of-the-art communication technologies in educational and learning institutions, prospective students, as well as current students in universities benefit immensely from using instant digital communication chats with others. For example, transitioning students from high schools to universities have a lot of challenges; students need to communicate instantly with college-career advisers, in order to have a proper guidance toward their major of choice and the right university. Similarly, current students at universities need advisers as well, to go through their degree for various tasks, such as motivation, counseling, registration, etc.

5.1.2.1   High School Chatbot Advising (Prospective Students)

Prospective students are pupils who are in the final stage of high school. These young students are interested in applying to universities to broaden their knowledge and shape their futures. Furthermore, according to Soppe et al. (2019), these students need to select their right majors and suitable universities because students who feel as if they don't fit their major or university are less likely to graduate on time. Therefore, students in high schools need to be advised and guided effectively before going through their final college-major choices. Despite the vital role of academic advisers in high schools, only a few researchers have studied and instigated dialogue systems and chatbots in this vital stage of education. Subsequently, most of what the authors have focused on studying are the impact of chatbots on students' admissions at colleges and universities. However, Assayed et al. (2023a) developed a machine learning chatbot called HSchatbot to assist students in some high schools to classify their enquiries based on types of their questions. Since most universities and colleges around the world receive thousands of applications yearly during a limited amount of time, which as a result, overwhelms admission officers with the many enquiries from students and parents, it's no doubt that having a suitable chatbot can handle those responses effectively and decrease the load on the staff. El Hefny et al. (2021) developed a chatbot called Jooka for supporting prospective students who are targeting the German University in Cairo (GUC). Moreover, Meshram et al. (2021) developed a chatbot called College Enquiry Chatbot that aims to answer any admission-related question such as admission requirements, documents required, college fees, courses that are offered, etc.; furthermore, the author highlighted the benefit that colleges get from students' enquiries as it can give them an indicator about the number of students that are interested to join the university locations on campus, as well as exposing them to the colleges and majors that are offered.

5.1.2.2   University Chatbot Advising (Matriculated Students)

Generally, universities refer the term matriculated to students who have officially enrolled and registered into a particular program or course (Drennan-Bonner, 2020; Prach, 2020). However, those students come to universities from different cultures and backgrounds, therefore having an instant adviser can play a vital role on their success (Sneyers & De Witte, 2018). Which is why advisers at universities can assist students in making the right decision in selecting the courses and monitoring the progress of students in order to ensure their success and graduation on time. Bilquise et al. (2022) developed a bilingual chatbot with two corpus files to store the English intents and the other to store the Arabic intents in order to support the current students in following the academic plan and consequently succeeding in the college. Another novel chatbot is developed by Le-Tien et al. (2022) for advising the matriculated students in Vietnamese universities to select the appropriate courses that match with their academic plan, and in due course, allowing students to conclude their major successfully.

5.2   CHALLENGES OF CHATBOT IN EDUCATIONAL ADVISING

According to the study that has been conducted by Miller et al. (2020), it is stated that communication and social skills are the most important characteristics in having an effective students' counselor or adviser. However, imitating human's personalities and behaviors remain the major challenges in developing the chatbot. Therefore, in this section, we will explain the biggest challenges of developing a chatbot for academic advising.

5.2.1   Interactive Student Experiences

The novelty of the advising chatbot should address the interaction with students as human-like, for instance, the chatbot can extract the emotions and the empathic feelings from the students' messages which can boost students' satisfaction in using it (Naous et al., 2020). Interestingly, Assayed et al. (2023b) developed a chatbot for recognizing students emotions during Covid-19, which can understand students

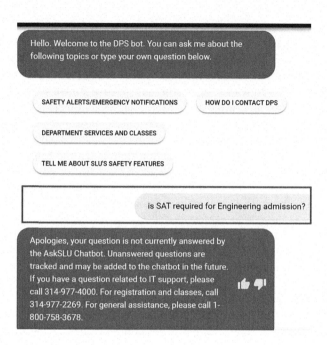

FIGURE 5.4 A rule-based chatbot from Saint Louis University response to student with unsatisfied answer.

expression by using different ML and NLP algorithms. Some chatbots in universities' websites use some particular keywords to find the student's answers and accordingly it will not be sufficient for students' satisfactions. These type of chatbots called a rule-based chatbot which programmed into predefines rules in order to be able to assist students for only particular topics. Figure 5.4 shows a rule-based chatbot called AskSLU from Saint Louis University, we tried to ask this question: Is SAT test required for engineering admission? The chatbot not be able to answer to the question successfully because it's not among the predefined rules in this chatbot and students cannot interact effectively with these type of chatbots. Accordingly, they will not be satisfied as they will lose the interest when there is no satisfied response. Moreover, a chatbot in Figure 5.5 called PantherBot from Chapman University shows a list of suggested answers with unempathetic response to student who is unable to afford the tuition and asking for financial aid.

5.2.2 OPEN SCOPE

Without a doubt, high school is one of the most crucial stages in students' lives, where in this stage, students begin the journey of shaping their futures. Ultimately, this leads to it being a stressful time for them, especially when they have concerns about applying to universities, application deadlines, admission tests, and selecting their majors. As a results, students are looking for precise and short answers from the

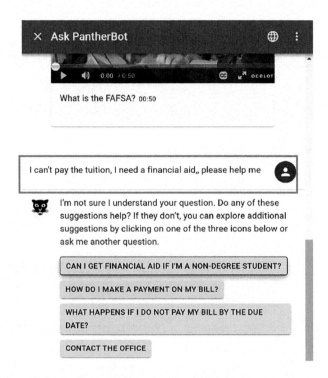

FIGURE 5.5 A chatbot called "PantherBot" from Chapman University response to student who is asking for a financial aid.

chatbot without any confusion as they would not be satisfied with open scope, unclear answers. Unfortunately, there are still some restrictions for using the open-domain chatbots. Skantz and Doğruöz (2023) evaluated the limitations of the open-domain chatbots compared to human-to-human dialogue by evaluating the interactions with the ChatGPT, in terms of serving as interactive search engine without engaging in small talk. Subsequently, they stated that training chatbots in open domain can cause a lack of coherent responses as the data is randomly connected without knowledge regarding the conversation or the people who it's supposed to be about. Therefore, users need to clarify details about their question in order to receive a clear answer. For example, Figure 5.6 shows an open reply from Durham University's chatbot as the parent asks about the requirements for applying to a computer engineering program for a student who graduated from a British curriculum high school; however, the response comes with four open different answers.

5.2.3 MULTIPLE LANGUAGE SUPPORT

Nowadays, a growing number of international schools and universities across the globe are inserting English medium instruction (EME) into learning and education, and it has become a global education phenomenon (Sánchez-García, 2020; Boruah

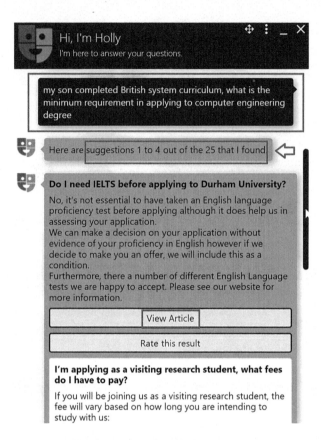

FIGURE 5.6   A chatbot from Durham University reply to parent who asks about the British HS curriculum requirement for applying to computer engineering.

& Mohanty, 2022). However, second language students might face challenges in communicating with teachers and peers (Aizawa & Rose, 2020). Therefore, students, as well as parents, need clear guidance and instructions by using multiple languages in order to help ensure the academic success of all students. In fact, most educational chatbots support English language enquires; however, some authors have been inspired to scope out bilingual advising chatbots that support the Arabic language (Bilquise et al., 2022, El Hefny et al., 2021). Nevertheless, different challenges of NLP in Arabic are highlighted from developers and researchers, where the ambiguity in the orthography, as well as, the dialectal variants pose the greatest challenges in Arabic NLP (Abdulkader et al., 2022; Almurayh, 2021; Abo et al., 2019)

5.3   CONCLUSION

Despite the fact that many researches have been done in educational chatbots and dialogue systems, but challenges in academic advising in particular are not elaborated and discussed enough. Prospective and matriculated students at universities need a clear advising to succeed in colleges and universities. Since the chatbots have varying level of complexities; several challenges are highlighted in this study, with considering the models and algorithms that are deployed into the chatbots. However, the lack of interactive students' experience is one of the most essential challenges for applying a chatbot in academic advising as it depends on how it allows students to communicate with chatbots as human-like. Students usually need short and clear answer without confusion; henceforth, it can lead us to the second challenge in having open-domain chatbot which can cause lack of coherent responses since the corpus are randomly collected without having knowledge about the conversation or the people who are supposed to be about. Finally, the second language students will be more satisfied in their experiences if they can be advised by using chatbot or a dialogue system with their own language.

REFERENCES

Abdulkader, Z. N., & Al-Irhayim, Y. F. M. (2022). A review of Arabic intelligent chatbots: Developments and challenges. *Al-Rafidain Engineering Journal (AREJ)*, *27*(2), 178–189.

Abo, M. E. M., Raj, R. G., & Qazi, A. (2019). A review on Arabic sentiment analysis: State-of-the-art, taxonomy and open research challenges. *IEEE Access*, *7*, 162008–162024.

Agarwal, R., & Wadhwa, M. (2020). Review of state-of-the-art design techniques for chatbots. *SN Computer Science*, *1*, 246 . https://doi.org/10.1007/s42979-020-00255-3

Aizawa, I., & Rose, H. (2020). High school to university transitional challenges in English Medium Instruction in Japan. *System*, *95*, 102390.

Almurayh, A. (2021). The challenges of using Arabic chatbot in Saudi Universities. *IAENG International Journal of Computer Science*, *48*(1), 190-201.

Assayed, S. K., Shaalan, K., & Alkhatib, M. (2023a). A chatbot intent classifier for supporting high school students. *EAI Endorsed Transactions on Scalable Information Systems*, *10*(3), 1-10.

Assayed, S., Shaalan, K., Al-Sayed, S., & Alkhatib, M. (2023b). Psychological emotion recognition of students using machine learning based chatbot. *International Journal of Artificial Intelligence and Applications (IJAIA)*, *14*(2), 29-39.

Bilquise, G., Ibrahim, S., & Shaalan, K. (2022). Bilingual AI-driven chatbot for academic advising. *International Journal of Advanced Computer Science and Applications*, *13*(8).50-57.

Bird, J. J., Ekárt, A., & Faria, D. R. (2021). Chatbot interaction with artificial intelligence: Human data augmentation with T5 and language transformer ensemble for text classification. *Journal of Ambient Intelligence and Humanized Computing*, *1*(1), 1–16.

Boruah, P., & Mohanty, A. (2022). English medium education in India: The neoliberal legacy and challenges to multilingual language policy implementation. In *Neoliberalization of English language policy in the Global South* (pp. 51–71). Cham: Springer International Publishing.

Drennan-Bonner, E. M. (2020). Increasing graduate yield with a transmedia campaign. (Master Thesis). Ball State University, Muncie, Indiana July 2020, (pp.1–40). .

El Hefny, W., Mansy, Y., Abdallah, M., & Abdennadher, S. (2021). Jooka: A bilingual chatbot for university admission. In Á. Rocha, H. Adeli, G. Dzemyda, F. Moreira, & A. M. Ramalho Correia (Eds.), *Trends and Applications in Information Systems and Technologies*. WorldCIST 2021. Advances in Intelligent Systems and Computing, vol 1367. Cham: Springer. https://doi.org/10.1007/978-3-030-72660-7_64

Haristiani, N. (2019, November). Artificial Intelligence (AI) chatbot as language learning medium: An inquiry. In *Journal of Physics: Conference Series* (Vol. 1387, No. 1, p. 012020). IOP Publishing.

Khan, S., & Rabbani, M. R. (2021). Artificial intelligence and NLP-based chatbot for islamic banking and finance. *International Journal of Information Retrieval Research (IJIRR)*, *11*(3), 65–77.

Lalwani, T., Bhalotia, S., Pal, A., Rathod, V., & Bisen, S. (2018). Implementation of a Chatbot System using AI and NLP. *International Journal of Innovative Research in Computer Science & Technology (IJIRCST)*, 6(3).

Le-Tien, T., Nguyen-DP, T., & Huynh-Y, V. (2022, January). Developing a Chatbot system using Deep Learning based for Universities consultancy. In *2022 16th International Conference on Ubiquitous Information Management and Communication (IMCOM)* (pp. 1–7). IEEE.

Meshram, S., Naik, N., Megha, V. R., More, T., & Kharche, S. (2021, August). College enquiry chatbot using rasa framework. In *2021 Asian Conference on Innovation in Technology (ASIANCON)* (pp. 1–8). IEEE.

Miller, S. M., Larwin, K. H., Kautzman-East, M., Williams, J. L., Evans, W. J., Williams, D. D., ... Miller, K. L. (2020). A proposed definition and structure of counselor dispositions. *Measurement and Evaluation in Counseling and Development*, *53*(2), 117–130.

Naous, T., Hokayem, C., & Hajj, H. (2020, December). Empathy-driven Arabic conversational chatbot. In *Proceedings of the Fifth Arabic Natural Language Processing Workshop* (pp. 58–68).

Prach, J. I. (2020). *College choice, consumer behavior, and gender enrollment patterns: A mixed methods case study of Marathon University*. Rowan University.

Prasannan, P., Joseph, S., & Rajeev, R. R. (2020, December). A chatbot in Malayalam using hybrid approach. In *Proceedings of the 17th International Conference on Natural Language Processing (ICON): System Demonstrations* (pp. 28–29).

Ranavare, S. S., & Kamath, R. S. (2020). Artificial intelligence based chatbot for placement activity at college using dialogflow. *Our Heritage*, *68*(30), 4806–4814.

Sánchez-García, D. (2020). Internationalization through language and literacy in the Spanish-and English-Medium education context. *Integrating Content and Language in Multilingual Universities*, 131–150.

Satheesh, M. K., Samala, N., & Rodriguez, R. V. (2020). Role of Ai-induced chatbot in enhancing customer relationship management in the banking industry. *ICTACT Journal on Management Studies*, 6(4), 1320–1323.

Skantze, G., & Doğruöz, A. S. (2023). The open-domain paradox for chatbots: Common ground as the basis for human-like dialogue. *arXiv preprint arXiv:2303.11708*.

Sneyers, E., & De Witte, K. (2018). Interventions in higher education and their effect on student success: A meta-analysis. *Educational Review*, *70*(2), 208–228.

Soppe, K. F. B., Wubbels, T., Leplaa, H. J., Klugkist, I., & Wijngaards-de Meij, L. D. N. V. (2019). Do they match? Prospective students' experiences with choosing university programmes. *European Journal of Higher Education*, *9*(4), 359–376.

Sun, L., Liu, Y., Joseph, G., Yu, Z., Zhu, H., & Dow, S. P. (2022, October). Comparing experts and novices for AI data work: Insights on allocating human intelligence to design a conversational agent. In *Proceedings of the AAAI Conference on Human Computation and Crowdsourcing* (Vol. 10, No. 1, pp. 195–206).

Thorat, S. A., & Jadhav, V. (2020, April). A review on implementation issues of rule-based chatbot systems. In *Proceedings of the international conference on innovative computing & communications (ICICC)*.

Vishwakarma, A., & Pandey, A. (2021). A review & Comparative analysis on various chatbots design. *International Journal of Computer Science and Mobile Computing*, *10*(2), 72–78.

6 Impact of AI-Based Chatbots on Faculty Performance in Higher Education Institutions

Shitika, Sushma Sharma and Monika Agarwal

6.1 INTRODUCTION

The success of an organization is significantly influenced by performance. This would be understood in terms of how well faculty perform in terms of their capacity to engage students in learning. Faculty performance can be influenced by various elements, including their level of experience, teaching strategies, classroom management abilities, and student engagement abilities. The usage of technology is one important issue, nevertheless, that can have an impact on teacher performance. The subject of education has undergone a recent transformation, and technology can greatly improve faculty effectiveness (Wang et al., 2018). For instance, technology can be utilized to make learning more dynamic and interesting, to make administrative duties more efficient, and to give students individualized feedback and support.

Using chatbots is one way that technology can be used to boost faculty performance. Chatbots are computer programs that can mimic human communication and can be used to give pupils immediate feedback and support. By lightening teachers' and educators' workloads, chatbots can aid in enhancing faculty performance. The importance of technology, particularly chatbots, in raising teacher performance is growing in the current digital era. Faculty can improve their performance and contribute to improving student outcomes by using technology to provide more personalized and engaging learning experience.

To analyze the variables affecting faculty members' acceptance and usage of this technology, researchers employed the unified theory of acceptance and use of technology (UTAUT) model developed by Venkatesh et al. in 2003. The four constructs in the UTAUT models are (i) performance expectancy, (ii) effort expectancy, (iii) social influence, and (iv) facilitating conditions.

Figure 6.1 shows the impact of AI chatbots on faculty performance with the help of the UTAUT model. Further, it explained that performance expectations, effort

DOI: 10.1201/9781003425809-6

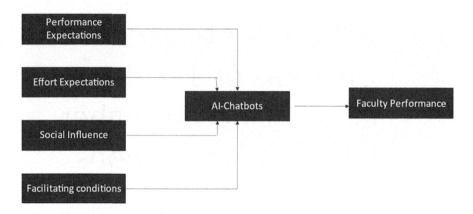

FIGURE 6.1   Conceptual framework

expectations, social influence, and facilitating conditions affect AI chatbots adoption and faculty performance in using information technology.

Researchers can first measure faculty members' expectations regarding how the technology will affect their performance in terms of performance expectancy. Surveys or interviews with faculty members can be used to gather information about their expectations for how the AI chatbot will improve their performance in research, teaching, or other professional endeavors(Jaradat and Banikhaled, 2013). Second, researchers might evaluate how faculty members expect the technology to be used (effort expectancy). Usability tests or surveys that evaluate how simple it is to use the AI chatbot can be used to do this (Salim, 2012). Third, researchers can examine how faculty members view the social influences (or norms) that surround the usage of technology. This can be accomplished by asking faculty members in surveys or interviews about their perspectives of what is expected of them by their peers, administrators, or other pertinent stakeholders regarding the employment of AI chatbots in academia (Kim and Lee, 2020). Fourth, researchers might evaluate the degree to which professors have access to the tools and assistance they need to apply the technology (facilitating conditions). This can be accomplished by asking faculty members about their opinions of the accessibility of instruction, technical assistance, or other resources required to operate the AI-chat (Ugur and Turan, 2018). By analyzing these factors, the UTAUT model can shed light by looking at how faculty members adopt and use of AI chatbots, as well as how these technologies affect their performance.

i)   The primary objective of this study is to know the enablers of AI chatbots on faculty performance by using the UTAUT model.

ii) The subsequent objective is to classify the variables into driving factors, linkage variables, and dependent variables. To better understand the various effects of the variables that improve faculty performance while utilizing AI chatbots in higher education institutions (HEIs), it is important to investigate and establish the contextual links among the variables.

This study specifically focuses on exploring the components and their contextual interactions of faculty performance as an integrated method because no prior research has identified and examined the elements influencing AI chatbots in an integrated manner. The remainder of the essay is structured as follows: The framework of the research methodology used in this study is presented in Section 2. Section 3 presents the interpretative structural modeling (ISM), and Cross Impact matrix multiplication applied to classification (MICMAC) analysis was applied to carry out established the relationship between faculty performance and AI chatbots. Section 4 discusses the major findings, while Section 5 concludes by outlining the research's implications, constraints, and potential future directions.

6.2 RESEARCH METHODOLOGY

ISM is a system that uses computers to establish and comprehend the basic connections between variables. It is based on graph theory and discrete mathematics. It aids in the creation of models that employ a relationship matrix to depict the relationship between several variables pointed at a common occurrence. Since the research aims to examine the elements and classify them into highly ordered lower-order variables in terms of drivers and dependence power, ISM is employed in this study. The directed graph can be used to determine the explain ability of such an objective. With brainstorming tools, several variables are identified. Thirteen variables were identified based on literature in Table 6.1, which can help to explore the relationship between AI chatbots and faculty performance. The relationship between these variables and the degree of complexity of these relationships was understood using ISM.

TABLE 6.1
Variables Identification

Variables	Abbreviation
Working from home	WH
Hedonic motivation	HM
Gender	G
Staff credentials	SC
Age	A
Knowledge of the subject matter	KSM
Teaching learning process	TLP
Extension activities	EA
Research contribution	RC
Performance expectancy	PE
Effort expectancy	EE
Facilitating conditions	FC
Social influence	SI

6.3   VARIABLES IDENTIFICATION

The success of an organization is significantly influenced by performance. HEIs are currently implementing a digital strategy. We might not have predicted its velocity over the last ten years, though. Chatbots are being employed more frequently at HEIs in the age of artificial intelligence to advance education by offering timely and individualized services to students and instructors, which can enhance faculty effectiveness and overall student success. Nassuora (2012) stated that leading universities and colleges have recently started implementing AI-based chatbots on their college search websites. This study investigates how faculty adopt technology and use chatbots to improve teaching and learning. The theory used for this study is reviewed in this section along with other hypotheses on technology acceptance. The UTAUT paradigm based on technology adoption has been suggested for the study to make it effective. Venkatesh et al. (2003) presented the UTAUT, an integrated theory of technology acceptance. According to Venkatesh et al. (2003), the model only fully accounts for around 50% of the variance in actual use and only about 70% of the variance in behavioral intention to use (Venkatesh et al., 2012). However, according to Dwivedi et al. (2019), the UTAUT model left out certain connections that might be important, hypothesized some connections that might not apply in all circumstances, and eliminated some components that might be essential for describing why information systems are accepted and used.

According to the UTAUT model, faculty members' behavioral intentions to use AI chatbots are closely related to their performance expectations, effort expectations, and social factors. Facilitating factors like availability of technology and technical help may have an impact on how faculty members employ AI chatbots. Faculty performance when employing AI chatbots can be impacted by variables including gender, age, and hedonic motivation. The UTAUT model's elements as well as additional potential usage and performance drivers, according to experts, should be taken into account while assessing the influence of AI chatbots on faculty performance. Overall, using AI chatbots has the potential to improve faculty productivity and performance, but it's crucial to carefully consider the effects of these tools and the variables that affect their performance. The following factors were identified as a measure driver of AI chatbots and faculty performance.

6.3.1   EMPLOYEE ATTITUDE

Using the UTAUT paradigm, several academics have investigated the connection between teacher performance and employee attitudes in the setting of AI chatbots. An application of the UTAUT model," and they discovered that performance expectancy and social influence were significant predictors of faculty attitudes toward chatbot technology.

6.3.2   HEDONIC MOTIVATION

Al-Emran et al. (2018) conducted a study on hedonic motivation and found to be a significant predictor of user acceptability in a study on the acceptance of AI chatbots in higher education. Overall, the research points to hedonic drive as a significant element in people's willingness to adopt and use technology, especially AI chatbots in higher education. Understanding the numerous aspects that affect user acceptance and adoption of technology can be facilitated by using the UTAUT model.

6.3.3 AGE

Yang et al. (2020) investigated the usage of AI chatbots in Chinese university libraries. They discovered that the intention to employ an AI chatbot was inversely correlated with age. However, they also discovered that perceptions of the AI chatbot's usability and convenience of use were more important predictors of the desire to utilize it than age.

6.3.4 GENDER

The gender element of faculty performance in the context AI chatbot is to look over the body of knowledge already written on the subject and pinpoint any research gaps. For instance, Zhang et al. (2019) discovered that while male faculty members tend to have higher performance expectations, female faculty members tend to perceive greater effort expectations when utilize chatbots. This shows that there might be disparities between genders in how useful and user-friendly AI chatbots are perceived.

6.3.5 STAFF CREDENTIALS

The gender element of faculty performance in the context AI chatbot is to look over the body of knowledge already written on the subject and pinpoint any research gaps. For instance, Zhang et al. (2019) discovered that while male faculty members tend to have higher performance expectations, female faculty members tend to perceive greater effort expectations when utilize chatbots. This shows that there might be disparities between genders in how useful and user-friendly AI chatbots are perceived.

6.3.6 KNOWLEDGE OF SUBJECT MATTER

The usage of AI chatbots in education and their effect on instructor performance have been studied by a few studies. For instance, Winkler and Sollner (2018) evaluated the effect of AI chatbots on teacher performance and showed that they can increase teacher performance by reducing the workload and boosting efficiency. Their study was published in Computers in Human Behavior.

6.3.7 TEACHING AND LEARNING PROCESS

Vafadar et al. (2021) looked at how AI chatbots affected student engagement and satisfaction. They discovered that the employment of chatbots boosted communication and collaboration between students and faculty members and had a favorable impact on student happiness and engagement.

6.3.8 EXTENSION ACTIVITIES

Several scholars have looked into the function of faculty performance and its factors in the context of extension activities. For instance, Li et al. (2005) looked into the effects of training, incentives, and social support on the effectiveness of extension agents in their study. They discovered that all three elements had a profound impact on their performance.

6.3.9 RESEARCH CONTRIBUTION

Koivisto (2023) looked into the variables that affect the acceptability and application of chatbots in customer support. According to their research, user attitudes and intentions toward using chatbots were highly influenced by performance expectancy, effort expectancy, and facilitating factors but not by social influence.

6.3.10 PERFORMANCE EXPECTANCY

Alam et al. (2021) are researchers who have contributed to the literature on AI chatbots and the UTAUT paradigm. Their study looked into the variables affecting the use of AI chatbots in higher education. They discovered that one of the most important elements influencing faculty members' adoption of AI chatbots was performance expectancy.

6.3.11 EFFORT EXPECTANCY

According to Amhag et al. (2021), faculty members' performance in terms of their willingness to use the technology was significantly impacted by how simple they believed AI chatbots to be to operate.

6.3.12 FACILITATING CONDITIONS

Chen and Chen (2020) investigated how enabling circumstances affected faculty members' acceptance of AI chatbots. The study emphasized the need of giving academic staff members technical assistance, education, and tools to help them better comprehend and utilize AI chatbots in their teaching.

6.3.13 SOCIAL INFLUENCE

Zhang et al. (2021) looked at how social influence affected faculty members' attitudes toward AI chatbots. The findings demonstrated that social influence has a substantial impact on faculty members' intentions to employ AI chatbots. The study sheds light on how important social impact is to faculty members' adoption of cutting-edge technologies like AI chatbots.

Overall, the researcher concluded that the performance of academics could be improved by using AI chatbots. The usefulness of AI chatbots in improving faculty performance depends on a variety of factors, including employee attitude, subject-matter expertise, teaching and learning processes, research contributions, and extension activities. This relationship may also be influenced by factors such as gender, age, staff qualifications, hedonic motivation, performance expectancy, effort expectancy, facilitating conditions, and social influence. Institutions can successfully adopt AI chatbots to increase teacher effectiveness, which will ultimately improve student results.

6.4 INTERPRETIVE STRUCTURAL MODELING (ISM) METHOD

ISM can be used to organize the complexity of these variables (Mandal and Deshmukh, 1994;). The fundamental concept behind ISM is to break down a complex issue into smaller, more manageable components using the expertise and real-world experience of expert participants. A multilevel structural model and several subsystems are built to accomplish this. The following steps are followed to identify the mutual interrelationship among the variables of performance and AI enablers:

Step 1: List the factors taken into consideration for the system under investigation. The systematic literature review approach was used to establish the obstacles to Green Lean implementation, which have been regarded as variables in the current work.

Step 2: Establishing a contextual relationship between the variables that have been identified.

Step 3: The creation of the structural self-interaction matrix (SSIM), which identifies pairwise interactions between variables, is the third step.

Step 4: Create a reachability matrix using the SSIM and test it for transitivity. According to the transitivity rule, if variable A is related to both variable B and variable C, then variable A must also be related to variable C.

Step 5: After using the transitivity rule, create the final reachability matrix. The reachability matrix obtained in Step 5 is divided into several levels then.

Step 6: Based on the final reachability matrix, create a directed graph and cut the transitivity linkages.

Step 7:The ISM-based model is created by swapping out variable nodes for statements.

Step 8: The ISM model created in Step 8 is checked for theoretical irregularities, and any adjustments are made as needed.

6.4.1 QUESTIONNAIRE DEVELOPMENT

Sixteen experts from various HEIs were contacted via email and in-person visits to further investigate the enablers of faculty performance in the context of artificial intelligence-based chatbots. They have been explained the AI chatbot method and its use for faculty and the study's goals during this initial encounter. Seven of the chosen experts agreed to participate in the study following several communications. A decision team of 7 people was established as a result to further investigate the links between AI-based bot adoption and faculty performance. All the participating experts had already implemented AI-based chatbots in their respective institutions or were in the process of doing so. Additionally, each of these specialists has more than 5 years of experience in the field of HEIs. Convincing these highly qualified individuals to engage in this study was one of the main challenges encountered in this investigation.

6.4.2 ESTABLISHING CONTEXTUAL RELATIONSHIP

To find the contextual links among the previously indicated variables, the ISM technique is based on the opinions of experts. Therefore, three expert meetings were scheduled as part of this research to establish this contextual relationship.

On a scale of low–moderate–high, the experts were asked to rate the significance and applicability of the 13 variables discovered by the SLR during the first meeting. The outcomes of this activity are shown in Table 6.1. The decision team's final meeting focused on analyzing and discussing the relationships in greater detail to establish the contextual links of the "leads to" type. This implied that one variable helps in achieving another variable. A contextual link between the variables of performance and chatbot adoption for performance was constructed based on this theory (Kumar et al., 2016) in Table 6.2.

6.4.3 SSIM DEVELOPMENT

After the "leads to" type contextual links had been constructed, the ISM method's next step involved creating an SSIM to represent the pairwise associations between

---

TABLE 6.2

Importance of Variables of Performance and Chatbot Adoption for Performance

S.no.	Variables	Importance
1	Employee attitude	High
2	Hedonic motivation	High
3	Age	High
4	Gender	High
5	Staff credentials	Moderate
6	Knowledge of the subject matter	Moderate
7	Teaching and learning process	High
8	Extension activities	Moderate
9	Research contribution	High
10	Performance expectancy	High
11	Effort expectancy	High
12	Facilitating conditions	High
13	Social influence	High

variables (i.e., barriers). Four symbols were employed to indicate the direction of these relationships, as follows:

V: variable I influences variable j;
A: variable j influences variable I;
X: variable i and Variable j influence each other; and
O: variable i and Variable j are unrelated.

The SSIM for these variables has been represented in Table 6.3 as follows:

6.4.4 FORMATION OF INITIAL REACHABILITY MATRIX

In this phase, V, A, X, and O are changed to 1 and 0 as appropriate for the particular scenario, converting the SSIM into a binary matrix known as the "initial reachability matrix." The following guidelines were followed throughout this conversion.

i. If the (i, j) entry in the SSIM was V, the (i, j) entry in the reachability matrix would be 1 and the (j, i) entry would be 0;

ii. If the (i, j) entry in the SSIM was A, the (i, j) entry would be 0 and the (j, i) entry would be 1;

TABLE 6.3
SSIM for Variables of Performance and Chatbot Adoption for Performance

Performance Indicators with AI (UTUAT Model)		13	12	11	10	9	8	7	6	5	4	3	2
1	Employee attitude	X	A	V	V	A	A	X	O	O	A	A	V
2	Hedonic motivation	V	A	X	X	V	X	X	A	O	O	O	
3	Gender	V	O	V	V	O	O	V	O	O	X		
4	Age	V	O	V	V	V	O	V	V	O			
5	Staff credentials	V	V	O	X	X	V	V	V				
6	Knowledge of the subject matter	X	O	O	V	X	A	X					
7	Teaching learning process	V	X	X	V	A	A						
8	Extension activities	X	A	A	V	X							
9	Research contribution	X	X	V	V								
10	Performance expectancy	O	A	X									
11	Effort expectancy	A	O										
12	Facilitating conditions	X											

iii. If the (i, j) value in the SSIM was X, the (i, j) entry would be 1 and the (j, i) entry would be 1;

iv. If the (i, j) value in the SSIM was O, the (i, j) entry would be 0 and the (j, i) entry would be 0.

Following these guidelines, Table 6.4 displays the initial reachability matrix.

6.4.5 FORMATION OF FINAL REACHABILITY MATRIX

The final reachability matrix for the ISM approach is created by applying the transitivity rule after the first reachability matrix has been created (In this instance, the transitivity rule was used to convert the initial reachability into the final reachability matrix for the variables of faculty performance and chatbot adoption, as shown in Table 6.5. This was done by Kannan et al. (2008).

6.4.6 LEVEL PARTITIONS

The reachability set and antecedent set for each Variable were identified from the final reachability matrix, as shown in Table 6.6 The variable itself and other variables that could aid in performance variables made up the antecedent set in a similar way. The top-level variables in the ISM hierarchy are the ones for which reachability and intersection sets are equal. The levels of each variable were reached by repeating this iteration. These levels contributed to the creation of the final interpretative structural model and the digraph.

6.4.7 FORMATION OF DIAGRAPH: AN ISM-BASED MODEL

Figure 6.2 displays the structural model that was produced from the final reachability matrix. An arrow pointing from variable I to variable j indicated the presence of a relationship between the two influencers. "Directed graph" or "diagraph" is the name given to the generated graph. The diagraph was ultimately transformed into the ISM model after the transitivity's were removed by the ISM technique.

6.4.8 MICMAC ANALYSIS

Investigating the influence and reliance of variables is the goal of the MICMAC analysis The driving and dependence powers of the investigated variables were used as the basis for this research.

Driving power is estimated by adding the entries of the interactions' potential in the rows, and dependence is computed by adding the entries of the interactions' potential in the columns, according to Kumar et al. (2016). Each variable's driving force is the variable that influences the other variables, and each variable's dependence power is the variable that is affected by the other variables. Figure 6.3 displays the driver power and dependence power of various barriers for additional MICMAC

TABLE 6.4

Initial Reachability Matrix

Variables	1	2	3	4	5	6	7	8	9	10	11	12	13	Driving Power
Employee attitude	1	1	0	0	0	0	1	0	0	1	1	0	1	6
Hedonic motivation	0	1	0	0	0	0	1	1	1	1	1	0	1	7
Gender	1	0	1	1	0	0	1	0	0	1	1	0	1	7
Age	1	0	1	1	0	1	1	0	1	1	1	0	1	9
Staff credentials	0	0	0	0	1	1	1	1	1	1	0	1	1	8
Knowledge of the subject matter	0	1	0	0	0	1	1	0	1	1	0	0	1	6
Teaching learning process	1	1	0	0	0	1	1	0	0	1	1	1	1	8
Extension activities	1	1	0	0	0	1	1	1	1	1	0	0	1	8
Research contribution	1	0	0	0	1	1	1	1	1	1	1	1	1	10
Performance expectancy	0	1	0	0	1	0	0	0	0	1	1	0	0	4
Effort expectancy	0	1	0	0	0	0	1	1	0	1	1	0	0	5
Facilitating conditions	1	1	0	0	0	0	1	1	1	1	0	1	1	8
Social influence	1	0	0	0	0	1	0	1	1	0	1	1	1	7
Dependence power	8	8	2	2	3	7	11	7	8	12	9	5	11	

TABLE 6.5
Final Reachability Matrix

Variables	1	2	3	4	5	6	7	8	9	10	11	12	13
Employee attitude	1	1	0	0	1*	1*	1	1*	1*	1	1	1*	1
Hedonic motivation	1*	1	0	0	1*	1*	1	1	1	1	1	1*	1
Gender	1	1*	1	1	1*	1*	1	1*	1*	1	1	1*	1
Age	1	1*	1	1	1*	1	1	1*	1	1	1	1*	1
Staff credentials	1*	1*	0	0	1	1	1	1	1	1	1*	1	1
Knowledge of the subject matter	1*	1	0	0	1*	1	1	1*	1	1	1*	1*	1
Teaching learning process	1	1	0	0	1*	1	1	1*	1*	1	1	1	1
Extension activities	1	1	0	0	1*	1	1	1	1	1	1*	1*	1
Research contribution	1	1*	0	0	1	1	1	1	1	1	1	1	1
Performance expectancy	1*	1	0	0	1	1*	1*	1*	1*	1	1	1*	1*
Effort expectancy	1*	1	0	0	1*	1*	1	1	1*	1	1	1*	1*
Facilitating conditions	1	1	0	0	1*	1*	1	1	1	1	1*	1	1
Social influence	1	1*	0	0	1*	1	1*	1	1	1*	1	1	1

usage. According to the driving power and dependence power of the variables, they have been classified into four different categories: Figure 6.3

   i. Autonomous variables: These are the variables with weak driving power and weak dependence power. These are represented in cluster I.
   ii. Dependent variables: These variables have weak driver potential but strong dependence power. These are classified in cluster II.
  iii. Linkage variables: These variables had both a powerful driving force and a powerful reliance. Cluster III contained a representation of these barriers.
  iv. Independent variables: Although these variables had a considerable driving force, their reliance power was limited. Cluster IV had a representation of these barriers.

6.5   DISCUSSION

Artificial intelligence has received an increasing interest in research as well as academics. Faculty members are the building blocks of institutions and universities.

TABLE 6.6

Level Partitioning

Elements (Mi)	Reachability Set R (Mi)	Antecedent Set A (Ni)	Intersection Set R (Mi)∩A (Ni)	Level
1	1, 2, 5, 6, 7, 8, 9, 10, 11, 12, 13,	1, 2, 3, 4, 5, 6, 7, 8, 9, 10, 11, 12, 13,	1, 2, 5, 6, 7, 8, 9, 10, 11, 12, 13,	2
2	1, 2, 5, 6, 7, 8, 9, 10, 11, 12, 13,	1, 2, 3, 4, 5, 6, 7, 8, 9, 10, 11, 12, 13,	1, 2, 5, 6, 7, 8, 9, 10, 11, 12, 13,	1
3	3, 4,	3, 4,	3, 4,	3
4	3, 4,	3, 4,	3, 4,	3
5	1, 2, 5, 6, 7, 8, 9, 10, 11, 12, 13,	1, 2, 3, 4, 5, 6, 7, 8, 9, 10, 11, 12, 13,	1, 2, 5, 6, 7, 8, 9, 10, 11, 12, 13,	1
6	1, 2, 5, 6, 7, 8, 9, 10, 11, 12, 13,	1, 2, 3, 4, 5, 6, 7, 8, 9, 10, 11, 12, 13,	1, 2, 5, 6, 7, 8, 9, 10, 11, 12, 13,	1
7	1, 2, 5, 6, 7, 8, 9, 10, 11, 12, 13,	1, 2, 3, 4, 5, 6, 7, 8, 9, 10, 11, 12, 13,	1, 2, 5, 6, 7, 8, 9, 10, 11, 12, 13,	1
8	1, 2, 5, 6, 7, 8, 9, 10, 11, 12, 13,	1, 2, 3, 4, 5, 6, 7, 8, 9, 10, 11, 12, 13,	1, 2, 5, 6, 7, 8, 9, 10, 11, 12, 13,	1
9	1, 2, 5, 6, 7, 8, 9, 10, 11, 12, 13,	1, 2, 3, 4, 5, 6, 7, 8, 9, 10, 11, 12, 13,	1, 2, 5, 6, 7, 8, 9, 10, 11, 12, 13,	1
10	1, 2, 5, 6, 7, 8, 9, 10, 11, 12, 13,	1, 2, 3, 4, 5, 6, 7, 8, 9, 10, 11, 12, 13,	1, 2, 5, 6, 7, 8, 9, 10, 11, 12, 13,	1
11	1, 2, 5, 6, 7, 8, 9, 10, 11, 12, 13,	1, 2, 3, 4, 5, 6, 7, 8, 9, 10, 11, 12, 13,	1, 2, 5, 6, 7, 8, 9, 10, 11, 12, 13,	2
12	1, 2, 5, 6, 7, 8, 9, 10, 11, 12, 13,	1, 2, 3, 4, 5, 6, 7, 8, 9, 10, 11, 12, 13,	1, 2, 5, 6, 7, 8, 9, 10, 11, 12, 13,	2
13	1, 2, 5, 6, 7, 8, 9, 10, 11, 12, 13,	1, 2, 3, 4, 5, 6, 7, 8, 9, 10, 11, 12, 13,	1, 2, 5, 6, 7, 8, 9, 10, 11, 12, 13,	1

Stakeholders are aware that faculty performance plays a crucial role in the process of knowledge creation. As an important intellectual capital, the adoption and usage of recent technological mechanisms become imperative for faculty members. The introduction of chatbots is one among these. These chatbots can help improve the efficiency of the teachers assisting them in the teaching–learning process, gaining knowledge, creating knowledge and a lot more. These chatbots can help in faster knowledge creation, knowledge dissemination, and enhancing extension activities for collaborations. It not only helps faculty members at the individual level but also will help the institutions to build their brands and gain recognition around the world. The integration of factors used to measure faculty performance and factors influencing the adoption of chatbots using the UTUAT model is not an easy task as many impending barriers may arise. However, identifying their contextual relationship can further help initiate and implement this model for better performance management. Through a thorough assessment of the academic literature, key variables to the

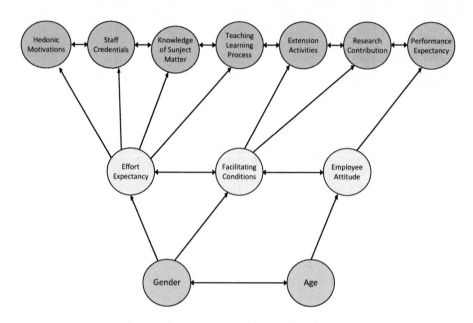

FIGURE 6.2   Diagraph representation of variables

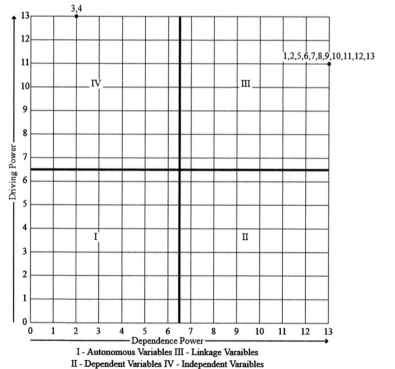

FIGURE 6.3   MICMAC analysis

adoption of AI chatbots for better performance were identified in the current study. These variables were further examined through discussions with professionals from academia as well as through an ISM analysis to look into how they interacted. As a first step to achieving their efficiency so that the implementation of chatbots to enhance the performance of faculty becomes a simpler practice, this study sought to learn about the variables that may enhance performance. Below is a discussion of some of the study's key findings.

Gender and age are the key independent variables. These demographic variables are included in the study purposively. Demographic variables play an important role when it comes to the adoption of technological changes. Introducing chatbots to enhance performance may reflect a significant impact based on these two important demographic variables. The pace of technological adoption varies for men and women; also, the same distinction can be made in terms of age groups (Oseni et al., 2015). It has been reported that despite proper training, employee attitude toward the adoption of such mechanisms varies across demographics. This has also been well represented by the diagraph and MICMAC analysis. In addition, the variables such as employee attitude, effort expectancy and facilitating conditions to adopt technology have high driving and dependence power. These variables have a greater impact on faculty performance. These variables act as linkage variables as shown in the diagraph. These can help boost faculty performance. The use of chatbots can help in improving facilitating conditions which thereby leads to better research contribution and participation in extension activities for community building. Similarly, introducing chatbots may increase effort expectancy in terms of result delivery which further helps in enhancing knowledge of the content. It can also make the teaching–learning process interactive and innovative. The variables such as "hedonic motivation," "performance expectancy," and "staff credentials" are at the topmost level of the diagraph. These variables are major contributors to the faculty performance yardstick. The success of faculty members is demonstrated by the effects of these parameters.

The outcome of the MICMAC study revealed that no autonomous variables exist. The lack of these variables in the current study demonstrates the significance of each one of the variables that were found. Therefore, the presence of any of them in this study's outlined variables may serve as a substantial variable in the implementation of chatbots for performance management and measurement.

The study's findings imply that some of the significant variables to measure the impact of AI chatbots on faculty performance are connected to the human category. This category comprises "motivation," "staff credentials," and "performance expectancy." Building a conducive environment that aids institutions in implementing and measuring the impact of AI-based chatbots requires trained human capital as a vital component. Additionally, studies have shown that the absence of human resources from inclusion in performance management and measurement can limit the chances of achieving more durable advantages.

Other important variables that must be included are technical, behavioral, and management variables, such as "employee attitude," "effort expectancy," and "gender." Several issues can also arise from "a lack of hedonic motivation," "lack of knowledge on the subject," and "performance expectancy."

To conclude, the present research focuses on identifying the variables which reflect the impact of AI-based chatbots on faculty performance. The inclusion of adoption variables derived from the UTUAT model of technology adoption and linking them to performance variables is the crucial aim of this study. Establishing contextual relationships among these sets of variables may help the investigators to improve performance assessment in their respective institutions.

6.6   CONCLUSION AND FUTURE RECOMMENDATIONS

To better understand the various implications of these factors on the implementation of this approach, this study explores the variables that boost the successful integration and implementation of chatbots for faculty performance measurement and establishes their contextual relationship. To achieve this, the first methodological step was to establish the variables that can help institutions effectively implement chatbots to enhance faculty performance. To do this, a thorough study of the academic literature was carried out. The ISM approach was used to study the thirteen variables after they had been discovered using this method to ascertain their contextual links and create a hierarchical structural model. Through a MICMAC analysis, the variables were divided into linkage and dependent obstacles. Consequently, two variables were assessed to be "independent" variables, eleven variables were classed as "linkage" barriers, and no variables were identified as "autonomous."

Therefore, this study enhances our knowledge by defining variables that will play a vital role in the implementation of chatbots for enhancing performance. It provides detailed knowledge by establishing a contextual relationship between variables of two different domains i.e., performance variables and variables of technology adoption based on the UTUAT model.

Overall, the study offers some insight into the application of chatbots for performance measurement and management, hence supporting its use. For this reason, it gives academicians reliable proof of the obstacles that can help the adoption of this strategy. Therefore, the future research goal arising from this research includes statistically verifying the ISM model suggested and empirically validating the variables found. The proposed ISM-based model offers a realistic depiction of the issue over the course of implementing chatbots for faculty performance enhancement.

However, statistical validation of this model is necessary. It is advised that this research be carried out using structural equation modeling (SEM) to validate this model. In the academic literature, the usage of SEM in the field of lean is widely established (Belekoukias et al., 2014).

REFERENCES

Alam, Mirza Mohammad Didarul, Mohammad Zahedul Alam, Syed Abidur Rahman, and Seyedeh Khadijeh Taghizadeh. "Factors influencing mHealth adoption and its impact on mental well-being during COVID-19 pandemic: A SEM-ANN approach." *Journal of Biomedical Informatics* 116 (2021): 103722, https://doi.org/10.1016/j.jbi.2021.103722

Al-Emran, Mostafa, Vitaliy Mezhuyev, and Adzhar Kamaludin. "Technology acceptance model in M-learning context: A systematic review." *Computers & Education* 125 (2018): 389–412, https://doi.org/10.1016/j.compedu.2018.06.008

Alshehri, S., R. Alghamdi, and A. Alqahtani. "Chatbots in education: A review of recent studies." *International Journal of Emerging Technologies in Learning (IJET)* 16, no. 10 (2021): 4–20.

Belekoukias, Ioannis, Jose Arturo Garza-Reyes, and Vikas Kumar. "The impact of lean methods and tools on the operational performance of manufacturing organisations." *International Journal of Production Research* 52, no. 18 (2014): 5346–5366, https://doi .org/10.1080/00207543.2014.903348

Chen, Lijia, Pingping Chen, and Zhijian Lin. "Artificial intelligence in education: A review." *IEEE Access* 8 (2020): 75264–75278, https://doi.org/10.1109/ACCESS.2020. 2988510

Dwivedi, Yogesh K., Nripendra P. Rana, Anand Jeyaraj, Marc Clement, and Michael D. Williams. "Re-examining the Unified Theory of Acceptance and Use of Technology (UTAUT): Towards a revised theoretical model." *Information Systems Frontiers* 21 (2019): 719–734, https://doi.org/10.1007/s10796-017-9774-y

Jaradat, Mohammed-Issa Riad Mousa, and Marie Banikhaled. "Undergraduate students' adoption of website-service quality by applying the Unified Theory of Acceptance and Use of Technology (UTAUT) in Jordan." *International Journal of Interactive Mobile Technologies* 7, no. 3 (2013): 22–29, http://dx.doi.org/10.3991/ijim.v7i3.2482

Kumar, S., S. Luthra, and A. Haleem. "Critical success factors of customer involvement in greening the supply chain: An empirical study." *International Journal of Logistics Systems and Management* 19, no. 3 (2016): 283–310, https://link.springer.com/10.1007 /978-3-031-21569-8_18

Kim, J., and K. S. S. Lee. "Conceptual model to predict Filipino teachers' adoption of ICT-based instruction in class: Using the UTAUT model." *Asia Pacific Journal of Education* (2020): 1–15.

Li, S., S. S. Rao, T. S. Ragu-Nathan, and B. Ragu-Nathan. "Development and validation of a measurement instrument for studying supply chain management practices." *Journal of Operations Management* 23, no. 6 (2005): 618–641, https://doi.org/10.1016/j.jom.2005 .01.002

Mandal, A., and S. G. Deshmukh. "Vendor selection using interpretive structural modelling (ISM)." *International Journal of Operations & Production Management* 14, no. 6 (1994): 52–59.

Nassuora, B. "Students acceptance of Mobile learning for higher education in Saudi Arabia." *International Journal of Learning Management Systems* 1, no. 1 (2012): 1–9.

Oseni, G. P. Corral, and P. Goldstein. "Winters explaining gender differentials in agricultural production in Nigeria." *Agricultural Economics* 46, no. 3 (2015): 285–310, https://doi .org/10.1111/agec.12166

Salim, B. "An application of UTAUT model for acceptance of social media in Egypt: A statistical study." *International Journal of Information Science* 2, no. 6 (2012): 92–105.

Ugur, N. G., and A. H. Turan. "E-learning adoption of academicians: A proposal for an extended model." *Behaviour & Information Technology* 37, no. 4 (2018): 393–405.

Vafadar, A., F. Guzzomi, A. Rassau, and K. Hayward. "Advances in metal additive manufacturing: A review of common processes, industrial applications, and current challenges." *Applied Sciences* 11 (2021): 1213, https://doi.org/10.3390/app11031213

Venkatesh, V., M. G. Morris, G. B. Davis, et al. "User acceptance of information technology: Toward a unified view." *MIS Quarterly* 27 (2003): 425–478.

Venkatesh, V., J. Y. Thong, and X. Xu. "Consumer acceptance and use of information technology: Extending the unified theory of acceptance and use of technology." *MIS Quarterly* (2012): 157–178.

Wang, K., C. Zhu, J. Tondeur, and K. Wang. "Using micro-lectures in small private online courses: What do we learn from students' behavioural intentions?" *Technology, Pedagogy and Education* 30 (2018): 427–442.

Winkler, R., and M. Söllner. "Unleashing the potential of chatbots in education: A state-of-the-art analysis." In *Academy of Management Annual Meeting (AOM)*, 2018.

Zhang, X., Y. Liu, J. Pu, L. Tian, S. Gui, X. Song, S. Xu, X. Zhou, H. Wang, W. Zhou, J. Chen, X. Qi, and P. Xie. "Depressive symptoms and quality of life among chinese medical postgraduates: A national cross-sectional study." *Psychology, Health & Medicine* 24 (2019): 1015–1027, https://doi.org/10.1080/13548506.2019.1626453

Zhang, L., I. Pentina, and Y. Fan. "Who do you choose? Comparing perceptions of human vs robo-advisor in the context of financial services." *Journal of Services Marketing* (2021). Ahead-of-print. https://doi.org/10.1108/JSM-05-2020-0162

7 Using AI-Powered Predictive Analytics Tools to Identify Students Falling Behind or Dropping Out

A. Reethika and P. Kanaga Priya

7.1 INTRODUCTION

7.1.1 STUDENT DROPOUT IN UNIVERSITY

Student dropout is a significant problem in universities worldwide, and it can have severe consequences for individual students, universities, and society as a whole. Students who quit college before finishing their degree or program of study are said to be dropouts. Dropping out of university can be a complex and multifaceted issue, and there can be various reasons why students may choose to leave their studies. Some common reasons for student dropout include financial difficulties, academic challenges, lack of motivation or interest, personal or family issues, feeling overwhelmed or unprepared, and social isolation. It is crucial to address these issues proactively and provide students with the necessary support and resources to overcome them. Universities can play a vital role in helping students succeed by offering a range of services and programs, such as financial aid, academic advising, counseling, and mentoring, to help students stay on track and complete their studies. Addressing the issue of student dropout is essential to ensuring that all students have access to higher education and can realize their full potential.

7.2 PROBLEM STATEMENT

There can be various reasons why students drop out of university, and these reasons can vary from one student to another. Some common problems that contribute to student dropout include:

DOI: 10.1201/9781003425809-7

1. Financial difficulties: Many students struggle with the high costs of tuition, textbooks, and living expenses, which can cause them to drop out or take a break from their studies.
2. Academic challenges: Some students may struggle to keep up with the demands of university-level coursework, particularly in subjects that are not aligned with their interests or strengths.
3. Lack of motivation or interest: Students who lack motivation or interest in their studies may find it challenging to stay engaged and may eventually drop out.
4. Personal or family issues: Students may face personal or family issues that make it difficult for them to continue their studies, such as health problems, family obligations, or other personal challenges.
5. Feeling overwhelmed or unprepared: Some students may feel overwhelmed by the demands of university life, such as managing coursework, extracurricular activities, and social life, and may not feel adequately prepared to handle these challenges.
6. Social isolation: Some students may feel socially isolated or disconnected from the university community, which can lead to feelings of loneliness and a lack of engagement in academic and social activities.
7. University dropout rates tend to be higher than high school dropout rates. Figure 7.1 shows the students dropout conditions, and Figure 7.2 describes the percentage of dropout due to various reasons. According to the National Center for Education Statistics, the overall college dropout rate in the United States is around 40%, while the high school dropout rate is around 6%. However, it is essential to note that these rates can vary significantly depending on factors such as race, ethnicity, socioeconomic status, and academic preparedness.

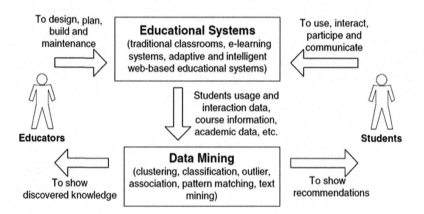

FIGURE 7.1 Predicting academic outcomes/other reason: A Survey from 2007 to 2018 (Source: https://link.springer.com/article/10.1007/s10758-020-09476-0)

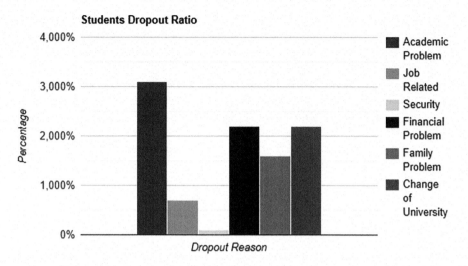

FIGURE 7.2 A dropout survey from 2017 to 2021 (Source: https://www.mdpi.com/2076 -3417/11/1/237)

7.2.1   State-of-Art and Related Work

1. "Predictors of dropout among high school students" by [1, 7]: This study found that student engagement and academic performance were the two main predictors of dropout.
2. "Exploring the complex nature of student dropout from university" by [2, 13]: Tinto's study identified several factors that contribute to student dropout, including academic preparation, financial difficulties, and a lack of social integration.
3. "High school dropout and the role of career and technical education: A survival analysis approach" by [3, 4, 6]: This study found that students who were enrolled in career and technical education programs were less prone to leave high school early.
4. "A longitudinal study of school belonging and academic motivation among secondary school students" by Goodenow (2021): This study found that students who felt a sense of belonging in their school were less likely to drop out.
5. "Why students drop out of school and what can be done" by Rumberger (2021): This review of research on student dropout identified several key factors, including academic preparation, school climate, family and community support, and individual factors such as motivation and engagement.
6. "Factors influencing high school dropout rates" by Li and Li (2020): This study found that factors such as low academic achievement, poverty, lack of parental involvement, and student misbehavior were significant predictors of high school dropout rates.

7. "Predictors of dropout for students in an online high school" by Sohn (2019): This study investigated the predictors of dropout for students in an online high school and found that factors such as academic performance, self-regulation, and online learning experience were significant predictors.

8. "Challenges of online learning and dropout rates in higher education" by [5, 9]: This study examined the challenges of online learning and the factors that contribute to dropout rates in higher education. The study found that factors such as lack of technical support, lack of motivation, and lack of interaction with peers and instructors were significant predictors of dropout rates in online courses.

9. "The impact of a comprehensive school counseling program on student dropout rates" by [8, 10]: This study examined the impact of a comprehensive school counseling program on student dropout rates and found that the program was associated with lower dropout rates and increased graduation rates.

10. "The role of perceived parental support in predicting high school dropout" by [11, 12]: This study investigated the role of perceived parental support in predicting high school dropout and found that students who perceived high levels of parental support were less likely to drop out of high school.

Overall, research on student dropout suggests that a combination of academic, social, and individual factors contribute to students leaving school before graduation. Understanding these factors and developing interventions to address them can help to reduce dropout rates and improve student success.

Overall, these studies suggest that a range of factors contribute to student dropout rates, including academic performance, socioeconomic status, online learning experience, parental support, and counseling support. Understanding these factors can help educators and policymakers develop targeted interventions to reduce dropout rates and improve student success.

7.3 PROPOSED WORK

Student dropout in universities is a major problem that affects the students, universities, and the society at large. The cost of education is increasing, and universities are under pressure to ensure that students complete their studies successfully. Therefore, it is necessary to identify students who are at risk of dropping out so that appropriate interventions can be put in place to prevent it. This proposed work aims to develop an AI predictive model that can predict student dropout in university.

The proposed work will use machine learning algorithms to develop a predictive model that can identify students who are at risk of dropping out. The dataset for the study will be obtained from the university's database, which will include student demographics, academic performance, and other relevant data as shown in Figure 7.3.

The study will adopt a supervised learning approach, which will involve training the AI model using historical data on student dropout. The data will be preprocessed

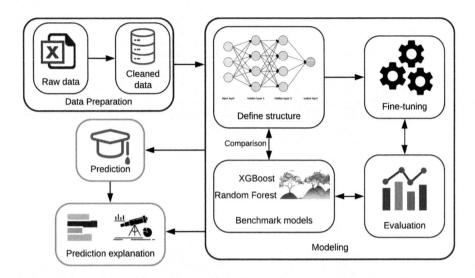

FIGURE 7.3 Deep learning with interpretability for predicting university dropout (Source: https://dl.acm.org/doi/abs/10.1145/3368308.3415382)

to remove missing values, outliers, and irrelevant features. The selected features will be fed into the machine learning algorithms, such as logistic regression, decision trees, and random forest, to develop the predictive model.

The flow of predicting student dropout in university using AI predictive methods can be divided into several stages, in Figure 7.4 as follows:

1. Data collection: Gathering pertinent information from the university's database is the first step. The data may include student demographics, academic performance, financial aid status, and other relevant information.
2. Data preprocessing: In this stage, the collected data are processed to remove missing values, outliers, and irrelevant features. The selected features will be transformed into a suitable format for the AI model.
3. Data splitting: Then, training and testing datasets are created from the preprocessed data. The testing dataset is used to assess the model's performance once the AI model has been trained.
4. Model selection: The next step is to select a suitable machine learning algorithm for the predictive model. Common algorithms used for student dropout prediction include logistic regression, decision trees, and random forest.
5. Model training: The AI model is trained using the selected algorithm on the training dataset. The model learns from the data and identifies patterns that can predict student dropout.
6. Model evaluation: The performance of the AI model is evaluated using various metrics such as accuracy, precision, recall, and F1-score. The model's effectiveness in predicting student dropout is measured using the receiver operating characteristic (ROC) curve.

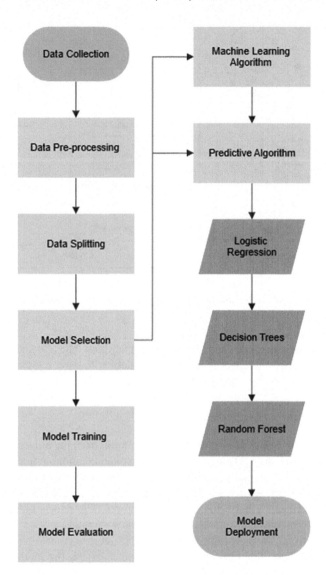

FIGURE 7.4 Flow of predicting university dropouts using prediction AI techniques (Source: Chart prepared by A. Reethika and P. Kanaga Priya)

7. Model deployment: The final stage is to deploy the trained AI model for prediction of student dropout. The model can be used to provide early warning signs to university authorities and instructors about students risk. This will enable universities to provide appropriate interventions to prevent student dropout and improve student success.

In summary, the flow of predicting student dropout in university using AI predictive methods involves collecting data, preprocessing the data, splitting the data, selecting a suitable algorithm, training the model, evaluating the model, and deploying the model. The ultimate goal is to provide a predictive tool that can help universities identify students who are at risk of dropping out and provide interventions to improve their academic success.

7.3.1 EVALUATION

The performance of the AI predictive model will be evaluated using various metrics such as accuracy, precision, recall, and F1-score. Figure 7.5 shows the model's effectiveness in predicting student dropout will be measured using the receiver operating characteristic (ROC) curve.

7.3.2 SOFTWARE TECHNIQUE

The choice of software tool for predicting student dropout in university using AI predictive methods can vary depending on the specific needs and preferences of the researcher. However, some commonly used software tools for developing and implementing AI models include Python-based frameworks like TensorFlow, Keras, and Scikit-learn, as well as R-based tools like Caret and H_2O. These tools provide a range of machine learning algorithms, data preprocessing capabilities, and evaluation metrics to support the development of accurate and reliable AI models for predicting student dropout in university.

Python-based frameworks like TensorFlow can be used to predict student dropout in university using AI predictive methods. TensorFlow is an open-source software library for dataflow and differentiable programming across a range of tasks, including machine learning, deep learning, and neural networks. It provides a range of tools and resources for developing AI models, including data preprocessing, model training, and evaluation metrics. Figure 7.6 shows the TensorFlow is a powerful and flexible tool for predicting student dropout in university using AI predictive methods, offering a range of algorithms, tools, and resources for developing and implementing accurate and reliable predictive models.

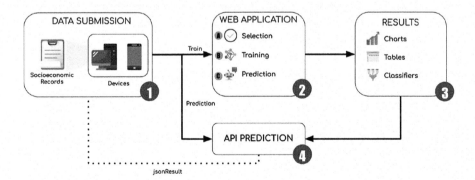

FIGURE 7.5 Dropout prediction using machine learning techniques based on socioeconomic data (Source: Chart prepared by A. Reethika and P. Kanaga Priya)

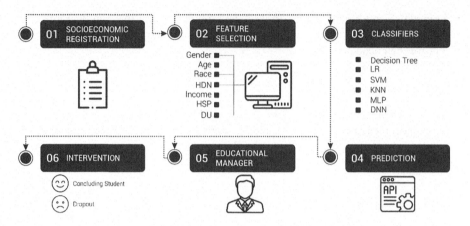

FIGURE 7.6   Prediction of dropout using TensorFlow (Source: Chart prepared by A. Reethika and P. Kanaga Priya)

7.4   RESULTS AND DISCUSSION

7.4.1   RESULT OF VARIOUS CATEGORIES

AI prediction methods can be used to analyze large amounts of data and identify patterns that may help predict student dropout rates. By analyzing data such as student attendance, grades, behavior, and demographic information, AI models can make predictions about which students are at the highest risk of dropping out.

Machine learning algorithms: Machine learning algorithms can be used to build predictive models based on historical data. These models can be trained to identify patterns in the data and make predictions about future events. For example, a machine learning algorithm could analyze a dataset of student grades, attendance, and demographic information to predict which students are most likely to drop out.

By using AI prediction methods, educators can identify students who are at the highest risk of dropping out and develop targeted interventions to help these students stay in school. For example, educators could use AI-generated insights to provide extra support to at-risk students, such as additional tutoring or mentoring, to help them stay on track and complete their education.

7.4.2   DROPOUT IDENTIFICATION IN PHYSICAL METHOD

Step 1: Data Collection

Information about students is gathered using ERP software. ERP software will gather all of the information about each and every student. Figure 7.7 shows the complete details about student.

Step 2: Mentor–Mentee Meeting

A mentor–mentee meeting is a scheduled session where a mentor and their mentee come together to discuss various topics related to the mentee's personal or

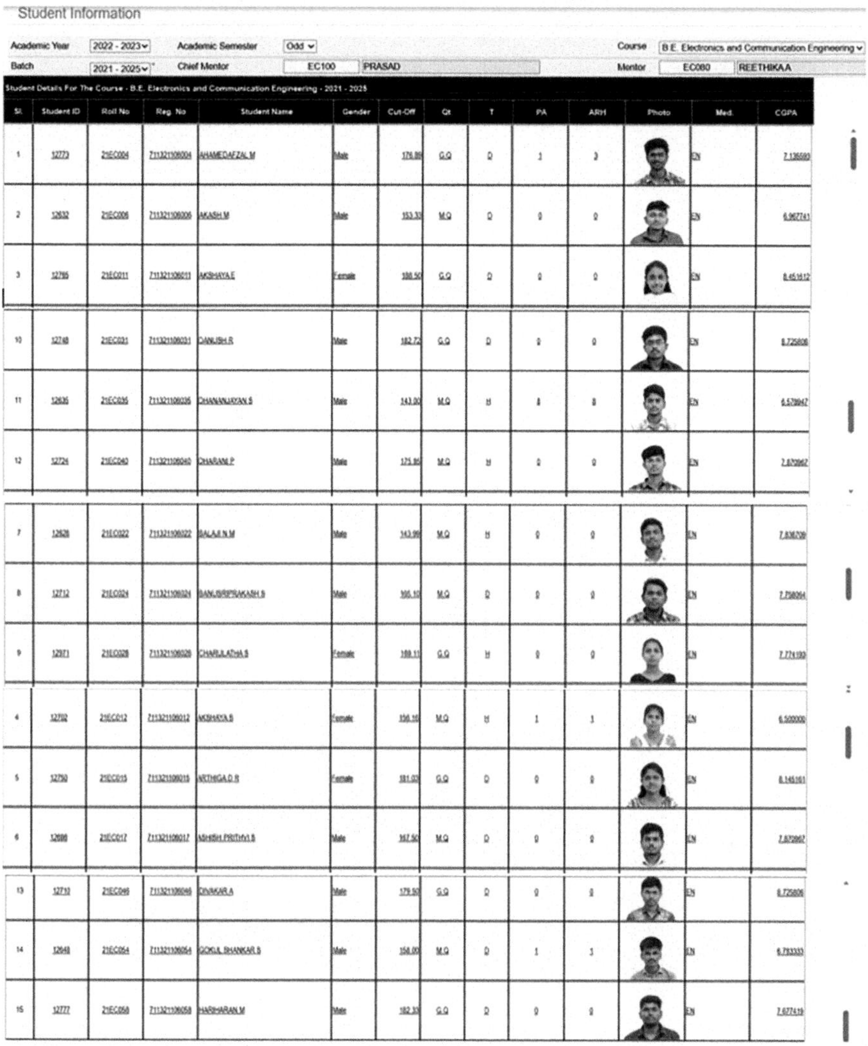

Student Information

Academic Year 2022 - 2023 | Academic Semester Odd | Course B.E. Electronics and Communication Engineering

Batch 2021 - 2025 | Chief Mentor EC100 PRASAD | Mentor EC080 REETHIKAA

Student Details For The Course - B.E. Electronics and Communication Engineering - 2021 - 2025

Sl.	Student ID	Roll No	Reg. No	Student Name	Gender	Cut-Off	Qt	T	PA	ARH	Photo	Med.	CGPA
1	12773	21EC004	711321106004	AHAMEDAFZAL M	Male	176.89	G.Q	D	1	3		EN	7.136593
2	12632	21EC006	711321106006	AKASH M	Male	153.33	M.Q	D	0	0		EN	6.967741
3	12765	21EC011	711321106011	AKSHAYA E	Female	188.50	G.Q	D	0	0		EN	8.451612
10	12748	21EC031	711321106031	DANUSH R	Male	182.72	G.Q	D	0	0		EN	8.725806
11	12635	21EC035	711321106035	DHANANJAYAN S	Male	143.00	M.Q	H	8	8		EN	6.578947
12	12724	21EC040	711321106040	DHARANI P	Male	175.86	M.Q	H	0	0		EN	7.870967
7	12626	21EC022	711321106022	BALAJI N M	Male	143.99	M.Q	H	0	0		EN	7.836709
8	12712	21EC024	711321106024	BANUSRIPRAKASH S	Male	165.10	M.Q	D	0	0		EN	7.758064
9	12971	21EC028	711321106028	CHARULATHA S	Female	169.11	G.Q	H	0	0		EN	7.774193
4	12702	21EC012	711321106012	AKSHAYA S	Female	156.10	M.Q	H	1	1		EN	6.500000
5	12750	21EC015	711321106015	ARTHIGA D R	Female	181.03	G.Q	D	0	0		EN	8.145161
6	12686	21EC017	711321106017	ASHISH PRITHVI S	Male	167.50	M.Q	D	0	0		EN	7.870967
13	12710	21EC046	711321106046	DIVAKAR A	Male	179.50	G.Q	D	0	0		EN	8.725806
14	12648	21EC054	711321106054	GOKUL SHANKAR S	Male	158.00	M.Q	D	1	1		EN	6.793333
15	12777	21EC058	711321106058	HARIHARAN M	Male	182.33	G.Q	D	0	0		EN	7.677419

FIGURE 7.7 Data generated in ERP software (Source: Prepared by A. Reethika)

professional development. The purpose of these meetings is to provide guidance, support, and advice to the mentee, as well as to help them achieve their goals and objectives.

Figure 7.8 shows the mentor mentee meeting of each student through mentor interaction.

During a mentor–mentee meeting, the mentor may provide feedback on the mentee's progress, discuss any challenges they may be facing, and offer advice and resources to help the mentee overcome those challenges. The mentor may also share

Minutes of Mentor Mentee Meeting - 3

Year / Sem	:	II / 3	Date & Time	:	03/10/2022 & 12.30 P.M
Batch	:	2021 - 2025	Venue	:	ECE Board Room
Mentor	:	REETHIKA A			

Agenda :

1. Dissemination of Institute vision and mission
2. Department Vision, Mission and PEO
3. Academic performance
4. NPTEL course
5. Co-curricular and Extra – curricular activities
6. Student discipline
7. Any other points

S.No	Roll No	Name of Student	CGPA	Arrears	Counselling
1	21EC004	AHAMEDAFZAL M	7.14	U21EC302	CIAT 1 performance is not satisfied and insisted to get pass in all the subjects in upcoming exam. Instructed to maintain subject notes regularly and coaching class has been scheduled. Informed to avoid taking leave. Instructed to get a good score on a weekly assignment on the NPTEL registered course. Appreciated the involvement participating in film club competitions
2	21EC006	AKASH M	6.97		CIAT 1 performance is not satisfied and insisted to get pass in all the subjects in upcoming exam. Instructed to maintain subject notes regularly and coaching class has been scheduled. Instructed to get a good score on a weekly assignment on the NPTEL registered course. Asked to participate in Co-curricular and extracurricular activities in and around the state/college
3	21EC011	AKSHAYA E	8.45		Appreciated CIAT 1 performance and instructed to do real time project. Instructed to get good score in weekly assignment of NPTEL registered course. Informed to participate in innovsense 2022 contest. Appreciated her involvement in extracurricular activity
4	21EC012	AKSHAYA S	6.50	U21EC302	CIAT 1 performance is not satisfied and insisted to get pass in all the subjects in upcoming exam. Instructed to maintain subject notes regularly and coaching class has been scheduled. Informed to avoid taking leave. Instructed to get a good score on a weekly assignment on the NPTEL registered course. Asked to participate in Co-curricular and extracurricular activities in and around the state/college
5	21EC015	ARTHIGA D R	8.15		Appreciated CIAT 1 performance and instructed to do real time project. Instructed to get good score in weekly assignment of NPTEL registered course. Informed to participate in innovsense 2022 contest. Appreciated her involvement in extracurricular activity
6	21EC017	ASHISH PRITHVI S	7.87		Appreciated CIAT 1 performance and instructed to do real time project. Instructed to get good score in weekly assignment of NPTEL registered course. Informed to participate in innovsense 2022 contest. Appreciated his involvement in extracurricular activity.
7	21EC022	BALAJI N M	7.64		Appreciated CIAT 1 performance and instructed to do real time project. Instructed to get good score in weekly assignment of NPTEL registered course. Informed to participate in innovsense 2022 contest. Appreciated his involvement volunteering in YRC club.
8	21EC024	BANUSRIPRAKASH S	7.76		CIAT 1 performance is not satisfied and need to concentrate more. Instructed to maintain subject notes regularly and coaching class has been scheduled. Instructed to get a good score on a weekly assignment on the NPTEL registered course. Informed to participate in innovsense 2022 contest.
9	21EC028	CHARULATHA S	7.77		Appreciated CIAT 1 performance and instructed to do real time project. Instructed to get good score in weekly assignment of NPTEL registered course. Informed to participate in innovsense 2022 contest. Appreciated her involvement in extracurricular activity Informed to prepare abstract for book chapter as soon as possible
10	21EC031	DANUSH R	8.73		Appreciated CIAT 1 performance and instructed to do real time project. Instructed to get good score in weekly assignment of NPTEL registered course Informed to participate in innovsense 2022 contest. Appreciated his involvement volunteering in YRC club. Informed to prepare abstract for book chapter as soon as possible
11	21EC035	DHANANJAYAN S	6.58	U21CY101, U21MA101, U21PH101, U21CSG02, U21EC302, U21EC303, U21EC304, U21ECG01	CIAT 1 performance is not satisfied and insisted to get pass in all the subjects in upcoming exam. Instructed to maintain subject notes regularly and coaching class has been scheduled. Informed to avoid taking on-duty during academic hours. Instructed to get a good score on a weekly assignment on the NPTEL registered course. Appreciated the involvement volunteering in YRC club
12	21EC040	DHARANI P	7.87		Appreciated CIAT 1 performance and instructed to do real time project. Instructed to get good score in weekly assignment of NPTEL registered course. Informed to participate in innovsense 2022 contest. Appreciated his involvement in extracurricular activity.
13	21EC046	DIVAKAR A	8.73		Appreciated CIAT 1 performance and instructed to do real time project. Instructed to get good score in weekly assignment of NPTEL registered course. Informed to participate in innovsense 2022 contest. Appreciated his involvement in appearing for government exam.
14	21EC054	GOKUL SHANKAR S	6.78	U21EC302	CIAT 1 performance is not satisfied and insisted to get pass in all the subjects in upcoming exam. Instructed to maintain subject notes regularly and coaching class has been scheduled. Informed to avoid taking on-duty during academic hours. Instructed to get a good score on a weekly assignment on the NPTEL registered course. Appreciated the involvement volunteering in rotract club
15	21EC058	HARIHARAN M	7.68		CIAT 1 performance is not satisfied and need to concentrate more. Instructed to maintain subject notes regularly and coaching class has been scheduled. Instructed to get a good score on a weekly assignment on the NPTEL registered course. Informed to pay the pending fee as soon as possible

FIGURE 7.8 Mentor–mentee meeting minutes generated by mentor through physical mode (Source: Prepared by A. Reethika)

their own experiences and insights to help the mentee gain a better understanding of their field or industry.

These meetings can take place in person or virtually, depending on the availability and preferences of the mentor and mentee. The frequency of the meetings can also vary, depending on the goals and needs of the mentee.

Overall, mentor–mentee meetings are an important part of the mentoring relationship, as they provide an opportunity for the mentor to offer personalized guidance and support to the mentee, helping them to grow both personally and professionally.

7.4.3 DROPOUT IDENTIFICATION USING AI PREDICTIVE METHOD

Student dropout identification is the process of analyzing data to predict which students are at the highest risk of dropping out of school. This analysis may involve machine learning algorithms, natural language processing, or deep learning techniques to identify patterns in student attendance, grades, behavior, and demographic information. By using these methods, educators can identify at-risk students and develop targeted interventions to help them stay in school. Mentor–mentee meetings are also an important part of the process, as they provide an opportunity for mentors to offer personalized guidance and support to students who are at risk of dropping out. Overall, student dropout identification is a crucial step in ensuring that all students have the opportunity to succeed in their education in Figure 7.9.

Using the same dataset, we have implemented in machine learning techniques. Result has been shown in Figure 7.10.

7.5 PERFORMANCE ANALYSIS

7.5.1 UNIVERSITY STUDENTS DROPOUT VS. NONDROPOUT

There are several differences between nondropout and dropout students. Here are some of the key comparisons by referring Figure 7.11:

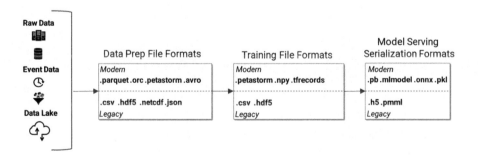

FIGURE 7.9 Raw data extracted from ERP login and processed through AI model (Source: Prepared by A. Reethika and P. Kanaga Priya)

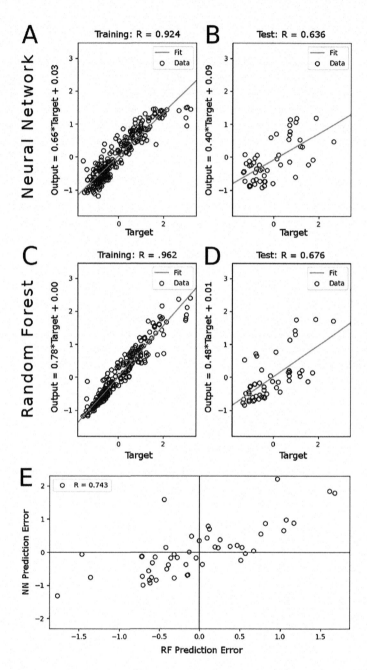

FIGURE 7.10 AI prediction method using TensorFlow (Source: Output prepared by A. Reethika and P. Kanaga Priya)

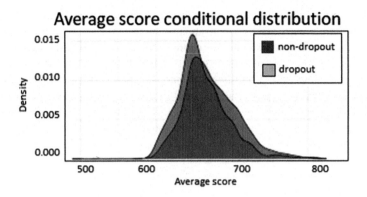

FIGURE 7.11   Performance chart of dropout vs. nondropout (Source: Chart prepared by A. Reethika and P. Kanaga Priya)

Academic performance: Nondropout students generally have better academic performance than dropout students. They have higher grades, better attendance, and are more likely to complete assignments on time.

Engagement: Nondropout students are more engaged in their education than dropout students. They participate in class discussions, ask questions, and are generally more interested in their coursework.

Support system: Nondropout students often have a stronger support system, both at home and at school. They may have parents or caregivers who are involved in their education, and they may have access to resources like tutoring or mentoring programs.

Socioeconomic status: Dropout rates are often higher among students from low-income families or disadvantaged communities. Nondropout students may come from more financially stable households and have access to resources that can support their academic success.

Future opportunities: Nondropout students are more likely to have access to future opportunities like college or career advancement. Dropping out of school can limit future opportunities and make it more difficult to achieve long-term goals.

Overall, nondropout students tend to have better academic performance, more engagement in their education, a stronger support system, and more future opportunities than dropout students.

7.6   CONCLUSION

The proposed work will develop an AI predictive model that can predict student dropout in university. The model will provide early warning signs to university authorities and instructors about students who are at risk of dropping out. This will enable universities to provide appropriate interventions to prevent student dropout and improve student success.

Some common reasons for dropping out of university include financial difficulties, personal or family issues, lack of motivation or interest in the subject matter, academic challenges, and feeling overwhelmed or unprepared for university-level studies.

It is worth noting that the factors that contribute to students dropping out of university are complex and multifaceted, and they can vary significantly from one student to another. Therefore, it is essential to address these issues proactively and provide students with the necessary support and resources to overcome them.

Both traditional and AI-based learning methods have their unique advantages and disadvantages, and they may appeal to different types of learners. Ultimately, the success of any learning program depends on various factors, such as the quality of teaching, the relevance of the curriculum, and the level of student engagement and motivation.

It is essential to address these issues proactively and provide students with necessary support and resources to overcome them. Universities can offer a range of services and programs, such as financial aid, academic advising, counseling, and mentoring, to help students stay on track and succeed in their studies.

REFERENCES

Antoni M, Drasch K, Kleinert C, Matthes B, Ruland M, Trahms A (2010) Arbeiten und Lernen im Wandel, Teil I: Überblick über die Studie (FDZ-Methodenreport 5/2010). Nürnberg: Forschungsdatenzentrum (FDZ) der Bundesagentur für Arbeit im Institut für Arbeitsmarkt- und Berufsforschung.

Barroso MF, Falcão EB (2004) Evasão universitária: o caso do Instituto de Física da UFRJ. In Anais do 9° encontro nacional de pesquisa em ensino de física. Federal University of Rio de Janeiro, Jaboticatubas, pp. 26–304.

Brasil (2016) SESu/MEC. Diplomação, Retenção e Evasão nos Cursos de Graduação em Instituições de Ensino Superior Públicas. http://www.andifes.org.br/wpcontent/files _flutter/Diplomacao_Retencao_Evasao_Graduacao_em_IES_Publicas-1996.pdf. Accessed 22 May 2017.

Brightspace (2020i) Monitor weekly success and risk in your class. https://documentation .brightspace.com/EN/insights/class_dashboard/instructor/understanding_class_ dashboard_1.htm. Accessed 17 September 2020.

Dancey C, Reidy J (2006) Estatística sem matemática para psicologia: usando SPSS para Windows. Porto Alegre: Artmed.

Eegdeman I, Meeter M, Van Klaveren C (2018) Cognitive skills, personality traits and dropout in Dutch vocational education. *Empirical Research in Vocational Education and Training*, 10(11), 18. https://doi.org/10.1186/s40461-01

Gong B, Nugent JP, Guest W, Parker W, Chang PJ, Khosa F, Nicolaou S (2019) Infuence of artifcial intelligence on canadian medical students' preference for radiology specialty: Anational survey study. *Academic Radiology*, 26(4), 566–577.

Itani A, Brisson L, Garlatti, S (2018) Understanding learner's drop-out in MOOCs. Lecture notes in computer science (Including subseries lecture notes in artifcial intelligence and lecture notes in bioinformatics), 11314 LNCS. https://doi.org/10.1007/978-3-030 -03493-1_25

Jivet I, Schefel M, Schmitz M, Robbers S, Specht M, Drachsler H (2020). From students with love: An empirical study on learner goals, self-regulated learning and sense-making of learning analytics in higher education. *Internet and Higher Education*. https://doi.org /10.1016/j.iheduc.2020.100758

Kizilcec RF, Pérez-Sanagustín M, Maldonado JJ (2016) Recommending self-regulated learning strategies does not improve performance in a MOOC. L@S 2016—Proceedings of the 3rd 2016 ACM conference on learning at scale. https://doi.org/10.1145/2876034.2893378

Padilla R, Netto SL, da Silva EAB. A survey on performance metrics for object-detection algorithms (Online, 2020), in the 27th International Conference on Systems, Signals and Image Processing (IWSSIP), pp. 237–242.

Rouder JN, Speckman PL, Sun D, Morey RD, Iverson G (2009) Bayesian t tests for accepting and rejecting the null hypothesis. *Psychonomic Bulletin and Review*, 16(2), 225–237. https://doi.org/10.3758/PBR.16.2.225

Xiao B, Wu H, Wei Y (2018) Simple baselines for human pose estimation and tracking, in 15th European Conference on Computer Vision (ECCV), Munich, pp. 472–487.

8 Augmented Reality in Education

An Immersive Experience Centered on Educational Content

Muhammad Abeer Irfan, Yaseen Irshad, Wahiza Khan, Abid Iqbal and Amaad Khalil

8.1 INTRODUCTION

The field of education is constantly evolving, and advancements in technology have allowed for new and innovative teaching and learning methods. One such advancement is the development of augmented reality (AR) technology, which has the potential to revolutionize the way students learn by providing a unique and interactive educational experience (Cascales et al., 2012).

With the help of augmented reality (AR) technology, the "AR-Learn" effort seeks to give students a thorough and immersive educational experience. This study aims to create 3D models of intricate tools and diagrams in various fields, such as biology, physics, engineering, etc., and enable students to interact with them in real-time using the cameras on their devices. We do this to give learners a more rational and appealing way to understand complex ideas. Our project aims to provide students with a deeper understanding of the subjects covered in their curriculum, to create a hands-on learning environment that allows students to explore and interact with 3D models at their own pace and to offer a unique and cutting-edge educational tool that can improve the overall learning experience.

AR-Learn fills the gap in the current offering of educational products by providing a more immersive and interactive learning experience. Traditional educational materials, such as textbooks and lectures, often rely on static 2D images, making it difficult for students to comprehend complex concepts fully. This work addresses and provides a solution to this problem by giving students access to interactive 3D models that they can manipulate and explore, allowing for a deeper and more intuitive understanding of the subject matter.

DOI: 10.1201/9781003425809-8

In this chapter, we will discuss the development and implementation of AR-Learn, its potential impact on education, and its effectiveness in enhancing students' learning experiences. We believe that by providing students with an immersive and interactive learning environment, we can help bridge the gap between traditional educational methods and modern technological advancements.

The field of education is constantly evolving, and advancements in technology have allowed for new and innovative teaching and learning methods. One such advancement is the development of augmented reality (AR) technology, which has the potential to revolutionize the way students learn by providing a unique and interactive educational experience (Cascales et al., 2012).

With the help of augmented reality (AR) technology, the "AR-Learn" effort seeks to give students a thorough and immersive educational experience. This study aims to create 3D models of intricate tools and diagrams in various fields, such as biology, physics, engineering, etc., and enable students to interact with them in real-time using the cameras on their devices. We do this to give learners a more rational and appealing way to understand complex ideas. Our project aims to provide students with a deeper understanding of the subjects covered in their curriculum, to create a hands-on learning environment that allows students to explore and interact with 3D models at their own pace, and to offer a unique and cutting-edge educational tool that can improve the overall learning experience.

AR-Learn fills the gap in the current offering of educational products by providing a more immersive and interactive learning experience. Traditional educational materials, such as textbooks and lectures, often rely on static 2D images, making it difficult for students to comprehend complex concepts fully. This work addresses and provides a solution to this problem by giving students access to interactive 3D models that they can manipulate and explore, allowing for a deeper and more intuitive understanding of the subject matter.

In this chapter, we will discuss the development and implementation of AR-Learn, its potential impact on education, and its effectiveness in enhancing students' learning experiences. We believe that by providing students with an immersive and interactive learning environment, we can help bridge the gap between traditional educational methods and modern technological advancements.

8.1.1 MIXED REALITY (MR)

Mixed reality (MR) is an advanced form of augmented reality (AR) that combines the elements of both virtual reality (VR) and AR technologies. Figure 8.1 depicts the taxonomy of the virtuality continuum as reported by (Milgram et al., 1995). In MR, virtual objects are anchored in the real world, allowing users to interact with them realistically. This technology creates an immersive experience for users, enabling them to interact with virtual objects as if they were real (Speicher et al., 2019).

The potential applications of MR are vast, ranging from education to entertainment and beyond. Using MR in education, designing engaging and interactive

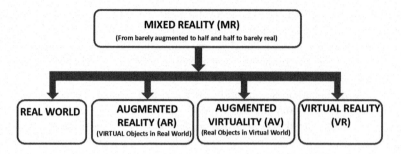

FIGURE 8.1 The reality–virtuality continuum consists of environments ranging from real to virtual and all possible variations and compositions of real and virtual objects in these environments (Milgram & Kishino, 1994)

lessons is possible. For example, MR can be used to create virtual laboratories for science classes, allowing students to conduct experiments in a safe and controlled environment. MR can also be used to create historical re-enactments or virtual tours of historical sites, bringing history to life in a way that was impossible in a traditional way. MR can also be used in healthcare for medical training, allowing medical professionals to practice surgeries virtually before performing them on patients. MR can also be used to create simulations of medical conditions, allowing medical professionals to understand better the conditions they are treating (Stretton et al., 2018).

In addition to education and healthcare, MR has potential applications in industries such as architecture, engineering, and construction. MR can be used to create virtual building plans, allowing architects and engineers to visualize their designs better and identify potential issues before construction begins. MR can also be used to create virtual walkthroughs of buildings, allowing clients to see what a finished building will look like prior to construction and receive feedback from the clients (Rokhsaritalemi et al., 2020).

Despite the potential benefits of MR, there are still some limitations and challenges to be addressed. One of the main challenges is the cost and accessibility of MR technology. MR hardware and software can be expensive, making it difficult for some organizations to implement them. Additionally, developing MR content requires specialized skills and knowledge, which can also be a barrier to adoption. Another challenge with MR is the potential for motion sickness or discomfort in some users. MR can disorient some people, leading to motion sickness or discomfort. This area is where further research is needed to understand better the causes of motion sickness and how to mitigate it in MR experiences.

In conclusion, MR is a powerful technology with vast prospective applications in education, healthcare, and other industries. While challenges are still to be addressed, the promising benefits make it an area worth exploring further. As technology continues to evolve, we will likely see even more exciting and innovative applications of MR in the future.

8.1.2 AUGMENTED REALITY (AR) AND VIRTUAL REALITY (VR)

AR and VR are two different technologies that offer unique experiences to users. The immersive technologies AR and VR both offer differ in a few ways. An in-depth comparison of AR and VR is given in this section. In contrast to VR, which entirely immerses the user in a virtual world, augmented reality overlaps digital content over a real-world environment. The degree of immersion each technology offers users is one of the main distinctions between AR and VR. Users can interact with the actual environment while viewing digital information in augmented reality, which offers a semi-immersive experience while allowing them to remain aware of their surroundings. Mobile devices, smart glasses, and other wearable gadgets that enable the user to view and interact with virtual content overlaid on the actual world are used to achieve this. AR is especially helpful when users need to access information while still engaging with their surroundings, like in the workplace or educational settings (Billinghurst, 2002; Jung & tom Dieck, 2018).

Contrarily, virtual reality (VR) offers a completely immersive experience by blocking out the real world and transporting users to a virtual setting. This is accomplished by using head-mounted displays (HMDs), which fully enclose the user's field of vision and frequently include speakers or headphones to deliver spatial audio. A sensation of presence and involvement that isn't attainable with conventional media can be achieved in a dynamic virtual world that is sensitive to user input. For training simulations, virtual tours, and gaming, VR is very useful because of its level of immersion. Both augmented reality and virtual reality are anticipated to play significant roles in various industries in the future.

In contrast to VR, which is predicted to develop in gaming, training, and virtual travel, augmented reality (AR) is likely to become increasingly common in contexts related to education, healthcare, and industry (Kyaw et al., 2019). Technology advancements, such as the development of more advanced HMDs and wearable gadgets, will likely substantially improve the capabilities and efficiency of both AR and VR. AR and VR provide distinctive advantages and drawbacks depending on the use case. Virtual reality (VR) offers a fully immersive experience that takes users to a virtual environment. In contrast, augmented reality (AR) offers a semi-immersive experience allowing users to interact with the real world. Both technologies are anticipated to play increasingly significant roles across various industries as technological improvements continue to improve their capabilities and effectiveness (Huang & Roscoe, 2021; Rojas-Sánchez et al., 2023).

Virtual reality (VR) and augmented reality (AR) technologies heavily rely on interaction. With AR, users can interact with digital content projected in the real world, providing a unique and immersive learning environment. Gesture recognition, voice commands, and other input techniques can all be used in this interaction. Real-time manipulation of virtual objects, the visualization of complex data, and more engaging research of various content types are all made possible by AR for learners. Employing specialized input devices, such as hand controllers, gloves, or haptic feedback devices, allow users to interact with a fully virtual environment in virtual reality (VR). Through this immersive learning environment, students can interact with a virtual world in a way that is not feasible through traditional media. Since the virtual environment can be completely transformed and users can engage with various objects, instances, and scenarios, VR has a much higher level of inter-activity than AR. The ability of AR interaction to be completely incorporated into the user's actual environment makes it possible for a more intuitive and natural expe-rience. This is one of the main benefits of AR interaction. Users can engage with digital content projected on actual items like exhibits, books, or posters meant to be instructional. This integration makes the development of interactive educational experiences more interesting and successful than conventional teaching techniques feasible.

On the other hand, virtual reality (VR) interaction enables students to interact with a digital environment that may replicate real-world circumstances, offer-ing a secure and realistic environment for instruction and practice. This kind of engagement is especially helpful in professions like medicine, where students can practice surgical techniques in a safe environment without the risk of endan-gering real patients. Gamers may manage and interact with the virtual environ-ment in a way that feels more natural and intuitive than conventional gaming controls because of the suitability of VR interaction for gaming (Checa et al., 2020; Tao et al., 2021).

Since both technologies have much potential for advancement in the future, the benefits of AR and VR engagement are not just restricted to the present. The ability of AR technology to recognize a larger variety of objects and situations, as well as to provide more seamless and natural interaction, is going to advance and become more sophisticated in the upcoming years. In terms of VR, it is expected that accessibility will increase as the cost of the necessary gear and software drops and the experience improves. Both technologies are anticipated to be used more frequently in various industries, such as entertainment, healthcare, and educa-tion. Augmented reality technology is widespread in the marketing, tourism, and education sectors. AR can be applied to the education sector to improve learning by making it more interactive and interesting. Students can learn more effectively by adding digital content to textbooks, posters, and other instructional materials. AR can be utilized in the marketing industry to develop personalized, interactive advertising campaigns that help businesses connect with their target audiences in new ways. AR can be used in the tourist sector to give visitors a better experi-ence at museums and historical sites. Comparing AR to VR, it also benefits from having a lower cost and being simpler to utilize. This is so that a wider range of consumers can employ AR, which can be deployed on already-existing devices like smartphones and tablets. Additionally, compared to VR, AR's technologi-cal specifications are less complicated and easier to construct. Because of this, organizations like businesses and educational institutions can adopt AR without substantially investing in technology or resources (Gudoniene & Rutkauskiene, 2019; Markel, 1972).

Both augmented and virtual reality are anticipated to be more frequently used in various industries. AR is expected to become a significant educational tool, enabling more dynamic and interesting learning opportunities. It is also anticipated to be utilized for work-related activities like remote collaboration, training, and maintenance. In order to support more sophisticated applications like virtual telepresence and remote surgery, VR is predicted to become more realistic and immersive. Additionally, it is anticipated to become more affordable and accessible, increasing its use to a wider spectrum of people (Berryman, 2012).

To sum up, AR and VR each has distinctive characteristics that make them effective in various applications. Virtual reality (VR) offers a fully immersive experience and more control over the user's environment, while augmented reality (AR) is more widely available and simpler to install. As these two technologies advance, it seems likely that they will be even more frequently used and integrated into various businesses, providing novel and creative methods to engage with the outside world. However, AR and VR have some drawbacks, including lesser immersion of AR compared to VR and its reliance on external devices. The disadvantages of VR include more expensive gear and development costs, the possibility of motion sickness, and the requirement for specialized physical space.

The rest of the chapter is arranged as follows: In Section 2, the literature review is provided. The methodology and core algorithms employed to develop AR-Learn are discussed in Section 3. Finally, the challenges and future directions of AR in education and its potential as a tool for personalized and immersive learning are provided in Section 4.

8.2 LITERATURE REVIEW

Augmented reality (AR) is a rapidly growing technology with much potential to revolutionize education. AR is an interactive and immersive technology that can provide learners with a unique learning experience by overlaying digital content in the real world. For example, AR provides object recognition industrial design, as shown in Figure 8.2. According to the literature, AR can improve students' engagement, motivation, and understanding of complex concepts. This section thoroughly reviews the relevant literature on AR and education, focusing on AR's advantages, potential limitations, and impact on student learning.

8.2.1 ADVANTAGES OF AR IN EDUCATION:

AR has several advantages that can enhance the teaching and learning experience. First, augmented reality (AR) can give students a practical educational experience that enables them to engage with digital content in real time, which can improve their understanding and retention of complex concepts, particularly in the STEM fields (science, technology, engineering, and mathematics) (Hwang et al., 2016). Second, AR can enhance learners' engagement and motivation by making learning more dynamic and enjoyable (Dunleavy et al., 2009). Third, AR can provide learners with personalized and adaptive learning experiences based on their needs and preferences (Hwang et al., 2016). Fourth, despite their location or socioeconomic standing, learners can access digital tools and resources through augmented reality (Jesionkowska et al., 2020).

FIGURE 8.2   Object recognition in industrial design using AR

8.2.2   AR IN EDUCATION: ITS LIMITATIONS

Although AR may have some advantages, there are also a few constraints that must be considered. First, implementing the necessary technological infrastructure for AR in various educational settings—including hardware, software, and connectivity—can be expensive and difficult (Jesionkowska et al., 2020). Second, some educators may find it difficult to include AR in the curriculum because constructing may take a lot of time and work (Dunleavy et al., 2009). Finally, some institutions may find it difficult to implement AR due to the possible need for specialized training and support for both educators and students (Hwang et al., 2016). The use of AR in educational settings has also raised concerns concerning possible diversions and safety risks (Jesionkowska et al., 2020).

8.2.3   EFFECTS OF AR ON LEARNING OUTCOMES

Numerous studies have examined how AR affects student learning in various educational contexts. According to a study in [10], AR helped students better understand scientific concepts and improved their learning drive. Similar findings were made by the authors of [4], who discovered that AR helped students remember and grasp basic anatomy principles. According to a study by Pellas et al. (2019), augmented reality (AR) increased students' interest and involvement in learning, particularly regarding geography and history, as shown in Figure 8.3. However, augmented reality's effects on student learning have been the subject of divergent results in several research (Xiong et al., 2021).

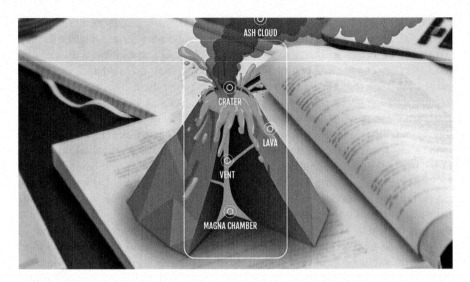

FIGURE 8.3   3D model of volcano eruption overlaid on the science textbook

The literature suggests that AR can potentially enhance teaching and learning experiences in various educational settings. However, it is important to consider the potential limitations and challenges associated with the use of AR and to ensure that it is implemented pedagogically sound and effective.

8.3 METHODOLOGY

This work has been divided into three main phases: image recognition, 3D modeling, and interactive design. Unity 3D game engine1 and the Vuforia2 augmented reality platform were used in the development of the AR-Learn project and were chosen because of their usability, dependability, and compatibility with a range of devices.

8.3.1 Software Tools

The following section contains details about these tools in more depth.

8.3.1.1 Vuforia

Vuforia was developed by Parametric Technology Corporation (PTC). It has become one of the most popular AR development platforms, with over 500,000 registered developers and over 275,000 applications created using Vuforia. It is an augmented reality software development kit (SDK) that allows developers to create mobile applications for various platforms, including iOS and Android. Vuforia uses computer vision technology to recognize and track images and objects in the real world, allowing digital content to be overlaid on top of them. This section provides a detailed overview of Vuforia, its features, and its applications in education.

The SDK includes various features and tools, including image recognition and tracking, 3D object recognition, text recognition, and Smart Terrain. One of the key features of Vuforia is its image recognition and tracking capabilities. With Vuforia, developers can create cross-platform applications that recognize and track real-world images, allowing digital content to be overlaid on top of them. This feature can create interactive educational content, such as textbooks and worksheets, that comes to life when visualizing on a mobile device. The ability of Vuforia to recognize 3D objects is another significant feature. With this functionality, developers can make applications that can recognize and track 3D objects in the physical world so that digital content can be overlaid on top of them. An 3D model of an automobile engine for industrial design using Vuforia Studio is shown in Figure 8.4. This capability can be utilized to develop engaging educational resources, such as virtual tours of historical landmarks or museums.

It also includes text recognition capabilities, which allow applications to recognize and track printed text in the real world. This useful feature can be used to create interactive educational content, such as language learning applications that provide real-time translations of printed text. In addition to these features, Vuforia includes Smart Terrain, which allows applications to recognize and track the shape and surface of real-world objects or scenes. This feature can create interactive educational experiences, such as virtual dissections of animals or geological surveys of landscapes. There are several uses for Vuforia in an educational setting. It can be used to produce multimedia exercises and manuals that improve learning and make it more immersive. Furthermore, it can be employed to create educational video games and simulations involving students learning difficult concepts. Moreover, it

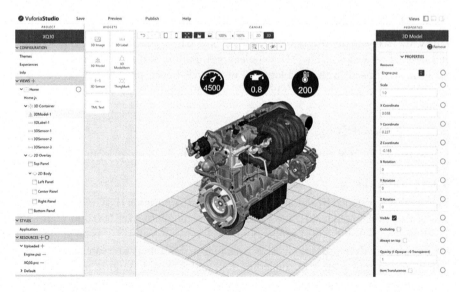

FIGURE 8.4   An instance of 3D model of automobile engine for industrial design using Vuforia Studio

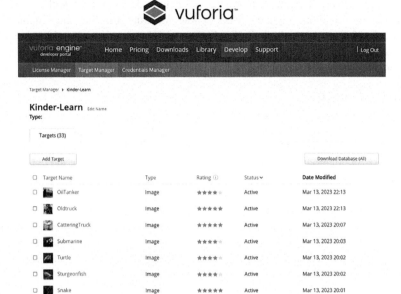

FIGURE 8.5   An insight of AR learning app for kindergarten

enables the development of virtual field trips that advise students to tour historical sites, museums, and other educational venues without leaving the classroom.

Here is an insight into an AR learning app for kindergarten children as shown in Figure 8.5.

Overall, Vuforia is a powerful AR development platform with numerous applications in education. Its image recognition and tracking capabilities, 3D object recognition, text recognition, and Smart Terrain make it a versatile and flexible tool for creating interactive educational content. The interface of the Vuforia engine, which is essential to the "AR-Learn" software's image recognition features, is shown in Figure 8.5. As AR technology continues to evolve and become more mainstream, we can expect to see even more innovative and engaging educational experiences created using Vuforia and other AR development platforms. In our work, Vuforia was used to produce the result. Using Vuforia's image recognition technology, we created an application that lets users aim their device's camera at a particular image or object and have the application superimpose pertinent digital material over the scene. As a result, we were able to give students a learning experience that was genuinely interactive and immersive.

We used Vuforia's Unity integration to add AR capability to our Unity-based application quickly. This integration helped us speed up our app's development by providing us with various tools and resources, including sample projects, Application Programming Interface (APIs), and plugins. Additionally, we could store and manage our image targets and related digital content in the cloud thanks to Vuforia's cloud recognition service. This made it simpler for us to update and change the content of our application without requiring users to download and install updates manually.

Vuforia played a crucial role in developing our educational application, providing us with the tools and resources necessary to create an engaging and interactive AR learning experience for our users.

8.3.1.2 Unity 3D

For the development of video games, mobile applications, and interactive experiences for a variety of platforms, including desktop, mobile, online, and console, Unity Technologies built the Unity3D game engine. Software developers can create immersive and interactive 3D and 2D experiences using this popular and potent game engine. In this chapter, we will go over numerous features of Unity3D, its background, and applications in developing games and other applications. Unity3D was first released in 2005 as a Mac OS X-exclusive game engine by Unity Technologies. It was designed to provide a simple, easy-to-use platform for developing 3D games and applications. In 2008, Unity3D was made available on Windows, and since then, it has gained much popularity due to its cross-platform support and ease of use. Unity3D has been used to develop various popular games, such as Rust, Hollow Knight, Hearthstone, Ori, and Blind Forest.

Unity3D is a robust game engine that offers a variety of features. These features make it simple for developers to develop games and applications for various devices, including support for many platforms like desktop, mobile, web, and console. Support for both 2D and 3D development, which enables the creation of various kinds of games and applications, support for several kinds of scripting languages, including C#, JavaScript, and Boo, which makes it simple for developers to generate original scripts and incorporate functionality into their games and applications, availability of an extensive asset library with a variety of elements that might be easily and quickly included in games and applications, such as 3D models, audio, and scripts. With the aid of a robust visual editor, developers may design and edit scenes, animations, and user interfaces without scripting any code. Additionally, an integrated physics engine enables the development of physics-based video games and software.

Unity3D is a popular game engine used to develop various games for different platforms. Unity3D is a popular option for game developers due to its simplicity and cross-platform compatibility. Games with excellent graphics, physics, and sound can be made with Unity3D, which improves the overall gaming experience. Unity3D is not only limited to game development but is also widely used in developing mobile applications and other interactive experiences. Unity3D's cross-platform support makes it easy for developers to create apps for multiple devices with a single code-base. Unity3D allows developers to create interactive and engaging applications with high-quality graphics and animations.

8.3.1.3 Scripting Backend of Unity

Scripting is a crucial aspect of game development, enabling developers to bring life to their creations. In Unity, a popular game engine, different scripting backends provide varying performance levels and compatibility with different platforms. This chapter will explore the scripting backends of Unity, highlighting their features, advantages, and use cases.

1) **Mono:** Mono is the default scripting backend in Unity, based on the open-source Mono framework. It offers cross-platform support and allows developers to write code in C#. Mono provides high compatibility with various platforms, including Windows, macOS, Linux, Android, iOS, etc. It benefits from a mature ecosystem and a vast community, making it a popular choice for Unity developers. There are numerous advantages to Mono, which are listed as follows:

   a) *Compatibility*: Mono offers excellent compatibility across different platforms, making porting games to multiple devices easier.

   b) *Performance*: Although not as performant as other scripting backends, Mono provides sufficient performance for most games, especially when optimized properly.

   c) *Large community:* Being widely used, Mono has a large community of developers who can offer support, share knowledge, and contribute to developing tools and libraries.

2) **Intermediate Language to C++ (IL2CPP):** Another Unity scripting backend translates the managed code (C# or other .NET languages) into platform-specific C++ code. It combines the benefits of managed code and native code, resulting in improved performance and platform compatibility. Following are some important features of IL2CPP.

   a) *Performance:* IL2CPP offers enhanced runtime performance compared to Mono. Converting code to C++ allows for more efficient execution and reduces memory overhead.

   b) *Platform compatibility:* IL2CPP supports a wide range of platforms, including all those supported by Mono, along with additional platforms such as consoles (PlayStation, Xbox, Nintendo Switch) and web platforms (WebGL).

   c) *Code obfuscation*: Since IL2CPP generates C++ code, it becomes harder for potential hackers to reverse-engineer or tamper with the game's code.

3) **Burst:** Burst is a high-performance scripting backend introduced in Unity 2018.1. It is specifically designed for CPU-intensive operations and works with the Unity Job System. Burst leverages the low-level virtual machine compiler to generate highly optimized machine code, significantly improving performance. A few of the Burst's characteristics are explained as follows:

   a) *Performance:* Burst is optimized for performance-critical code. Generating highly efficient machine code can deliver substantial speed gains for computationally intensive tasks.

   b) *Job system integration*: Burst works seamlessly with the Unity Job System, allowing developers to write highly parallelized code and leverage multicore processors effectively.

c) *Simplified development:* Burst simplifies the process of achieving performance optimizations as it automatically applies various optimization techniques under the hood.

Understanding the different scripting backends of Unity is crucial for game developers to choose the appropriate one based on their project requirements. Mono offers excellent compatibility and a mature ecosystem, while IL2CPP provides improved performance and wider platform support. Burst, however, is ideal for CPU-intensive operations and offers significant performance gains when used in conjunction with the Unity Job System. By utilizing the appropriate scripting backend, developers can enhance their Unity games' performance, compatibility, and overall quality.

8.3.1.4 Relationship Between Scripting Backends and the AR Learn application

We examined the various Unity scripting backends in Section 8.3.1.2.1, emphasizing their benefits. Analyze the value of the scripting backend regarding the creation of the AR Learn application, which uses augmented reality (AR) technology to turn kids' excessive screen time into something imaginative and productive. The choice of a scripting backend is a key factor in defining the efficiency, compatibility, and overall user experience of the AR Learn application. Unity has a variety of scripting backends, including Mono, IL2CPP, and Burst, all of which have particular strengths and potential impacts on the performance of an application.

a) **MONO for Cross-Platform Support:** For developing the AR Learn app, the Mono scripting backend—which is Unity's default option—is an excellent selection. Mono's cross-platform compatibility guarantees that the programs may be deployed easily across numerous devices, including smartphones, tablets, and even PCs, as it targets learners who may use a variety of gadgets and operating systems. This makes the software easily accessible and widely available for students to use on their favorite devices.

b) **Enhanced Performance and Platform Compatibility with IL2CPP:** Performance becomes essential for the AR Learn application to deliver an engaging and immersive AR experience. Developers may use the IL2CPP scripting backend's enhanced runtime speed, which translates to smoother animations, faster loading times, and fewer lags during AR interactions. Furthermore, IL2CPP's increased platform compatibility enables the application to reach more consumers by supporting new platforms like game consoles and web platforms. Thus, the AR Learn application's accessibility and audience increase since children can use it on various gadgets.

c) **Burst for Optimized CPU-Intensive Operations:** Burst, Unity's high-performance scripting backend, can significantly improve several parts of the AR Learn application's functionality, even though it may not substantially rely on CPU-intensive processes. For instance, Burst with the Unity Job System can significantly increase performance if the program contains intricate calculations or simulations. This allows resource-intensive applications like complex physics simulations or real-time data processing to be carried out effectively, improving the user experience.

In conclusion, Unity3D is a powerful and popular game engine employed in developing video games and software. Its numerous capabilities, including cross-platform compatibility, 2D, and 3D support, many scripting languages, a sizable content store, a visual editor, and an integrated physics engine, make it a top choice for developers. Unity3D has been used to develop several well-known games and applications for various platforms. It is the most suitable choice for developers to build interactive and captivating consumer experiences because of its cross-platform support and ease of usage.

8.3.2 IMAGE RECOGNITION AND TRACKING

The first step in the development of AR-Learn was to create an image recognition system that could recognize 2D images and overlay them with 3D models. We used the Vuforia platform to create the image recognition system. Vuforia provides a comprehensive set of tools to recognize and track various types of images. To create the image recognition system, we used an edge detection algorithm to identify the boundaries of the 2D images. This allowed us to identify the specific image the user pointed their camera at. Once the image was identified, we used Vuforia's object recognition algorithm to match the image to a 3D model in our database.

8.3.3 IMAGE DETECTION USING VUFORIA ENGINE

Vuforia uses this algorithm to identify images and objects in the real world that trigger the display of AR content. The algorithm uses various computer vision techniques such as feature detection, image processing, and pattern recognition to match the real-world image with the image in the app database. Additionally, we have used the tracking algorithm to track the position and orientation of the device in real time. We use marker-based and natural feature tracking to track the device's movements and update the AR content accordingly. Figure 8.6 shows the tracking process. All the different crosses are the tracking points through which a point cloud analyses the scene and creates AR upon it, the big red circle shows the point at which AR gets augmented. Next, we rendered the 3D models and other AR content in real time using Unity. A combination of rendering techniques such as rasterization, raytracing, and shading are available to create realistic 3D graphics. We then employed the physics engine algorithm of Unity to simulate physics and collisions in the AR environment. It computes the motion and interactions of objects based on their mass, velocity, and other physical properties. Finally, both Vuforia and Unity combine the real-world view seamlessly with virtual AR content. The algorithm calculates the AR content's position, size, and orientation relative to the real-world view and adjusts it in real time as the device moves.

FIGURE 8.6 Object tracking: cross marks (trackers) of various features of a scene/object; the red circle represents the placement area of its 3D model

The Vuforia engine uses a patented visual simultaneous localization and mapping (VSLAM) algorithm to identify and track the targets. VSLAM is a simultaneous localization and mapping (SLAM) algorithm commonly used in robotics and computer vision applications. The VSLAM algorithm used in Vuforia analyzes the visual features of the target image and compares them to a preexisting database of target images. The algorithm can handle various lighting conditions, camera positions, and orientations, making it suitable for various AR applications. The VSLAM algorithm in Vuforia is supported by additional techniques, such as geometric constraints and machine learning-based techniques, to improve its accuracy and robustness. These techniques work together to provide a reliable and efficient image recognition and tracking system.

The technical formulas employed in VSLAM can be extremely complicated and vary depending on the application. A high-level description of the VSLAM method is that it estimates the camera's pose (position and orientation) in relation to the target image and updates the estimate as the camera moves and the image varies. A set of nonlinear equations need to be solved in order to accomplish this, which can be done using optimization methods like the Gauss-Newton (Burke & Ferris, 1995) [14] method and the Levenberg-Marquardt algorithm (Moré, 2006).

8.3.3 FEATURE DETECTION AND MATCHING ALGORITHM

The main goal of this algorithm is to identify distinctive features in an image and match them across different images, enabling accurate tracking of objects in real-world environments. The feature detection stage involves identifying regions in an image that are distinctive and repeatable, regardless of changes in lighting, scale, and orientation. This process involves analyzing the image to find key or interest points defined by certain properties such as high contrast or unique texture. There are various feature detection algorithms used in computer vision, including Harris corner detection (Sánchez et al., 2018), scale-invariant feature transform (SIFT) (Markel, 1972), speeded up robust features (SURF) (Bay et al., 2006), and oriented FAST and rotated BRIEF (ORB) (Rublee et al., 2011).

In the Harris corner detection algorithm (Sánchez et al., 2018), the corners are identified as points with high eigenvalues of the autocorrelation matrix, which is computed based on the gradient of the image. The SIFT algorithm (Markel, 1972) identifies key points by finding local maxima/minima of the difference of Gaussian functions in scale space. The SURF algorithm (Bay et al., 2006) uses HAAR wavelet responses for feature detection. The ORB algorithm uses the FAST algorithm (Rosten & Drummond, 2006) for corner detection and BRIEF (Calonder et al.) for feature descriptor generation.

After detecting features in each image, the matching stage involves identifying corresponding features in different images. This process involves computing a descriptor for each feature, which captures its unique characteristics and then comparing the descriptors across different images to find the best matches. There are two main approaches for feature matching: brute-force matching and nearest-neighbor matching.

8.3.4 3D MODELING

In the project's second stage, the images that the image recognition system recognized were turned into 3D models. The 3D models were made using Unity's 3D modeling tools. Careful consideration was taken during creation to guarantee that each model accurately represented the real thing.

We employed a number of methods, including 3D scanning, photogrammetry, and manual modeling, to generate the 3D models. Photogrammetry was used to make representations of abstract items, while 3D scanning was used to create extremely accurate models of complicated objects. For artifacts that were difficult to scan or reconstruct photogrammetrically, manual modeling was employed to create models. The 3D modeling stage is shown in Figure 8.7. Various motherboard parts were added to the scene during this stage. These parts were either extensively modeled in Cinema 4D or extracted from various online sources. This 3D program was used to produce specific materials that gave the target models depth and realism. The model has been created as Filmbox (FBX) files, a flexible 3D model format that enables animation and baked materials, to make it easier to incorporate AR features. These FBX files were then integrated into Unity after being exported, where they served as the basis for adding the AR application capabilities. The result of this comprehension approach is a carefully detailed and visually appealing 3D model, further increasing the immersive and interactive features of our designed application.

In this method, the geometric information has been extracted from photographs or digital images. It uses mathematical algorithms to create accurate 3D models or maps of objects, structures, and landscapes. To create accurate 3D models of

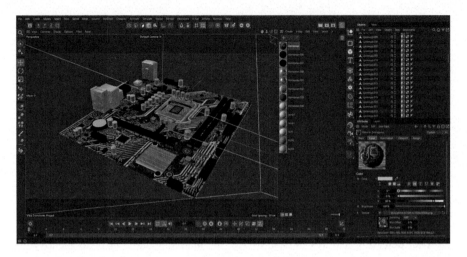

FIGURE 8.7   Different components of motherboard showcased during 3D modeling phase in Cinema 4D

the study area, photogrammetry techniques were employed using a combination of aerial and ground-based imagery. A DJI Phantom drone was used to capture high-resolution aerial photographs, while a handheld digital camera was used for ground-based shots. Bundle adjustment and triangulation algorithms were used to optimize camera parameters and determine the position of features in 3D space. Image matching was employed to identify corresponding points in the images, and a structure from motion algorithm (Westoby et al., 2012) was used to reconstruct the 3D scene. The resulting dense point cloud was then processed using a mesh reconstruction algorithm to generate a 3D mesh, which was textured using a texturing algorithm to create a realistic representation of the study area. In a photogrammetric project, we used bundle adjustment, an iterative optimization algorithm to refine the positions and orientations of cameras and 3D points. The goal of bundle adjustment is to minimize the reprojection error, which is the difference between the predicted image coordinates of a 3D point and its measured coordinates in the image. The equations used in bundle adjustment are typically based on a nonlinear least-squares optimization problem. The adjustment minimizes the sum of squared errors of the observations over all images, as shown in Equation (8.1).

$$\min_{P,X} \sum_{i=1}^{n} \sum_{j=1}^{m} X_{ij} - X_{ij}(P, X^2 \tag{8.1}$$

where P represents the set of camera parameters (position and orientation) for each image, 3D point coordinates are represented by X, and n is the total number of images. m is the number of observed points in an image. X_{ij} is the measured image point, and $\hat{X}_{ij}(P,X)$ is the predicted image point for the corresponding 3D point based on camera parameters P and X.

To determine the position of a point in 3D space, we used the triangulation method, which computes the intersection of multiple lines of sight from different camera positions. This is done using Equations 8.2, 8.3, and 8.4.

$$\frac{x_i - X_{c,i}}{f_i} = \frac{x_j - X_{c,j}}{f_j} \qquad (8.2)$$

$$\frac{y_i - Y_{c,i}}{f_i} = \frac{y_j - Y_{c,j}}{f_j} \qquad (8.3)$$

$$\frac{z_i - Z_{c,i}}{f_i} = \frac{z_j - Z_{c,j}}{f_j} \qquad (8.4)$$

Here, $x_i, y_i,$ and z_i represent the 3D coordinates of the point of interest, while the orientation and position of the camera are denoted by $x_{c,i}, y_{c,i},$ and $z_{c,i}$. The 3D coordinates of the same point of interest in camera j is represented as $x_j, y_j,$ and z_j. However, the camera is denoted by $x_{c,j}, y_{c,j},$ and $z_{c,j}$.

8.4   INTERACTIVE DESIGN

Designing an interactive user interface for the AR-Learn program was the final stage of the project. We designed a simple and user-friendly user interface (UI) using Unity's user interface abilities. Users can interact with the 3D models through the interface and examine all the models' properties. We combined Unity's user interface capabilities with custom programming to build the interactive user interface. We also added animations and physics simulations to give consumers a more realistic experience.

Several algorithms are used by Unity to create 3D tracking, augmented reality, and real-time renderings, such as simultaneous localization and mapping (SLAM) [23]. We used SLAM to track the camera's movement and map the environment in real time. This is a core task in our work as it allows virtual objects to be accurately placed in the real world. SLAM uses feature detection and matching to create a point cloud of the environment, which is used to track the camera's position and orientation.

The overall procedure for building an AR application is shown in Figure 8.8. In order to begin, the camera is turned on and pointed in the direction of the desired image or subject (if object identification is desired). The camera then starts the detection procedure to find the presence of the picture or object. The application moves on to the tracking phase after a successful detection. Trackers capture and attach to selected pixel groups throughout the scene during tracking. These trackers act as anchor points, making tracking the target's precise location and rotation possible. The phase of real-time augmentation starts once tracking is established. 3D models and other virtual content are superimposed on the tracked surface by the AR application. Users are given an immersive and interactive experience related to

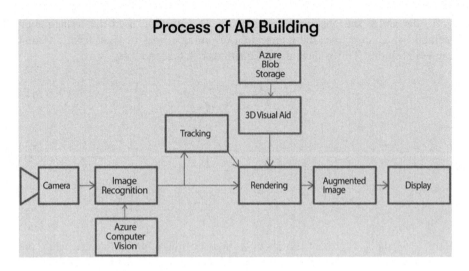

FIGURE 8.8   Flowchart of AR building process

blending the actual and virtual worlds. It is significant to highlight that the complex algorithms behind the scenes allow for the seamless and immediate execution of the entire operation. These algorithms use strong computational approaches to guarantee precise tracking, fluid augmentation, and seamless mixing of the AR Learn application's virtual and real aspects.

The various stages involved in the development of AR Learn are depicted in the flowchart shown in Figure 8.9. The selection and declaration of target images, which identify the images that will cause the recognition of matching 3D models, and building the recognition mechanism come after choosing the images. This entails putting algorithms and methods into place to make it possible for the AR application to recognize and track the targeted images in real-time precisely. We concentrate on building 3D models that correspond to the specified images simultaneously. These models have been carefully produced and are intended to accurately depict the desired items or characters that will be enhanced during the AR experience.

To achieve optimum performance within the AR environment, the 3D models go through optimization processes, including lowering polygon counts and fine-tuning the overall topology. The 3D models are smoothly combined with the designated target images once they are prepared for integration. In order to achieve the augmented reality effect, the models and images must be aligned during this integration phase. To create an accurate and engaging AR experience, the team carefully perfects the alignment and visual elements. After extensive testing and improvement, the final stage is to build the AR Learn app into an APK file. The AR Learn application may be downloaded and installed on Android devices using this APK file, allowing users to take advantage of its AR-enhanced learning experience. In order to provide an entertaining and instructive augmented reality experience, AR Learn combines the choice of target images, recognition techniques, production and optimization of 3D models, integration of models with images, and the final deployment of the mobile application.

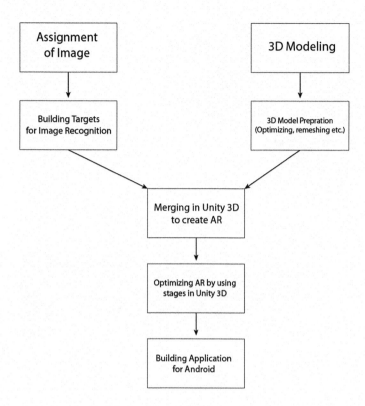

FIGURE 8.9   Flowchart of AR application building for Android

8.5   RESULTS AND DISCUSSION

The outcomes are covered in this section. Students at the university and college levels tested the AR-Learn software, and the findings were overwhelmingly favorable. The application was recognized for being imaginative and offering students a good time while learning. Additionally, it was noticed that when utilizing the AR-Learn app, the students were more attentive and interested during their learning sessions. The feedback from the students, parents, and teachers was outstanding, as they found the program very useful and exciting. The AR Learn application is demonstrated in action in Figure 8.10. It shows how seamlessly we integrated augmented reality capabilities into our application. The illustration shows how 3D chocolate chip cookies were meticulously planned during the application's development phase and then added to a selected image, giving a visually appealing effect. Users can bring an object or scene to life by pointing their cellphones at it while running our developed "AR-Learn" program. The application's intriguing use of augmented reality technology improves the user experience overall and offers young children an immersive and interactive learning environment.

Figure 8.11 is a 3D model of a phoenix that has been animated in a 3D system, and the animation track is then rendered in Unity. After successfully testing the

FIGURE 8.10   Demonstration of seamless integration of AR features of chocolate chip cookies

animation, we can export the model to Unity's augmented reality features and use it in our augmented reality applications. The curves in Figure 8.11 show the animation curves used in our application's animation process. In order to determine the interpolation between two keyframes, these curves are a necessary tool. We can change the timing and pace of the animations by adjusting these curves. We can make seamless transitions and give the animations a realistic feel by using methods like easing in and out. The animations become more fascinating, interesting, and user-engaging mainly due to the precise use of animation curves, improving overall visual appeal.

Figure 8.12 shows an instance of our suggested animation method, illustrating the complex mechanisms involved in bringing the objects to life. Each diamond-shaped element in our animation workflow is a keyframe, which is a fundamental building component. These keyframes integrate to produce exciting animations by assigning particular values to properties at specific times. Figure 8.12 also demonstrates how the 3D models were strategically placed with keyframes to allow for fluid motion and effective communication. Our application can create exciting and engaging experiences that attract young learners through the power of motion, thanks to our precise approach to animation.

Figure 8.13 provided an insightful perspective on our meticulous material development procedure. We used a variety of channels, including Albedo, displacement, and bumps, to produce astonishing visual effects. These channels enabled us to produce complex textures that gave our 3D model depth and realism. Additionally, we

FIGURE 8.11   3D model of a phoenix animated in a 3D software and the track in being played in unity; the model is then export to the AR functionality of Unity and our designed application

thoroughly optimized the appearance of our model, making it appear more photorealistic and similar to real-life objects by using various roughness maps. Our application's overall quality and immersive experience were greatly improved by the meticulous attention to detail in creating the materials.

Figure 8.14 shows a 3D model of a vibrant town with anime-inspired design features. Colorful 3D models and animations, such as a moving tram and other

FIGURE 8.12   Material creation process of a helicopter model

FIGURE 8.13   Vibrant town with an anime-inspired aesthetics

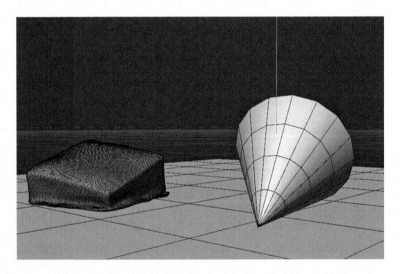

FIGURE 8.14   A demonstration of using Unity 3D's robust physics engine for the soft body (on the left side) and rigid body (on the right side)

interesting 3D objects, bring the environment to life. This specific rendering was a valuable test render during the application's development phase for augmented reality learning. It was essential to our iterative approach since it helped us identify and solve challenges while looking for creative alternatives to improve the user experience.

The featured graphics in Figure 8.14 explore how Unity 3D's powerful physics engine is used. We utilize the bullet engine in our proposed program, a popular physics simulation engine used by numerous 3D software applications. We were able to generate realistic physics simulations for the rigid and soft bodies on the left and right sides of Figure 8.14 by utilizing the physics engine. By accurately simulating the physical behavior of the items, these simulations give users a more engaging and participatory experience. Our intended 3D models were completed with expertly made animations, bringing them to life and boosting the application's interactivity by giving them a sense of realism.

In conclusion, the results of this study suggest that the AR-Learn application is a promising tool for improving student learning experiences in subjects such as engineering, biology, and physics. The positive feedback from students, parents, and teachers indicates that AR technology has the potential to revolutionize the way students learn and help make learning more accessible and interactive. Future research can further investigate the impact of AR technology on student learning outcomes and explore its potential applications in other fields. The feedback and learning outcomes obtained from the students, parents, and teachers indicate that the use of AR in education can significantly impact student engagement and knowledge retention. Despite AR's positive outcomes and advantages in education, the development and implementation of AR-based educational technologies are not without their limitations and challenges. One major challenge we encountered while developing our AR-based software was the availability of resources and expertise in developing countries. The development of AR applications requires specialized technical skills and equipment, which may not be readily available in these countries. We had to invest in resources and seek out expert help to overcome this challenge.

The expense of creating our application was another challenge we had to overcome. When complex features and functionalities are needed, AR development might be expensive. This might be difficult for educational institutions and students in developing countries with inadequate resources. Platforms were one problem; the software was developed for Android systems, but it needs to be rebuilt for iOS platforms. Since iOS and Android have distinct architectures, we must perform operations from scratch to make them compatible with iOS devices.

Additionally, it's important to ensure all students have access to AR-based devices regardless of socioeconomic standing. The digital gap that could result from some students' lack of access to the tools or internet connectivity needed for AR-based learning could restrict the potential benefits of AR in education. Despite these challenges, we believe the advantages of AR-based learning rise above their drawbacks. With the use of our software, we were able to show how AR may promote participation, deepen understanding of complex concepts, and improve learning outcomes for students. It is crucial to address challenges and strive toward making augmented reality (AR) technology more accessible and cheaper for all students, particularly those in developing nations, as it continues to advance.

8.6   CONCLUSION AND FUTURE WORK

We proposed a novel idea of using AR technology in the field of education; we built an application called "AR-Learn" to enhance the learning capabilities of the students. The learning environment we established with our program is interesting and stimulating, which can aid learners in better information retention. The study's findings showed that the application had a favorable effect on students' learning outcomes, with users reporting increased focus and engagement. Overall, this study shows how AR technology may be used in education and emphasizes the need for more innovation in this area. It is crucial to investigate the possible uses of augmented reality (AR) technology in education and to keep enhancing its efficiency as it becomes more widely available. This initiative acts as a springboard for additional study and advancement in the area of augmented reality-based learning.

Our future goal is to soon transform our AR tool into a VR, which can give consumers a more immersive experience. A 3D environment must be made, the program must be optimized for VR, and VR-specific features must be integrated to turn the AR-Learn project into a VR experience. Developing a 3D environment is the first stage in transforming the AR-Learn app into a VR app. Software like Unity 3D, which was used in building the AR-Learn app, can be used for this. The 3D models used in the AR-Learn software would need to be optimized for VR setup. This is due to the fact that in order to give a more realistic experience, VR needs more intricate 3D models. Users should be able to interact with the 3D models in a virtual reality environment. The application must be VR-optimized in the next step. As a result, the software must be created to function with VR headsets like the Oculus Rift or HTC Vive. The software must have its aesthetics and user interface modified for virtual reality (VR) devices and its performance must be enhanced for the VR platform. This phase requires a thorough assessment of the application's performance capabilities and the hardware specifications for VR devices. Adding VR-specific functionality is the last part of transforming the AR-Learn application to VR software. Unique capabilities that VR devices offer, including hand tracking and motion control, can improve the user experience. These functionalities should be incorporated into the app's interface so that users can engage with it in interesting and creative ways. For instance, users can browse the app with hand gestures rather than a touchscreen interface.

Even though the AR-Learn app has shown that it can improve student engagement and learning, there is still an opportunity for development. One of its limitations is that our study only included a small sample of students. Future research might benefit from using a larger and more varied sample size. Furthermore, only a few themes are covered by the application's content; however, future upgrades may add more topics to the database. The accessibility of the app is an additional aspect that needs improvement. Despite the fact that the software may be used on any camera-equipped smartphone, some students could not have access to one, which would limit their ability to use the program to its full potential. The app's accessibility could be improved in the future by offering different access methods to the material, including through a desktop or laptop computer.

Overall, the AR-Learn app has shown its potential to promote student learning and engagement, but there are still ways to make it more usable and advantageous to a wider range of students.

REFERENCES

Bay, H., Tuytelaars, T., & Van Gool, L. (2006). Surf: Speeded up robust features. *3951*, 404–417. https://doi.org/10.1007/11744023_32

Berryman, D. R. (2012). Augmented reality: A review. *Medical Reference Services Quarterly*, *31*(2), 212–218. https://doi.org/10.1080/02763869.2012.670604

Billinghurst, M. (2002). Augmented reality in education. *New Horizons for Learning*, *12*(5), 1–5. https://doi.org/10.240.194.115

Burke, J. V., & Ferris, M. C. (1995). A Gauss—Newton method for convex composite optimization. *Mathematical Programming*, *71*(2), 179–194. https://doi.org/10.1007/bf01585997

Calonder, M., Lepetit, V., Strecha, C., & Brief, F. (2010). Binary robust independent elementary features. *Proceedings of the European Conference on Computer Vision*. https://link.springer.com/chapter/10.1007/978-3-642-15561-1_56

Cascales, A., Laguna, I., Pérez-López, D., Perona, P., & Contero, M. (2012). Augmented reality for preschoolers: An experience around Natural Sciences educational contents. *Spdece*, *113*, 122. https://doi.org/10.1007/978-3-642-39420-1_12

Checa, D., Bustillo, A., & Applications. (2020). A review of immersive virtual reality serious games to enhance learning and training. *Multimedia Tools*, *79*, 5501–5527. https://doi.org/10.1007/s11042-019-08348-9

Dunleavy, M., Dede, C., Mitchell, R., & Technology. (2009). Affordances and limitations of immersive participatory augmented reality simulations for teaching and learning. *Journal of Science Education*, *18*, 7–22. https://doi.org/10.1007/s10956-008-9119-1

Gudoniene, D., & Rutkauskiene, D. (2019). Virtual and augmented reality in education. *Baltic Journal of Modern Computing*, *7*(2), 293–300. https://doi.org/10.22364/bjmc.2019.7.2.07

Huang, W., & Roscoe, R. D. (2021). Head-mounted display-based virtual reality systems in engineering education: A review of recent research. *Computer Applications in Engineering Education*, *29*(5), 1420–1435. https://doi.org/10.1002/cae.22393

Hwang, G.-J., Wu, P.-H., Chen, C.-C., & Tu, N.-T. (2016). Effects of an augmented reality-based educational game on students' learning achievements and attitudes in real-world observations. *Interactive Learning Environments*, *24*(8), 1895–1906. https://doi.org/10.1080/10494820.2015.1057747

Jesionkowska, J., Wild, F., & Deval, Y. (2020). Active learning augmented reality for STEAM education—A case study. *Education Sciences*, *10*(8), 198. https://doi.org/10.3390/educsci10080198

Jung, T., & tom Dieck, M. C. (2018). *Augmented Reality and Virtual Reality*. https://doi.org/10.1007/978-3-319-64027-3

Kyaw, B. M., Saxena, N., Posadzki, P., Vseteckova, J., Nikolaou, C. K., George, P. P., . . . Zary, N. (2019). Virtual reality for health professions education: Systematic review and meta-analysis by the digital health education collaboration. *Journal of Medical Internet Research*, *21*(1), e12959. https://doi.org/10.2196/12959

Markel, J. (1972). The SIFT algorithm for fundamental frequency estimation. *IEEE Transactions on Audio Electroacoustics*, *20*(5), 367–377. https://doi.org/10.1109/tau.1972.1162410

Milgram, P., & Kishino, F. (1994). A taxonomy of mixed reality visual displays. *IEICE TRANSACTIONS on Information Systems, 77*(12), 1321–1329. https://doi.org/10.1117/12.197321

Milgram, P., Takemura, H., Utsumi, A., & Kishino, F. (1995, December). Augmented reality: A class of displays on the reality-virtuality continuum. In *Telemanipulator and Telepresence Technologies* (Vol. 2351, pp. 282–292). Spie. https://doi.org/10.1117/12.197321

Moré, J. J. (2006). The Levenberg-Marquardt algorithm: Implementation and theory. *Numerical Analysis: Proceedings of the Biennial Conference Held at Dundee*, June 28–July 1, 1977. https://doi.org/10.1007/bfb0067700

Pellas, N., Fotaris, P., Kazanidis, I., & Wells, D. (2019). Augmenting the learning experience in primary and secondary school education: A systematic review of recent trends in augmented reality game-based learning. *Virtual Reality, 23*(4), 329–346. https://doi.org/10.1007/s10055-018-0347-2

Rojas-Sánchez, M. A., Palos-Sánchez, P. R., & Folgado-Fernández, J. A. (2023). Systematic literature review and bibliometric analysis on virtual reality and education. *Education Information Technologies, 28*(1), 155–192. https://doi.org/10.1007/s10639-022-11167-5

Rokhsaritalemi, S., Sadeghi-Niaraki, A., & Choi, S.-M. (2020). A review on mixed reality: Current trends, challenges and prospects. *Applied Sciences, 10*(2), 636. https://doi.org/10.3390/app10020636

Rosten, E., & Drummond, T. (2006). Machine learning for high-speed corner detection. *Computer Vision–ECCV 2006: 9th European Conference on Computer Vision, Graz, Austria*, May 7–13. Proceedings, Part I 9. https://doi.org/10.1007/11744023_34

Rublee, E., Rabaud, V., Konolige, K., & Bradski, G. (2011). ORB: An efficient alternative to SIFT or SURF. *2011 International Conference on Computer Vision*. https://doi.org/10.1109/iccv.2011.6126544

Sánchez, J., Monzón, N., & Salgado De La Nuez, A. (2018). An analysis and implementation of the harris corner detector. *Image Processing On Line*. https://doi.org/10.5201/ipol.2018.229

Speicher, M., Hall, B. D., & Nebeling, M. (2019). What is mixed reality? *Proceedings of the 2019 CHI Conference on Human Factors in Computing Systems*. https://doi.org/10.1145/3290605.3300767

Stretton, T., Cochrane, T., & Narayan, V. (2018). Exploring mobile mixed reality in healthcare higher education: A systematic review. *Research in Learning Technology, 26*, 2131–2131. https://doi.org/10.25304/rlt.v26.2131

Tao, G., Garrett, B., Taverner, T., Cordingley, E., & Sun, C. (2021). Immersive virtual reality health games: A narrative review of game design. *Journal of NeuroEngineering and Rehabilitation, 18*, 1–21. https://doi.org/10.1186/s12984-020-00801-3

Westoby, M. J., Brasington, J., Glasser, N. F., Hambrey, M. J., & Reynolds, J. M. (2012). 'Structure-from-motion' photogrammetry: A low-cost, effective tool for geoscience applications. *Geomorphology, 179*, 300–314. https://doi.org/10.1016/j.geomorph.2012.08.021

Xiong, J., Hsiang, E.-L., He, Z., Zhan, T., & Wu, S.-T. (2021). Augmented reality and virtual reality displays: Emerging technologies and future perspectives. *Light: Science & Applications, 10*(1), 216. https://doi.org/10.1038/s41377-021-00658-8

9 University 4.0 and Competences of Future
A Review

Astadi Pangarso

9.1 INTRODUCTION

The fourth industrial revolution has altered many facets of society, including education. Universities in particular are implementing new technologies and instructional methods to prepare students for a labor market that is constantly evolving. This new phase in the evolution of education is known as University 4.0. Universities utilize digital technologies to transform instruction, learning, research, and administration in University 4.0.

University 4.0 is founded on the principles of Industry 4.0, which includes automation, the Internet of Things, artificial intelligence, and other emergent technologies. University 4.0 integrates these technologies into various aspects of the university, including instruction, research, and administration. This new phase of university transformation is intended to equip students with the digital economy-relevant skills and competencies they need to thrive.

As the labor market evolves, employers are increasingly seeking candidates with relevant digital economy skills. University 4.0 is intended to impart these skills to students. The success competencies will continue to evolve, and universities must continue to adapt to satisfy the needs of their students and the job market.

The emergence of University 4.0 has brought significant changes to the landscape of higher education, emphasizing the need for students to possess future-ready competencies. Nevertheless, despite the growing interest in this field, previous research published in Scopus-indexed journals has revealed voids in our understanding of the specific skills students need to succeed in the University 4.0 era.

The emergence of University 4.0 has caused a shift in the landscape of higher education, emphasizing the need for students to possess future-ready skills. Previous studies have identified research deficits on the specific competencies students need to succeed in the University 4.0 era despite the growing interest in this field. Consequently, this paper aims to identify and address the research gaps in the extant literature concerning future competencies in University 4.0. This paper is written in the order presented by Rocco et al. (2023), which begins with an introduction, method, findings, discussion, and conclusion.

DOI: 10.1201/9781003425809-9

9.2   METHOD

To address the research questions and achieve the objectives of this study, a systematic literature review (SLR) type literature review was employed (Kraus et al., 2022; Snyder, 2019). According to Lim et al. (2022), SLR is the initial impetus for empirical research, allowing it to exist alone as a study (Kraus et al., 2022; Lim et al., 2022). This SLR nomenclature focuses on hybridization within the domain, specifically between University 4.0 and future competencies. In addition, this SLR contains a critical evaluation of an inductive reasoning strategy (triangulation) that employs a combination of protocols and procedures with 16 process sequences as described below:

(1) Search database. This research data is comprised of Scopus database-derived scientific research publication documents. It should be noted that at least two databases, Scopus and Web of Science/ (WoS), provide data on scientific research publication documents and are highly regarded internationally (Pangarso, 2021; Pangarso, Sisilia, & Peranginangin, 2022; Pangarso, Sisilia, Setyorini, et al., 2022). Due to the author's restricted access to the WoS database, research data for this SLR paper is obtained solely from the Scopus database.

(2) Search keywords and (3) Boolean operators. An initial search of the Scopus database using the keyword pairs: "university 4.0" and "competence" OR "competency" and 0- documents were found. Figure 9.1 depicts the results of an initial search of the Scopus database using the keyword combinations "university 4.0" and "competence" OR "competency."

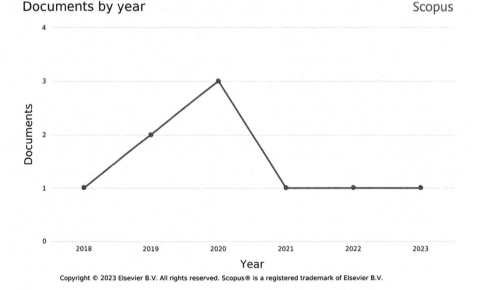

Documents by year   Scopus

FIGURE 9.1   Documents by year based on a search of the Scopus database for the keyword combination "university 4.0" AND "competence" OR "competency" (Source: Scopus.com)

(4) Search period. Figure 9.1 shows that the search for scientific research publication documents utilizing the Scopus database began in 2018 and will continue until 2023. On May 5, 2023, the SLR data document search was conducted.

(5) Search field. Search for documents using the Scopus database's "article title, abstract, and keywords" fields.

(6) Subject area. Figure 9.2 depicts a Scopus database document search based on subject area.

(7) Publication type. Publication-type SLRs are published documents, (8) none of which are currently in press or proof.

(8) Document type. Figure 9.3 depicts a Scopus database document search based on type.

(9) Source type. Figure 9.3 depicts a Scopus database document search based on source.

(10) Language. For the language of the five documents, there are seven in English, one in Spanish, and one in Russian. All of nine SLR documents will undergo further analysis because there are still manuscripts with abstracts written in English. Then, all nine documents proceed to the subsequent phase.

(11) Quality filtering. All documents are published in journals, conference proceedings and book series/chapter that are not marked as predatory, discontinued, or cancelled. Then, all nine documents proceed to the subsequent phase.

(12) Document relevance. According to the abstracts and keywords of the nine documents, the combination of "university 4.0" AND "competence" OR

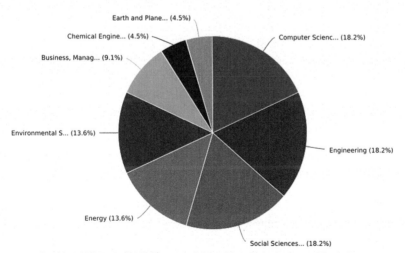

Documents by subject area   Scopus

Earth and Plane... (4.5%)
Chemical Engine... (4.5%)
Business, Manag... (9.1%)
Computer Scienc... (18.2%)
Environmental S... (13.6%)
Engineering (18.2%)
Energy (13.6%)
Social Sciences... (18.2%)

FIGURE 9.2 Documents by subject area based on a search of the Scopus database for the keyword combination "university 4.0" AND "competence" OR "competency" (Source: Scopus.com)

Documents by type   Scopus

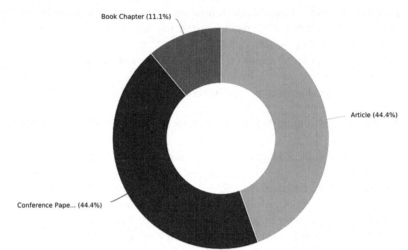

Book Chapter (11.1%)

Article (44.4%)

Conference Pape... (44.4%)

FIGURE 9.3 Documents by type based on a search of the Scopus database for the keyword combination "university 4.0" AND "competence" OR "competency" (Source: Scopus.com)

"competency" is still explicitly written. Then, all nine documents proceed to the subsequent phase.

(13) Screening process. Through a screening process based on documents that can be downloaded in their entirety and in full English, only four documents advance to the next phase.

(14) Exclusion–inclusion criteria and (16) codebook building is based on a comprehensive examination of all manuscripts using the keyword combination "university 4.0" AND "competence" OR "competency" to search each manuscript. The author only reviewed each highlighted sentence in relation to the keyword bundle to ensure that "university 4.0" AND "competence" OR "competency" was discussed. In the end, a total of four documents that had passed the 16-step SLR procedure were obtained for additional analysis and synthesis. Even if there aren't many documents produced by the SLR process to use as data samples for additional analysis, this can still be done (Pangarso, 2021; Pangarso, Sisilia, & Peranginangin, 2022; Pangarso, Sisilia, Setyorini, et al., 2022).

To analyze the results of four documents that have passed through the 16 processes above, they are then objectively analyzed using:

1. Bibliometric by analyzing performance and science mapping using VoSViewer (van Eck & Waltman, 2010) and ScienceScape (ScienceScape, n.d.).
2. Content analysis by quantifying a specific unit of analysis with the summative approach.

9.3 FINDINGS AND DISCUSSION

The four documents that passed the 16-stage SLR process were Aladyshkin et al. (2020), Madaliyeva et al. (2020), Jugembayeva et al. (2022), and Jugembayeva & Murzagaliyeva (2023).

Here is the SLR document description as shown in Table 9.1. According to Table 9.1, the following description applies to Scopus-indexed research publication documents that pass the SLR procedure. In terms of authorship, multi authorship still predominates. Researchers from developing nations, particularly Kazakhstan, continue to dominate the field for newly developed nations such as Russia. The balance between conceptual and empirical content in published articles creates a need for research in the form of literature reviews. This paper contributes to the completion of the body of knowledge concerning University 4.0 and future competencies in the form of SLR, which, according to Scopus database information, has never existed before. The form of empirical research is still exclusively quantitative, so qualitative and mixed-method research are still viable options. Furthermore, from the publication type, all documents have gone through an academic peer review process, giving greater confidence in the quality of scientific publications. Lastly, about publication outlets, the SLR results document is also quite excellent; it merely leaves room for more reputable publication outlets, such as those that publish in world-renowned journals, have restricted access (free), and are indexed by Scopus Q1 with WoS impact factor.

Additionally, Figure 9.5 shows the first data extraction and bibliometric analysis.

In addition to bibliometrics, ScienceScape includes SLR data processing, as shown in Figure 9.6.

According to Scopus citation data for the four documents that passed the SLR process, only two have received citations. This consists of performance-based bibliometric analysis. The two documents consist of articles from Jugembayeva et al. (2022) and Aladyshkin et al. (2020) with a total of 3 and 18 Scopus citations, respectively.

After performance analysis, a science mapping analysis is conducted using VosViewer and ScienceScape to process data. Figure 9.4 reveals that there are two main themes, red and green, represented by the colors red and green. The red theme contains eleven subthemes: advanced technology, learning, training, instruction, digital (infrastructure, learning, transformation, and literacy), Education 4.0, and Industry 4.0. The green theme comprises higher education, the global challenge, environmental technology, the fourth generation, and sustainable development. Figure 9.4 reveals an intriguing fact: the connection between the red and green themes is established through one of the green teas, namely higher education. University, as we all know, is an institution of higher education. Higher education in the context of University 4.0 can be interpreted as a center with objectives related to sustainable development, a global challenge, by presenting environmental technology. The concept of University 4.0 is closely related to sustainable development goals (SDG) and plays a significant role in achieving them. Moreover, the red theme relates more to the significant function of higher education institutions/universities 4.0 in preparing

TABLE 9.1
The SLR Documents Description

No	Name of author/s, year	Number of author/s	Author/s national origin	Article types (such as empirical, conceptual, position, theoretical, and literature reviews)	Type of empirical investigation (qualitative, quantitative, or combined methods)	Type of publication (peer-reviewed vs. non-peer-reviewed, academic vs. professional vs. popular)	Publishing outlet
1	Aladyshkin et al. (2020)	5	Russia	Conceptual	-	Peer reviewed, academic	Lecture Notes in Networks and Systems (Q4)
2	Madaliyeva et al. (2020)	5	Kazakhstan	Conceptual	-	Peer reviewed, academic	E3S Web of Conferences
3	Jugembayeva et al. (2022)	3	Kazakhstan	Empirical	Quantitative	Peer reviewed, academic	Sustainability (Q1)
4	Jugembayeva and Murzagaliyeva (2023)	2	Kazakhstan	Empirical	Quantitative	Peer reviewed, academic	Sustainability (Q1)

Documents per year by source   Scopus

Compare the document counts for up to 10 sources.Compare sources and view CiteScore, SJR, and SNIP data

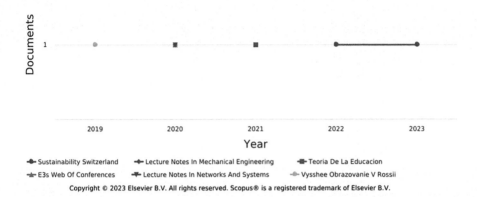

FIGURE 9.4   Documents by source based on a search of the Scopus database for the key-word combination "university 4.0" AND "competence" OR "competency" (Source: Scopus .com)

competent human resources to participate in Industry 4.0 in the future. Advanced technology in a digital infrastructure that facilitates learning, training, and teaching activities is required to develop competent human resources. Therefore, universities must implement digital technologies that promote digital literacy to modernize their institutions. With digital transformation, it is anticipated that a culture of digital literacy learning will emerge.

Figure 9.5 complements Figure 9.4 by displaying the essential competencies pro-duced by University 4.0, which include abstract-logical reasoning, creativity, and critical thinking. Regarding the future competencies that must be considered by uni-versities 4.0, imagination is also crucial. From Figure 9.5, we also obtained a sum-mative content analysis based on University 4.0 and competence-related keywords as follows: abstract-logical thinking

(1 paper); creativity (1 paper); critical thinking (1 paper); digital economics (1 paper); digital infrastructure (1 paper); digital learning (1 paper); digital literacy (1 paper); digital transformation (1 paper); e-learning (1 paper); education 4.0 (1 paper); engineering education

(1 paper); imagination (1 paper); industry 4.0 (1 paper); integration processes (1 paper); key competencies (1 paper); modern technologies (1 paper).

9.3.1   IMPLICATIONS

Based on the two types of bibliometric analysis and content analysis, this paper has implications/contributions both theoretically and practically.

A. The theoretical implications of this paper are as follows:

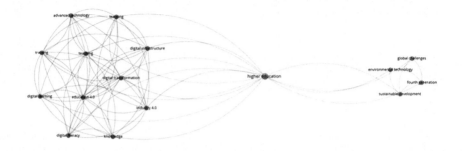

FIGURE 9.5　Bibliometric analysis using VosViewer (Source: VosViewer)

(i) discovering total sixteen thematic knowledge clusters objectively; (ii) elucidating nomological networks of sixteen themes with significance to university Industry 4.0 contributions to SDGs and the provision of qualified human resources to participate in Industry 4.0; (iii) monitoring the evolutionary nuances of research on University 4.0 and future competencies is still extremely limited, creating opportunities for future study; (iv) identifying knowledge gaps with potential for future research regarding the sixteen themes of University 4.0 and future competencies.

B. The practical implications of this paper are as follows:

(i) objectively evaluating and reporting research output and influence based on bibliometric and content analysis of four documents that passed the SLR process; (ii) Scopus is the only database used to determine the scope of SLR coverage. Scopus is one of the databases that provide credible international scientific publication documents; (iii) universities as higher education institutions must still undergo digital transformation to detect irregularities.

9.4　CONCLUSION

The following are some of the future competencies that are relevant in University 4.0:

Digital literacy: Digital literacy is the ability to use digital technologies effectively. In University 4.0, students must be proficient in using digital technologies to access, analyze, and synthesize information.

Critical thinking and problem-solving: University 4.0 emphasizes critical thinking and problem-solving skills. Students need to be able to analyze complex problems, evaluate evidence, and develop creative solutions.

Innovation and creativity: University 4.0 encourages innovation and creativity. Students need to be able to generate new ideas, develop prototypes, and test and refine solutions.

The limitations of this SLR study include the fact that the research data originates from a single database, Scopus. It is recommended that future research utilize

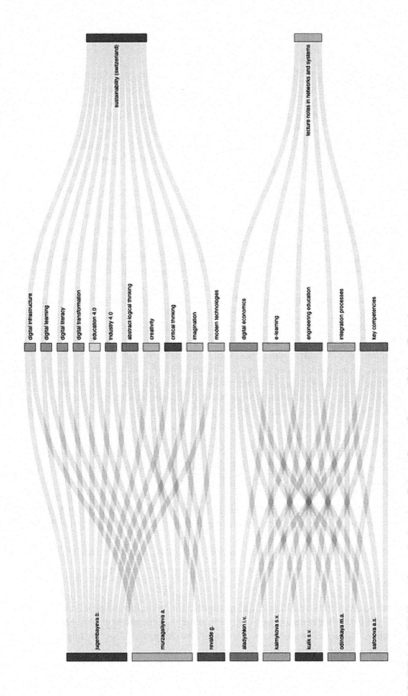

FIGURE 9.6 Bibliometric analysis using ScienceScape (Source: ScienceScape)

the WoS database to reduce outcome bias. Opportunities exist for future empirical research, mainly qualitative and blended methods.

REFERENCES

Aladyshkin, I. V., Kulik, S. V., Odinokaya, M. A., Safonova, A. S., & Kalmykova, S. V. (2020). Development of Electronic Information and Educational Environment of the University 4.0 and Prospects of Integration of Engineering Education and Humanities. In *Lecture Notes in Networks and Systems* (Vol. 131, Issue March, pp. 804–811). https://doi.org/10.1007/978-3-030-47415-7_86

Jugembayeva, B., & Murzagaliyeva, A. (2023). Physics Students' Innovation Readiness for Digital Learning within the University 4.0 Model: Essential Scientific and Pedagogical Elements That Cause the Educational Format to Evolve in the Context of Advanced Technology Trends. *Sustainability (Switzerland), 15*(1). https://doi.org/10.3390/su15010233

Jugembayeva, B., Murzagaliyeva, A., & Revalde, G. (2022). Pedagogical Model for Raising Students' Readiness for the Transition to University 4.0. *Sustainability (Switzerland), 14*(15). https://doi.org/10.3390/su14158970

Kraus, S., Breier, M., Lim, W. M., Dabić, M., Kumar, S., Kanbach, D., Mukherjee, D., Corvello, V., Piñeiro-Chousa, J., Liguori, E., Palacios-Marqués, D., Schiavone, F., Ferraris, A., Fernandes, C., & Ferreira, J. J. (2022). Literature Reviews as Independent Studies: Guidelines for Academic Practice. *Review of Managerial Science, 16*(8), 2577–2595. https://doi.org/10.1007/s11846-022-00588-8

Lim, W. M., Kumar, S., & Ali, F. (2022). Advancing Knowledge through Literature Reviews: "What", "Why", and "How to Contribute." *Journal: The Services Industries Journal, Forthcoming*, 1–33. https://doi.org/10.1080/02642069.2022.2047941

Madaliyeva, Z., Kassen, G., Sadykova, N., Baimoldina, L., & Zakaryanova, S. (2020). Resources and Competencies as Major Determinants of University Models 4.0. *E3S Web of Conferences, 159*. https://doi.org/10.1051/e3sconf/202015909001

Pangarso, A. (2021). A Socio-Economic Proposed Theoretical Framework for Responding to The Covid-19 Outbreak. *E3S Web of Conferences, 317*, 01084. https://doi.org/10.1051/e3sconf/202131701084

Pangarso, A., Sisilia, K., & Peranginangin, Y. (2022). Circular Economy Business Models in the Micro, Small, and Medium Enterprises: A Review. *Etikonomi, 21*(2), 313–334. https://doi.org/10.15408/etk.v21i2.24052

Pangarso, A., Sisilia, K., Setyorini, R., Peranginangin, Y., & Awirya, A. A. (2022). The Long Path to Achieving Green Economy Performance for Micro Small Medium Enterprise. *Journal of Innovation and Entrepreneurship, 11*(1), 1–19. https://doi.org/10.1186/s13731-022-00209-4

Rocco, T. S., Plakhotnik, M. S., McGill, C. M., Huyler, D., & Collins, J. C. (2023). Conducting and Writing a Structured Literature Review in Human Resource Development. *Human Resource Development Review, 22*(1), 104–125. https://doi.org/10.1177/15344843221141515

ScienceScape. (n.d.). Retrieved May 7, 2023, from https://medialab.github.io/sciencescape/

Snyder, H. (2019). Literature Review as a Research Methodology: An Overview and Guidelines. *Journal of Business Research, 104*(August), 333–339. https://doi.org/10.1016/j.jbusres.2019.07.039

van Eck, N. J., & Waltman, L. (2010). Software Survey: VOSviewer, a Computer Program for Bibliometric Mapping. *Scientometrics, 84*(2), 523–538. https://doi.org/10.1007/s11192-009-0146-3

10 Technology-Enabled Integrated Fusion Teaching for University 4.0

Rajesh Tiwari, Bimal Anjum, Himanshu Kargeti and Dr. Ashulekha Gupta

10.1 INTRODUCTION

Technology has played an important role in the evolution of business, countries, and life styles. University-driven education system has largely remained isolated from technology disruptions. The traditional business models have become obsolete and noncompetitive in the era of technology-driven ecosystem. University education system has to adapt to technology-driven model to remain relevant for the society. The transformation of ideal image of universities is driving the transformation of universities. Covid pandemic has provided an opportunity for rapid disruptions along with gradual changes (Chaka, 2020a). Researchers and policy makers have ignored reforms in higher education. Ignoring fundamental issues for reforming higher education would be a big mistake (Greenwood, 2007). Higher education institutions can play a crucial role for sustainable development (Giesenbauer & Muller-Christ, 2020). This chapter is an attempt to review the literature on University 4.0 in light of technology-enabled teaching. This chapter begins with an overview of overview Education 4.0. The second and third section of the chapter presents with advantages and challenges of University 4.0. Research methodology is discussed in forth section. Findings of bibliometric analysis is presented in fifth section. Sixth and seventh sections of the chapter focus on discussion and conclusion. Education 4.0 is aligned with Industry 4.0 in adoption of emerging technologies like automation, artificial intelligence, cloud computing, Internet of Things, blockchain (Chaka, 2020b). The Education 4.0 is confined to limited countries and limited institutions (Chaka, 2022).

10.2 ADVANTAGES OF UNIVERSITY 4.0

University 4.0 puts student as the key focus of all learning endeavours. The student-centric approach will enhance the learning outcomes for the students (Sharma, 2019).

DOI: 10.1201/9781003425809-10

The personalised learning flexibility gives the edge to students to develop a more efficient portfolio of skills. Teachers will be able to enhance productivity by reducing the administrative work load by optimal usage of technology and automation. The general administrative operations will become streamlined and reduce the cost of operation in long run. The university management will be able to develop more efficient business model (Sharma, 2019). Optimal utilization of resources with focus on efficiency reduces wastage and positively impacts sustainability (Padmalosan et al., 2023). It was argued by Drucker that university and higher education is in danger. The library in University 4.0 will be open access without barriers of time and distance through digital medium. The University 4.0 will be better connected with external environment and will be a living platform for creation and dissemination of ideas (Contreras et al., 2020). Technology enabled teaching is more effective than traditional teaching (Mistry and Pandya, 2020).

10.3   CHALLENGES OF UNIVERSITY 4.0

Economically weaker section students would not be able to access technology-enabled learning resources. Faculty training for technology-enabled teaching is a concern. Technology-enabled delivery of practical courses need to be evaluated. Poor internet connection and device availability are a concern for technology-enabled teaching (Mahajan et al., 2023). Poor infrastructure needs to be addressed for technology-enabled teaching. Health issues due to long screen time will limit the adoption of technology-enabled teaching. Lack of hands-on experience will impact career growth (Onyema et al., 2020). Decline in revenues of universities is a concern which needs to be addressed (Regehr, 2013). Uniform strategies for digitisation will not deliver desired results. Technology in absence of good governance leads to failure of policies (Tiwari et al., 2020). Satisfaction of users is crucial for continuous adoption of technology-enabled services (Chand et al., 2022).

10.4   METHOD

The Scopus database was used for the bibliometric analysis. The keywords used to extract documents were "technology enabled teaching" OR "university 4.0" OR "ICT Enabled Teaching" OR "Fusion Teaching" OR "sustainable teaching." The date of search was April 20, 2023. In total, 154 documents were obtained in the initial stage. Exclusion criteria were applied to screen documents. Language was the first exclusion criteria. Documents other than English were excluded. After first stage of exclusion, 146 documents were extracted. Second criteria of exclusion selected was type of document. Review (3), editorial (1), erratum (1), letter (1), and retracted (1) documents were screened in second stage of exclusion. Then, 139 documents were extracted after second stage of exclusion. The 139 documents comprised of article (80), conference paper (45), book chapter (11), and book (3). The third stage of exclusion comprised of one-to-one screening of the documents to exclude documents not focused on the research area under consideration. Sixteen documents were excluded in third stage of exclusion. Finally, 123 documents were selected for bibliographic analysis.

10.5 RESULTS

There is a sudden increase in research publications after the onset of Covid pandemic. The publications were less than five till 2018, except 2015, which witnessed six publications. Rapid rise in publications is witnessed since 2019. Fourteen documents were published in 2019, followed by 16 in 2020. Twenty-six documents were published each in 2021 and 2022. Three documents have been published in 2023 till April 20, 2023. Covid-19 pandemic has made technology integration into teaching across the world, due to lock down and Covid restrictions.

10.5.1 CITATION ANALYSIS

Out of 46 countries, 27 countries met the threshold for minimum ten citations. Singapore the most prominent country for technology-enabled teaching for sustainability for University 4.0 with 99 citations and 33 citations per document, followed by United States with 97 citations and 12 documents. Russian Federation is third most cited country, followed by Canada. Russian Federation has published highest documents (13), followed by China, India, and United States with 12 each. India has 15 citations from 12 documents. The research on technology-enabled teaching for University 4.0 is focused in countries with established technology interface and a vibrant education sector. Along with developed economies, emerging economies have also shown interest in research on technology-enabled teaching. The link strength is zero. There is lot of scope for collaborative research between different countries.

Out of 233 organisations, 22 met the threshold of 15 citations. Singapore Management University is the prominent organisation with 88 citations. National Yunlin University of Science and Technology, Taiwan has second highest citation (55), followed by Kazan Federal university, Russian Federation with 41 citations. Most of the organisations have published just one document. There is no link strength. The technology-enabled teaching for University 4.0 is an emerging area of research. University of Toronto was fourth most cited organisation, followed by Cornell University; University of Bremen; Institute for Research and Development "UTRIP," Slovenia; Institute of Education and Sciences, Portugal; University of Latvia, Latvia; and Tainan University of Technology, Taiwan.

Out of 96 sources, only 19 sources met the threshold of ten citations. Sustainability (Switzerland) is the leading journal with 19 documents and 126 citations. *Computers in Human Behavior* has 88 citations from one document. *Journal of Teacher Education for Sustainability* was third most cited journal followed by *Social Work Education, Action Research, Lecture Notes in Networks and Systems, International Journal of Engineering and Advanced Technology, Proceedings - 2018 IEEE Industrial Cyber-Physical Systems, ICPS 2018, Nursing Education Perspectives, British Journal of Educational Technology,* and *International Journal of Engineering Pedagogy.*

Out of 122 documents, 79 meet the threshold of at least one citation. "Enhancing students' learning process through interactive digital media: New opportunities for collaborative learning" published in *Computers in Human Behavior* is the most cited article by Gan B., Menkhoff T., and Smith R (2015). Article titled "Trends in higher education in Canada and implications for social work education" by Regehr (2013) has 36 citations. Third most cited article is "Teaching/learning action research requires fundamental reforms in public higher education" authored by Greenwood (2007). "University 4.0: Promoting the transformation of higher education institutions toward sustainable development" is the fourth most cited document authored by Giesenbauer and Muller-Christ (2020). Fifth most cited document was "Promoting sustainable social emotional learning at school through relationship-centered learning environment, teaching methods and formative assessment," followed by "Effective teaching and activities of excellent teachers for the sustainable development of higher design education," "Digital transformation of a university as a factor of ensuring its competitiveness," "Interaction between education and business in digital era," "Development of electronic information and educational environment of the University 4.0 and prospects of integration of engineering education and humanities," and "A matter of life and death: end-of-life simulation to develop confidence in nursing students."

10.5.2   COCITATION ANALYSIS

The cocitation analysis is done with full counting method, using cited references as unit of analysis. Out of 4437 references, only 22 met the threshold of two citations. Out of 22, only eight items were connected. Cocitation of sources was done with a threshold of minimum five citations. Out of 3,089 sources, 70 met the threshold. Out of 70, 67 were connected. *Sustainability* is the top cocited source with 88 citations and link strength of 926, followed by *Journal of Cleaner Production* with a citation of 46, a link strength of 782. *International Journal of Sustainability in Higher Education* is the third top cocited source with a citation of 27 and link strength of 571 as shown in Table 10.5. *Computers in Human Behavior* was sixth most cocited journal followed by *IEEE Transactions on Education, Educational Technology & Society, Higher Education* and *Journal of Computer Assisted Learning.*

10.5.3   COAUTHORSHIP ANALYSIS

Coauthorship analysis for countries was done with a threshold of minimum four documents and one citation. Out of 48 countries, 15 met the criteria. Out of 15 countries, only five were connected. China has a link strength of three, followed by United States and Australia with a link strength of two. Slovenia has a link strength of one. Russian Federation has 13 documents, followed by India, China, and United States with 12 documents.

10.5.4   CO-OCCURRENCE ANALYSIS

Co-occurrence analysis is conducted with a threshold of minimum five occurrences. Out of 881 keywords, 20 met the threshold. Co-occurrence map is depicted in Figure 10.1.

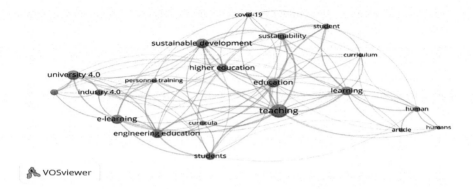

FIGURE 10.1 Co-occurrence map of keywords (Source: Chart is designed by Rajesh Tiwari, Bimal Anjum, Himanshu Kargeti, Ashulekha Gupta)

Teaching was the top cited keyword with 34 occurrences. Sustainable development and University 4.0 had 20 occurrences. E-learning and education had 19 occurrences each. The sustainability has attracted the attention of researchers in higher education. Covid pandemic has brought sustainability to the forefront of research. The technology-enabled teaching is primarily focussed on University 4.0 and sustainability. Engineering education has been the prominent area of research.

10.5.5 BIBLIOGRAPHIC COUPLING

Bibliographic coupling was conducted using VOSviewer using document as the unit of analysis with full counting method. Out of 122 documents, 52 documents were connected.

10.5.5.1 Cluster I: Sustainable Teaching

Cluster I was focussed on sustainable teaching. Cluster I comprised of 15 items. Lai and Peng (2019) is the most cited article of this cluster with 21 citations and a link strength of two. Dai (2019) is second most cited article with 13 citations and a link strength of two. Bucea-Manea-Toniş (2022) had five citations and a link strength of two. Attitude of teacher toward sustainability influences the sustainable teaching. Sustainable teaching is required for sustainable development (Lai & Peng, 2019). Dai and Hwang (2019) found that education for sustainable development is still is infancy. Sustainable teaching has the potential for provide pathways to students to explore sustainability. Bucea-Manea-Tonis et al. (2022) found that technology-enabled teaching by incorporating digital resources is needed for sustainability of universities and deliver learner-centric quality programs.

10.5.5.2 Cluster II: Technology-Enabled Teaching

Cluster II was focussed on technology-enabled teaching. Cluster II comprised of 10 documents. Gan, Menkhoff, and Smith (2015) is the most cited article of this cluster with 88 citations and a link strength of two. Kerroum (232020) is the second most cited article with 15 citations and a link strength of two. Krajcovic (2021) is the third most cited article with 8 citations and a link strength of two. Bachir (2019a) had four citations but a link strength of ten. Bachir and Abenia (2019) had two citations and a link strength of seven. Gan et al. (2015) observed that collaborative learning supported by technology-enabled teaching enhances learning outcomes. Kerroum et al. (2020) recommended digital approach for transformation of university to satisfy the stakeholder expectations. Krajcovic et al. (2021) found technology-driven teaching to be more effective in knowledge transfer and retention. Virtual reality model was recommended for better learning outcomes. Bachir et al. (2019) examined technology interface in universities and recommended cyber physical system for transformation of a university to University 4.0. Universities have to align themselves with Industry 4.0 to provide learning in a hybrid mode utilising virtual and physical delivery modes. Bachir and Abenia (2019) recommended technology-enabled teaching supported by Internet of Everything.

10.5.5.3   Cluster III: Social-Cultural Orientation

Cluster III was focussed on sociocultural orientation for transformation of universities. Cluster III comprised of 10 documents. Regehr (2013) is the most cited article in this cluster with 36 citations and a link strength of one. Ferreira (2020) is the second most cited article with 24 citations and a link strength of two. Hakansson Lindqvist (2019) is the third most cited article with 17 citations and a link strength of eight. Regehr (2013) highlighted the issue of declining revenues amid rising accountability of universities. It was recommended that creativity is needed for adoption of technology in universities. Social and emotional aspects must be integrated into teaching to make it sustainable. Hakansson (2019) argued that leadership and attitude toward technology-enabled teaching influences outcomes of technology adoption and sustainability.

10.5.5.4   Cluster IV: Collaborations

Cluster IV focussed on evaluation of the role of collaboration for transformation of universities. Cluster IV comprised of nine documents. Wen (2017) is the most cited article in this cluster with seven citations and a link strength of one. Indrajit (2021) is the second most cited article with six citations and a link strength of seven. Wessels (2022) is the third most cited article with citation of two and a link strength of seven. Wen and Wu (2017) evaluated training needs of teachers. It was found that evaluation of teacher should be done independently to enhance self-reflection about their teaching and suggest ways to improve their teaching. Domain-specific and research-oriented training will enhance quality of teaching. Self-reflection will enhance sustainability. Indrajit et al. (2021) argued that collaboration with stakeholders, resource sharing, and optimal usage of technology is required transformation of universities to University 4.0 in alignment with Industry 4.0. Gorina and Polyakova (2021) viewed collaboration as a way forward to transform university and contribute in sustainable development. Wessels and van Wyk (2022) proposed macro and micro renewal model for University 4.0. collaboration of policy makers at country

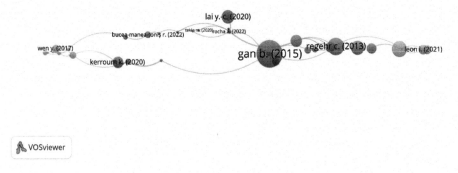

FIGURE 10.2   Network map of bibliographic coupling (Source: Chart is prepared by Rajesh Tiwari, Bimal Anjum, Himanshu Kargeti, Ashulekha Gupta)

level and institution level is needed for synchronising the transformation. At micro level, understanding of student demographics, training and sensitivity of teachers, and flexibility of leadership is needed for transforming the universities according to Industry 4.0.

10.5.5.5   Cluster V: Pedagogy

Cluster V focussed on pedagogy for University 4.0. Cluster V comprised of eight documents. Giesenbauer (2020) is the most cited article of this cluster with 31 citations and link strength of nine. Leon (2021) is the second most cited article with 11 citation and link strength of four. Alonso-García (2021) is the third most cited document in this cluster with 10 citations and link strength of two. Giesenbauer and Muller-Christ (2020) supported networking for transformation. Leon et al. (2021) suggested BIM pedagogy for teaching to manage issues due to pandemic. Alonso-Garcia et al. (2021) examined pedagogy of remote teaching during Covid pandemic. It was found that pedagogy and evaluation needs improvement to achieve sustainability. Pedagogy for University 4.0 should focus on debate, discussion involving various stakeholders (Rosak-Szyrocka et al., 2022). The network map of bibliographic coupling is shown in Figure 10.2.

10.6   DISCUSSION

The emergence of Industry 4.0 in developed economies is getting reflected in emergence of research interest for university 4.0. The university 4.0 is aligned with Industry 4.0. The need for creative thinking human resource for managing complex problems will drive university 4.0. The sudden increase in research interest for university 4.0 after onset of Covid pandemic indicates the paradigm shift higher education sector. The availability of digital infrastructure and devices is supporting integration of technology-enabled teaching for university 4.0. Singapore emerged as the top cited country, followed by United States. European countries are amongst the prominent countries for research interest in technology-enabled teaching for university 4.0. India with 12 documents shows the potential for university 4.0. Being the youngest country on account of demographic profile, India has the potential for leveraging demographics with digital ecosystem for university 4.0. Singapore Management University, Singapore is the prominent university for citation. University 4.0 and technology-enabled teaching has been ignored by researchers. Most of the organisations have published only 1 document. There is lot of scope for further research and collaborations between different universities. Technology-enabled teaching and university 4.0 is been considered as potential source to enhance sustainability. Sustainability (Switzerland) is the most prominent journal with 19 articles and 126 citations. The research interest is broad base with articles being published in diverse academic fields ranging from computers, engineering, teaching, nursing and social sciences. Availability of digital ecosystem provides a cost effective and feasible manner to transform traditional universities to digital driven university 4.0. Role of teachers is prominent for realisation of university 4.0 (Lai & Peng, 2019). Teaching was found to be the most frequently occurring keyword, followed by sustainable development. The disruptions in technology, business and societal relationships have led to creation of new ways of production, resource utilisation, evaluation and innovation. Transformation in teaching will drive the transformation of universities. Universities failing to align with Industry 4.0 will be driven out by market forces. Researchers have given highest preference to sustainability issues while exploring university 4.0. The cluster I was the largest cluster with 15 articles, focussed on sustainability. Attitude, pedagogy should be oriented towards sustainability. Technology-enabled teaching is necessary condition for university 4.0. Cluster II was focussed on technology-enabled teaching. Technology in isolation is not sufficient for transformation of universities. Cluster III highlighted the importance of sociocultural orientation for university 4.0. The transformation needs a customised approach that suits the sociocultural and economic requirements of the university. Universities need to evolve as open systems to align with the requirements of Industry 4.0 and contribute towards sustainability. Cluster IV signified the role of collaboration with other stakeholders and institutions for transformation of universities. Technology infrastructure is useful only when used with appropriate pedagogy. Cluster V focussed on pedagogy and operations of university. Pedagogy needs to evolve to give space for self-reflection, discussion, collaboration and optimal utilisation of digital infrastructure.

There is an opportunity to explore technology-enabled fusion teaching model of Tiwari et al. (2023). The technology-enabled fusion teaching integrates assessment with teaching. The real time assessment provides opportunity for self-reflection. Fusion teaching integrates digital resources in the classrooms. The learning outcomes of technology-enabled fusion teaching is significantly better than traditional teaching. Traditional exam system promotes rote learning (Nargund-Joshi et al., 2011; Upadhyay, 2014). Fusion teaching takes into consideration integration of various stakeholders in design, delivery and evaluation of learning activities.

10.7 CONCLUSION

This chapter explored technology-enabled fusion teaching for University 4.0 using bibliometric analysis of articles published in Scopus database. In total, 123 documents from Scopus database were used for the bibliometric analysis using VOSviewer. Science mapping was adopted for bibliometric analysis. The technology-enabled teaching and University 4.0 have attracted the attention of researchers in developed economies. Covid pandemic has enhanced the research interest as institutions and countries struggle with sustainability issues. Sharp rise in publication in University 4.0 after the onset of Covid highlights the vulnerability of traditional universities is a disruptive world. The research publications from different institutions and regions parts lacks collaboration. The bibliographic coupling resulted in five clusters. Sustainability, technology-enabled teaching, sociocultural orientation, collaboration, and pedagogy were the major themes of research in University 4.0. Sustainable education system needs to address emotional stability and ability to solve complex problems by reforming traditional assessment with a comprehensive assessment integrating emotional and social attitudes of learner. University 4.0 needs integration of policy framework, leadership involvement, technology infrastructure, teacher and student readiness, self-reflection-based learning, and assessment and collaboration with stakeholders to transform traditional universities to an open system working in sync with Industry 4.0 to support sustainable development.

REFERENCES

Alonso-García, M., Garrido-Letrán, T. M., & Sánchez-Alzola, A. (2021). Impact of COVID-19 on educational sustainability. Initial perceptions of the university community of the University of Cádiz. *Sustainability*, 13(11), 5938. https://doi.org/10.3390/su13115938

Bachir, S., & Abenia, A. (2019). Internet of everything and educational cyber physical systems for university 4.0. In *Computational Collective Intelligence: 11th International Conference, ICCCI 2019, Hendaye, France, September 4–6, 2019, Proceedings, Part II 11* (pp. 581–591). Springer International Publishing. https://doi.org/10.1007/978-3 -030-28374-2_50

Bachir, S., Gallon, L., Abenia, A., Aniorté, P., & Exposito, E. (2019). Towards autonomic educational cyber physical systems. In *2019 IEEE SmartWorld, Ubiquitous Intelligence & Computing, Advanced & Trusted Computing, Scalable Computing & Communications, Cloud & Big Data Computing, Internet of People and Smart City Innovation (SmartWorld/SCALCOM/UIC/ATC/CBDCom/IOP/SCI)* (pp. 1198–1204). IEEE. https://doi.org/10.1109/SmartWorld-UIC-ATC-SCALCOM-IOP-SCI.2019 .00223

Bucea-Manea-Țoniș, R., Vasile, L., Stănescu, R., & Moanț ă, A. (2022). Creating IoT-enriched learner-centered environments in sports science higher education during the pandemic. *Sustainability*, 14(7), 4339. https://doi.org/10.3390/su14074339

Chaka, C. (2020a). Higher education institutions and the use of online instruction and online tools and resources during the COVID-19 outbreak-An online review of selected US and SA's universities. https://doi.org/10.21203/rs.3.rs-61482/v1

Chaka, C. (2020b). Skills, competencies and literacies attributed to 4IR/Industry 4.0: Scoping review. *IFLA Journal*, 46(4), 369–399. https://doi.org/10.1177/0340035219896376

Chaka, C. (2022, April). Is education 4.0 a sufficient innovative, and disruptive educational trend to promote sustainable open education for higher education institutions? A review of literature trends. In *Frontiers in Education* (Vol. 7, p. 226). Frontiers. https://doi.org /10.3389/feduc.2022.824976

Chand, K., Tiwari, R., & Sapna. (2022). Effect of perception and satisfaction on preference for mobile wallet. *FIIB Business Review.* https://doi.org/10.1177/23197145221077365

Contreras, G. S., Cepa, C. B. M., Fernández, I. S., & Escobar, J. C. Z. (2020). Higher education in the face of the push of new technologies. Virtual, augmented and mixed reality in the teaching environment. *Contemporary Engineering Sciences*, 13(1), 247–261. https://doi.org/10.12988/ces.2020.91601

Dai, Y., & Hwang, S. H. (2019). Technique, creativity, and sustainability of bamboo craft courses: Teaching educational practices for sustainable development. *Sustainability*, 11(9), 2487. https://doi.org/10.3390/su11092487

Ferreira, M., Martinsone, B., & Talic, S. (2020). Promoting sustainable social emotional learning at school through relationship-centered learning environment, teaching methods and formative assessment. *Journal of Teacher Education for Sustainability*, 22(1), 21–36. https://doi.org/10.2478/jtes-2020-0003

Gan, B., Menkhoff, T., & Smith, R. (2015). Enhancing students' learning process through interactive digital media: New opportunities for collaborative learning. *Computers in Human Behavior*, 51, 652–663. https://doi.org/10.1016/j.chb.2014.12.048

Giesenbauer, B., & Müller-Christ, G. (2020). University 4.0: Promoting the transformation of higher education institutions toward sustainable development. *Sustainability*, 12(8), 3371. https://doi.org/10.3390/su12083371

Gorina, L., & Polyakova, E. (2021). University 4.0 within the context of the sustainable development of higher education. In *E3S Web of Conferences* (Vol. 250, p. 04002). EDP Sciences. https://doi.org/10.1051/e3sconf/202125004002

Greenwood, D. J. (2007). Teaching/learning action research requires fundamental reforms in public higher education. *Action Research*, 5(3), 249–264. https://doi.org/10.1177/1476750307081016

Hakansson Lindqvist, M. (2019). School leaders' practices for innovative use of digital technologies in schools. *British Journal of Educational Technology*, 50(3), 1226–1240. https://doi.org/10.1111/bjet.12782

Indrajit, R. E., Wibawa, B., & Suparman, A. (2021). University 4.0 in developing countries: A case of Indonesia. *International Journal of Sociotechnology and Knowledge Development (IJSKD)*, 13(3), 33–59. https://doi.org/10.4018/IJSKD.2021070103

Kerroum, K., Khiat, A., Bahnasse, A., & Aoula, E. S. (2020). The proposal of an agile model for the digital transformation of the University Hassan II of Casablanca 4.0. *Procedia Computer Science*, 175, 403–410. https://doi.org/10.1016/j.procs.2020.07.057

Krajcovic, M., Gabajova, G., Matys, M., Grznar, P., Dulina, L., & Kohar, R. (2021). 3D interactive learning environment as a tool for knowledge transfer and retention. *Sustainability*, 13(14), 7916. https://doi.org/10.3390/su13147916

Lai, Y. C., & Peng, L. H. (2019). Effective teaching and activities of excellent teachers for the sustainable development of higher design education. *Sustainability*, 12(1), 28, https://doi.org/10.3390/su12010028

Leon, I., Sagarna, M., Mora, F., & Otaduy, J. P. (2021). BIM application for sustainable teaching environment and solutions in the context of COVID-19. *Sustainability*, 13(9), 4746. https://doi.org/10.3390/su13094746

Mahajan, R., Kumar, S., & Agrawal, M. (2023). Online teaching effectiveness: Lessons from Indian universities during the Covid-19 pandemic. *Global Business and Organizational Excellence.* https://doi.org/10.1002/joe.22207

Mistry, P., & Pandya, R. (2020). Web-based learning: Problems and tip-off students. *Mukt Shabd Journal*, IX(V), 2687–2697. https://doi.org/09.0014.MSJ.2020.V9I5.0086781.10300

Nargund-Joshi, V., Rogers, M. A. P., & Akerson, V. L. (2011). Exploring Indian secondary teachers' orientations and practice for teaching science in an era of reform. *Journal of Research in Science Teaching*, 48(6), 624–647. https://doi.org/10.1002/tea.20429

Onyema, E. M., Eucheria, N. C., Obafemi, F. A., Sen, S., Atonye, F. G., Sharma, A., & Alsayed, A. O. (2020). Impact of Coronavirus pandemic on education. *Journal of Education and Practice*, 11(13), 108–121. https://doi.org/10.7176/JEP/11-13-12

Padmalosan, P., Vanitha, S., Kumar, V. S., Anish, M., Tiwari, R., Dhapekar, N. K., & Yadav, A. S. (2023). An investigation on the use of waste materials from industrial processes in clay brick production. *Materials Today: Proceedings*. https://doi.org/10.1016/j.matpr.2023.01.238

Regehr, C. (2013). Trends in higher education in Canada and implications for social work education. *Social Work Education*, 32(6), 700–714. https://doi.org/10.1080/02615479.2013.785798

Rosak-Szyrocka, J., Apostu, S. A., Ali Turi, J., & Tanveer, A. (2022). University 4.0 sustainable development in the way of society 5.0. *Sustainability*, 14(23), 16043. https://doi.org/10.3390/su142316043

Sharma, P. (2019). Digital revolution of education 4.0. *International Journal of Engineering and Advanced Technology*, 9(2), 3558–3564. https://doi.org/10.35940/ijeat.A1293.129219

Tiwari, R., Chand, K., & Anjum, B. (2020). Crop insurance in India: A review of Pradhan Mantri Fasal Bima Yojana (PMFBY). *FIIB Business Review*, 9(4), 249–255. https://doi.org/10.1177/2319714520966084

Tiwari, R., Agrawal, P., Singh, P., Bajaj, S., Verma, V., & Chauhan, A. S. (2023). Technology enabled integrated fusion teaching for enhancing learning outcomes in higher education. *International Journal of Emerging Technologies in Learning*, 18(7), 243–249. https://doi.org/10.3991/ijet.v18i07.36799

Upadhyay, S. (2014). Rethinking the education system in India: A critical analysis. *Asian Man (The)-An International Journal*, 8(1), 55–71. https://doi.org/10.5958/0975-6884.2014.00007.3

Wen, Y., & Wu, J. (2017). A study on Singapore Chinese language teachers' professional proficiency and training needs for sustainable development. *Journal of Teacher Education for Sustainability*, 19(2), 69–89. https://doi.org/10.1515/jtes-2017-0015

Wessels, L., & van Wyk, J. A. (2022). University 4.0: A conceptual model for South African Universities and the fourth industrial revolution. In *Africa and the Fourth Industrial Revolution: Curse or Cure?* (pp. 33–66). https://doi.org/10.1007/978-3-030-87524-4_3

11 Using Artificial Intelligence Tools in Higher Education

Zeynep Aytaç

11.1 INTRODUCTION

Nowadays, technology has revolutionized education, offering numerous options to enhance students' research skills through personalized digital learning tools (Singh, 2018). By using technology, students can learn faster, broaden their perspective (Havenstein, 2008), and have a positive and engaging learning experience. Additionally, technology can increase the effectiveness of teaching (Ellison, Steinfield, & Lampe, 2007), provide guidance, and serve as an information retrieval tool. Overall, integrating technology into education can greatly benefit students who are adept at learning through technology-based approaches. Also, digital learning tools offer another approach that can significantly enhance students' education. Tools that employ AI technology have the capability to collect data from their environment, which is then processed to generate outputs that are tailored to the specific environment. AI encompasses a broad range of analytical methods, with machine learning, deep learning and natural language processing being among the most prominent (Zawacki-Richter, Marín, Bond, & Gouverneur, 2019).

Higher education has seen a rise in the utilization of digital learning tools due to the advancements in technology and changes in educational practices. Ørnes et al. (2015) outline five key reasons, from a teacher's perspective, for incorporating digital tools into their teaching practice. These reasons comprise of promoting diversified teaching methods, supplementing academic resources, boosting students' autonomy in learning, facilitating effective student monitoring, and ultimately leading to an enhanced learning experience for students.

Artificial intelligence is employed across various domains, such as business and healthcare (Lin et al., 2021), transportation and traffic, entertainment and sports, and information production and industry (Niemi & Liu, 2021). The integration of artificial intelligence technologies has commenced in the creation and application of digital educational resources. AI's influence is significant in the field of education, where it manifests in various AI-powered tools like automated grading systems and intelligent tutoring systems (ITS) (Montebello, 2018; Wang & Zhao, 2020).

 DOI: 10.1201/9781003425809-11

11.2 ARTIFICIAL INTELLIGENCE IN EDUCATION (AIED)

The origins of AI can be traced back to the 1950s when John McCarthy arranged a two-month workshop at Dartmouth College in the United States, during which he first introduced the term "artificial intelligence" in 1956 (Russel & Norvig, 2010, p. 17). Baker and Smith (2019) offer a comprehensive definition of AI as "computers that carry out cognitive functions commonly associated with the human mind, specifically learning and problem-solving." They further clarify that AI is not a single technology but instead an encompassing term that encompasses various technologies, such as data mining, machine learning, neural networks, algorithms and natural language processing.

Research on the use of AI in education (AIEd) has been ongoing for approximately three decades. Since its establishment in 1997, the International AIEd Society has been publishing the *International Journal of AI in Education* and is currently organizing the 20th annual AIEd conference this year (Zawacki-Richter, Marín, Bond, & Gouverneur, 2019).

Over the past few years, there has been a notable increase in the utilization of artificial intelligence in education, and this trend has attracted significant interest and focus. The 2022 Horizon report highlights the utilization of artificial intelligence in learning analytics concentrates on the ability of institutions to employ AI to arrange, examine, and comprehend data for decision-making purposes and to aid in facilitating student achievement. In this manner, AI serves as a tool that the institution can utilize to effectively and efficiently handle the copious amounts of data obtained through its various systems and platforms. The emphasis of AI for learning tools is centered on the direct interaction between students and AI-based tools and technologies as part of their learning environments and experiences. When AI is employed in this capacity, it becomes a reliable companion and assistant to students as they navigate their way through various college experiences. It provides guidance through tasks, facilitates the development of beneficial behaviors and thinking, and offers automation and efficiency as an advantage to the institution's interactions with its students. Although AI applications in both of these areas are still developing, there is significant potential for growth and impact that presents higher education and teaching and learning professionals with reasons for both optimism and caution in both the immediate and distant future (Educause, 2022). The report (Educause, 2019) indicates that AI in education is predicted to expand by 43% between 2018 and 2022, with even greater growth anticipated in AI applications pertaining to teaching and learning, as predicted by the Horizon Report 2019 Higher Education Edition.

In 2021, the size of the worldwide market for AI in education was assessed to be USD 1.82 billion. It is projected to experience a compound annual growth rate of 36% from 2022 to 2030. During the pandemic, there was a notable increase in the demand for creative AI-powered education solutions. A 2021 survey conducted by the University Professional and Continuing Education Association revealed that 51% of US faculty members have greater trust in online education compared to their pre-outbreak level (GVR [Grand View Research]), 2022). In 2021, the learning platform and virtual facilitators segment accounted for more than 45% of the market revenue, and it is expected to maintain its dominance throughout the forecast period. This segment's growth can be attributed to the increasing adoption of digital education and learning technologies worldwide. The market is categorized into several applications, including intelligent tutoring system (ITS), learning platform and virtual facilitators, fraud and risk management, smart content and others.

In addition, virtual facilitators assist students in addressing complex real-world social problems by providing them with guidance and skills related to social development. The smart content segment is projected to experience the highest compound annual growth rate of 37.8% during the forecast period. This growth can be attributed to the increasing adoption of smart content, which streamlines the time-consuming task of creating exercises for both students and teachers. To make these exercises more engaging, technologies such as natural language processing and computer vision are increasingly being utilized.

11.3   TREND OF ARTIFICIAL INTELLIGENCE IN EDUCATION

The integration of AI in education aims to enhance the learning experience for students, teachers, and educators. Numerous companies are developing innovative AI-based solutions and services that can be integrated with different educational platforms. Furthermore, the rising popularity of online education for skill development is driving the demand for AI in education. In addition, academic studies in the field of artificial intelligence in education have been increasing rapidly in recent years.

Figure 11.1 depicts the publication trend between 1999 and 2019, indicating that the number of AIEd publications has generally increased during the years under examination. During the evolution of the published article output, it can be observed that there were three stages, with the first stage spanning from 1999 to 2002, which

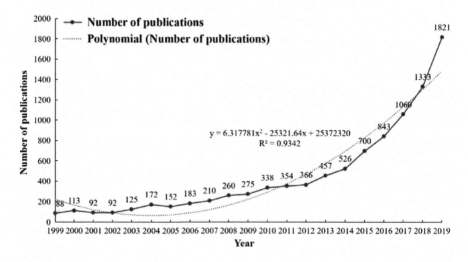

FIGURE 11.1   Publication trend of AIEd between 1999 and 2019 (Source: Chen, Xie, & Hwang, 2020).

exhibited a relatively sluggish growth trend. Between 2003 and 2011, the second stage of publication evolution demonstrated a consistent growth trend, while the third stage, spanning from 2012 to 2019, was characterized by a rapid increase in the number of published articles. The study's findings indicate that the growing global interest in the use of AI in educational settings has resulted in a significant surge in AIEd publications, with over 74% of the literature being released between 2012 and 2019. These results suggest that AIEd is a rapidly expanding research field.

Out of the 9560 publications related to AI in education, the term "education" appears the most, with 1001 publications, accounting for 10.47% of the total. Other frequently used keywords include "machine learning" (8.37%), "robotics" (7.71%), "artificial intelligence" (6.98%), "deep learning" (3.76%), "system" (2.98%), and "educational robotics" (2.90%) (Chen, Xie, & Hwang, 2020).

11.4 ARTIFICIAL INTELLIGENCE TOOLS IN EDUCATION

AI has been incorporated into numerous tools utilized for various purposes within educational settings. The focus of the present study is on four AI-based tools, namely intelligent tutoring systems, chatbots, automated assessment systems, and dashboards. These tools have been singled out due to their prevalence as the most commonly utilized AI-based technologies within the education sector (Celik, 2023; Chen et al., 2022). Luckin et al. (2016) have classified the current AI technologies in education into three groups: intelligent support for collaborative learning, intelligent virtual reality, and personal tutors.

In this study, artificial intelligence tools used in education were examined in five main domains. These are learning platforms, intelligent tutoring system (ITS), chatbots, automated assessment systems, and intelligent virtual reality (IVR). Furthermore, additional tools employed artificial intelligence in education have been reviewed.

11.4.1 LEARNING PLATFORMS

Online platform equipped with a virtual tutoring system can facilitate professional development courses. Numerous free and open courses are currently available, offering a range of engaging and structured features and content. Many of these courses, such as those found on Udemy, MOOCs Google AI, Khan Academy, Alison, edX, Coursera, and Udacity, have integrated AI technology into their offerings (Zhang, 2021). Altitude Learning, Carnegie Learning, Knewton's Alta, and Cognii Virtual TA are some examples of educational platforms.

- Altitude Learning is an e-learning platform that prioritizes student-centered education with the primary objective of enabling students to drive their own learning process through a personalized educational journey. By providing options for individual or group assignments, the AI tool facilitates a student-centered approach to learning that incorporates the latest research on effective teaching methods. Additionally, its intuitive interface and evaluation system promote self-directed learning and help students develop valuable skills.

- Carnegie Learning, an education technology and curriculum solutions provider, utilizes AI and machine learning in its learning platforms for high school and college-level students. The platforms provide distinctive solutions for math, world languages and literacy. One of its notable software, the MATHia, was developed by academicians from Carnegie Mellon University.

- Knewton's Alta is a leading AI-powered tool for higher education that provides a comprehensive courseware solution for students. The platform combines openly available content and adaptive learning technology to deliver a highly personalized learning experience. Alta tool comprises all the necessary instructional content, including text, videos, examples, and assessments required for a particular course. Additionally, the tool offers multiple courses in a variety of disciplines, including math, statistics, chemistry, and economics, to cater to the diverse needs of learners. Overall, Knewton's Alta serves as a powerful tool for personalized and effective higher education.

- Cognii Virtual TA is a virtual tutoring platform that utilizes AI technology to provide personalized learning experiences for students. Using advanced machine learning algorithms, Cognii Virtual TA is able to assess each student's strengths and weaknesses, offering targeted instruction and real-time feedback to promote academic growth and success. This AI-powered platform serves as a powerful tool for enhancing the quality of education, providing students with tailored support to help them reach their full potential.

11.4.2 Intelligent Tutoring Systems (ITS)

Intelligent tutoring systems (ITS) have the ability to simulate individualized personal tutoring. ITS can assess the unique learning journey of each student, choose appropriate content, offer cognitive support and guidance, and facilitate conversation to keep the student engaged using algorithms and neural networks. ITS is immense, particularly in institutions that offer distance learning and have numerous students enrolled in their modules, making it feasible to provide personal tutoring on an individual level (Richter et al., 2019). By lessening the workload of teachers, intelligent tutoring systems provide them with additional time to dedicate to instruction (Mohamed & Lamia, 2018). Computer systems known as intelligent tutoring systems consist of four primary components: a tutoring model, a domain model, an interface model and a student model. These components work together to provide students with immediate and adaptive feedback or instruction during the learning process (Graesser, Conley, & Olney, 2012; Mcroy & Freedman, 2000). Simulated human tutorial dialogue is a crucial component of tutoring instruction for intelligent tutoring systems. According to a study conducted by Chi, Jordan, and VanLehn (2014), intelligent tutoring systems that incorporated tutorial dialogue outperformed conventional step-based ITSs. AutoTutor is an intelligent tutoring system that utilizes tutorial dialogue and natural language to emulate human tutoring. Its purpose is to encourage students to articulate and clarify their understanding of the fundamental concepts of domain knowledge. Intelligent tutoring systems that incorporate conversational dialogue are a distinct subset of ITSs known as dialogue-based ITSs (Rus & Stefanescu, 2016). As per the pedagogical evaluation, the learning outcomes achieved by AutoTutor were found to be similar to those attained by human educators (Graesser, 2016; Nye et al., 2014). The two most commonly discussed and utilized intelligent tutoring systems (ITS) in the field of education are ALEKS (Doignon & Falmagne, 1999) and Cognitive Tutor (Anderson et al., 1995; Ritter, Anderson, Koedinger, & Corbett, 2007). Also, Querium, an AI-driven tool, offers customized and intelligent guidance to students through its tutoring services.

- Cognitive Tutor utilizes technology in the realm of mathematics education by delivering personalized instruction based on the analysis of problem-solving approaches in geometry and algebra courses (Ritter, Anderson, Koedinger, & Corbett, 2007).[*][†]

11.4.3 CHATBOTS

Chatbots serve as virtual assistants for both students and educators, enabling them to engage in conversations through either written or spoken interactions. Teachers have the ability to initiate a dialogue with chatbots using voice commands or by typing text (Luo et al., 2019). Teachers can receive updates on students' learning progress through notifications sent by chatbots (Chocarro et al., 2021). The capability of chatbots to communicate in a natural way makes them useful tools. One example is the text-based chatbot system "Pounce," which was implemented at Georgia State University to assist students with administrative tasks such as registration, admission, and financial aid (Greenhow et al., 2020). The other examples of AI-based chatbots are ChatGPT, Perplexity and Ivy.

- One of the chatbots used in education is ChatGPT. ChatGPT is a chatbot powered by generative AI that engages in natural and human-like conversations with users. The chatbot has been trained using data from a vast array of sources found online, and it has been taught by humans to communicate with users in an authentic manner.
- Perplexity is a chatbot that utilizes generative AI to facilitate conversational interactions between users and the chatbot. One unique feature of

---

[*] ALEKS is an intelligent assessment and learning system that operates online and encompasses a wider variety of subjects, such as mathematics, science, statistics, and business, and is designed for higher education and K-12 (Baxter & Thibodeau, 2011; Grayce, 2013).

[†] Querium provides an AI-powered platform that supports students in developing skills, assisting them for their academic and professional careers. The system adopts a personalized approach, offering customized lessons and systematic tutoring guidance. The artificial intelligence virtual tutor is a standout feature of the platform, enhancing the quality, speed and analysis of student learning while boosting student outcomes. Research has demonstrated the positive impact of this tool, which effectively supports and guides students toward mastering critical skills

Perplexity is its ability to cite sources in its responses, providing users with clickable links that offer additional context and information.

- Ivy comprises a range of chatbot AI tools tailored to support universities and colleges with various aspects of their operations, including application forms, enrollment, tuition costs, deadlines, and other administrative tasks. One of Ivy's distinctive features is its capability to design recruitment campaigns by leveraging data analysis. The AI tool can offer students vital information about loans, scholarships, grants, tuition payments, and more. Furthermore, its capacity to create customized chatbots for each department makes it applicable across the organization.

11.4.4 AUTOMATED ASSESSMENT SYSTEMS

Automated assessment systems, also referred to as automated grading systems, have the ability to identify and evaluate student responses automatically. Automated speech recognition and natural language processing which are subfields of AI, are commonly employed in the automation of these systems (Ahn & Lee, 2016). As examples of Automated Evaluation Systems, Gradescope and Eklavvya AI Proctoring have been examined.

- Gradescope is an educational tool that simplifies the grading process for teachers by providing a single platform for grading paper-based exams, online homework, and project submissions. The tool employs a blend of machine learning and artificial intelligence techniques to facilitate quick and efficient grading, thereby reducing the workload and effort required by teachers.
- Eklavvya AI Proctoring is a web-based system that utilizes AI technology to monitor students during online assessments, identifying any instances of malpractice. By analyzing the facial expressions and behavior of students, Eklavvya AI proctoring can accurately detect any irregularities during the assessment process. This AI-powered proctoring system serves as a powerful tool for ensuring academic integrity and maintaining the fairness and validity of online assessments.

11.4.5 INTELLIGENT VIRTUAL REALITY

Virtual reality has been defined in several ways, including as an interface between humans and computers that replicates genuine environments and facilitates participant engagement, as a three-dimensional digital realm that precisely mimics real-world surroundings, or as cyberspace (Gorman, Meier, & Krummel, 1999). The incorporation of artificial intelligence into augmented reality technology results in an "intelligent" virtual reality system. In the field of dental education, there has been a significant surge in the adoption and utilization of virtual reality (VR), mixed reality (MR), augmented reality (AR), and haptic technology over the past few years (Saghiri et al., 2022).

One application of intelligent virtual reality (IVR) is to involve and direct students in genuine virtual reality and learning environments based on games. In virtual or remote laboratories, virtual agents have the potential to serve as instructors, assistants, or even peers for students (Perez et al., 2017).

In bioscience education, VR has the ability to function as a tool for active learning and improve the educational experience by promoting active engagement and self-directed learning among students, through its highly interactive software. This is significant because medical and bioscience education frequently necessitates students to have hands-on interaction with objects, such as organs, to enhance their comprehension through self-directed inquiry and exploration of their structure (Fabris, Rathner, Fong, & Sevigny, 2019).

Numerous tools that can be integrated into educational courses have been created utilizing VR technology. Tools such as Nearpod, Unimersive, CBC VR, Sesqui VR, Veative, YouTube 360 Videos, EON Reality-Education, and NYT VR Virtual Reality are a few examples of virtual reality applications in education.

11.4.6 THE OTHER TOOLS IN AIED

The integration of AI-powered systems and applications in education offers students the benefit of immediate and responsive support. With the help of AI, students can receive instant responses to their queries and concerns, enabling them to resolve issues promptly. In addition, AI provides personalized, conversational assistants that can assist students with their assignments. This feature allows for flexible learning, enabling students to learn at their own pace and on their own schedule. Overall, the incorporation of AI in education serves as a powerful means of improving the learning experience and promoting academic success. The following is a list of other AIEd tools utilized in higher education or on an individual basis.

- Quillbot is a tool that assists in the paraphrasing and rewording of text. By analyzing a vast selection of synonyms, Quillbot can suggest alternative wording options to find the most appropriate words for the desired fluency, vocabulary, tone, and style.
- Yippity is a tool that can automatically transform any text or website into a quiz format. By analyzing the submitted text, Yippity generates questions and answers that can be copied and pasted into various quiz tools or flash-card applications.
- Curipod can create an interactive slide deck on a particular topic within seconds. This tool includes features such as polls, word clouds, open-ended questions, and a drawing tool.
- With the assistance of AI, Grammarly serves as an online writing assistant that aids in the creation of clear and error-free text. This tool can be integrated into various applications, including email clients, productivity suites, and social media platforms. By utilizing AI technology, Grammarly can check grammar, spelling, style, tone, and other elements to improve the overall quality of the written content.
- The YouTube Summary with ChatGPT is a Chrome Extension that provides users with quick access to summaries of the YouTube videos they are watching,

powered by OpenAI's ChatGPT AI technology. This free extension helps users save time and accelerate learning. To view the AI summary, users can click on the transcript and summary and then click on the ChatGPT icon.

- With Speechify, users can easily convert text into a natural-sounding voice across various devices, including Google Chrome, Apple devices, and Android devices. Whether it's text in a document, PDF, webpage, or book, Speechify can transform it into speech, making it easier to listen to the content on the go.

- DALL-E 2 is an innovative AI system that can generate realistic images and artwork based on natural language descriptions. By understanding the relationship between images and their accompanying text, DALL-E 2 leverages a technique called "diffusion" to transform a random pattern of dots into a recognizable image. This method involves gradually modifying the initial pattern toward an image as the AI recognizes key features mentioned in the corresponding text description.

- Nuance offers speech recognition software that provides to the needs of both faculty and students. With its Dragon Speech Recognition product, the company provides a fast transcription service that can handle up to 160 words per minute. This feature is particularly useful for students who struggle with writing or typing. Additionally, the software supports voice commands, enabling users to navigate through documents seamlessly. This feature is especially beneficial for students with accessibility needs.

- Knowji is a prominent AIEd tool that specializes in teaching vocabulary through a visually engaging and auditory application. It incorporates the latest educational research to provide language learners with various methods to accelerate their learning process. Knowji uses an advanced algorithm that employs a spaced repetition technique to track and predict a student's recall of each word. This feature is particularly useful as it enables users to learn more effectively over time. The AI-powered tool carefully monitors a student's progress and predicts when they are likely to forget a word, providing timely reminders to reinforce the learning process.

- SciSpace Copilot is a robust AI-powered application that assists scientists and researchers in navigating the vast scientific literature. By leveraging advanced natural language processing algorithms, the program analyzes scientific publications and extracts valuable information. This feature allows researchers to quickly and efficiently identify the most significant and relevant research papers in their field, saving valuable time and effort. Overall, SciSpace Copilot serves as a powerful tool for researchers seeking to streamline their literature review process.

11.5 CONCLUSION

The potential of Artificial Intelligence in education lies in its ability to provide students with personalized learning experiences, enable teachers to grade assignments with greater speed and accuracy, and offer immediate feedback and support to students. By leveraging the power of AI, education can be made more effective and efficient, creating a more dynamic and engaging learning environment for students. AI is an ideal tool for improving the personalized learning experience of students. Its customized training materials are designed to accommodate various learning styles. By utilizing machine learning, a hyperpersonalization model is used to create a customized profile for each student. This approach allows the lessons to be broken down into smart notes, facilitating better understanding and comprehension for the student. Overall, AI offers a powerful means of enhancing personalized learning and promoting academic success.

In this study, a comprehensive review has been presented regarding the extensive range of AI technologies and tools that can be utilized in higher education to assist students, faculty, and administrators. These were categorized into five main domains (learning platforms, intelligent tutoring system, chatbots, automated assessment systems, and intelligent virtual reality). The framework, which was formulated based on the review, enhances comprehension and conceptualization of the tools and technologies of AI in education. This study also reviews platforms and tools that can be utilized to create intelligent support systems for students and to facilitate personalized and adaptive learning environments by providing principles for their learning. The potential of AI-based tools and services to assist students, faculty, and administrators across the student journey is substantial. AI applications will be one of the most significant technological concerns in education for the next two decades.

REFERENCES

Ahn, T. Y., & Lee, S. M. (2016). User experience of a mobile speaking application with automatic speech recognition for EFL learning. *British Journal of Educational Technology*, *47*(4), 778–786. https://doi.org/10.1111/bjet.12354

Anderson, J. R., Corbett, A. T., Koedinger, K. R., & Pelletier, R. (1995). Cognitive tutor: Lesson learned. *Journal of the Learning Sciences*, *4*, 167–207. https://doi.org/10.1207/s15327809jls0402_2

Baker, T., & Smith, L. (2019). Educ-AI-tion rebooted? Exploring the future of artificial intelligence in schools and colleges. Retrieved from Nesta Foundation website: https://media.nesta.org.uk/documents/Future_of_AI_and_education_v5_WEB.pdf

Baxter, R. J., & Thibodeau, J. C. (2011). Does the use of intelligent learning and assessment soft-ware enhance the acquisition of financial accounting knowledge? *Issues in Accounting Education*, *26*, 647–656. https://doi.org/10.2308/iace-50052

Celik, I. (2023). Towards Intelligent-TPACK: An empirical study on teachers' professional knowledge to ethically integrate artificial intelligence (AI)-based tools into education. *Computers in Human Behavior*, *138*, 107468.

Chen, X., Xie, H., & Hwang, G. J. (2020). A multi-perspective study on artificial intelligence in education: Grants, conferences, journals, software tools, institutions, and researchers. *Computers and Education: Artificial Intelligence*, *1*, 100005.

Chen, X., Zou, D., Xie, H., Cheng, G., & Liu, C. (2022). Two decades of artificial intelligence in education. *Educational Technology & Society*, *25*(1), 28–47.

Chi, M., Jordan, P., & VanLehn, K. (2014). When is tutorial dialogue more effective than step-based tutoring? In *Intelligent Tutoring Systems: 12th International Conference, ITS 2014, Honolulu, HI, USA, June 5-9, 2014*. (pp. 210–219). Springer International Publishing.

Chocarro, R., Cortiñas, M., & Marcos-Matás, G. (2021). Teachers' attitudes towards chatbots in education: A technology acceptance model approach considering the effect of social language, bot proactiveness, and users' characteristics. *Educational Studies*, 1–19. https://doi.org/10.1080/03055698.2020.1850426

Doignon, J. P. & Falmagne, J. C. (1999). *Knowledge spaces*. Berlin: Springer.

EDUCAUSE. (2019). Horizon report: 2019 higher education edition. Retrieved from Educause Learning Initiative and The New Media Consortium website: https://library.educause.edu/-/media/files/library/2019/4/2019horizonreport.pdf

EDUCAUSE. (2022). Horizon report | Teaching and learning edition. Retrieved from Educause Publications website: https://library.educause.edu/resources/2022/4/2022-educause-horizon-report-teaching-and-learning-edition

Ellison, N., Steinfield, C., & Lampe, C. (2007). The benefits of Facebook 'friends': Exploring the relationship between college students. Use of online social networks and social capital. *Journal of Computer Mediated Communication*, *12*(4), 1143–1168. https://doi.org/10.1111/j.1083-6101.2007.00367.x

Fabris, C. P., Rathner, J. A., Fong, A. Y., & Sevigny, C. P. (2019). Virtual reality in higher education. *International Journal of Innovation in Science and Mathematics Education*, *27*(8).

Gorman, P. J., Meier, A. H., & Krummel, T. M. (1999). Simulation and virtual reality in surgical education: Real or unreal?. *Archives of Surgery*, *134*(11), 1203–1208.

Graesser, A. C. (2016). Conversations with AutoTutor help students learn. *International Journal of Artificial Intelligence in Education*, *26*, 124–132.

Graesser, A. C., Conley, M. W., & Olney, A. M. (2012). Intelligent tutoring systems. In S. Graham & K. Harris (Eds.), *APA educational psychology handbook, vol. 3. Applications to learning and teaching* (pp. 451–473). Washington, DC: American Psychological Association.

Grayce, C. J. (2013). A commercial implementation of knowledge space theory in college general chemistry. In J. C. Falmagne, D. Albert, C. Doble, D. Eppstein, & X. Hu (Eds.), *Knowledge spaces* (pp. 93–113). Berlin: Springer-Verlag.

Greenhow, C., Galvin, S. M., Brandon, D. L., & Askari, E. (2020). A decade of research on K–12 teaching and teacher learning with social media: Insights on the state of the field. *Teachers College Record*, *122*(6), 1–72.

GVR [Grand View Research]. (2022). AI in education market size & share report, 2022–2030 website. https://www.grandviewresearch.com/industry-analysis/artificial-intelligence-ai-education-market-report#

Havenstein, H. (2008). Companies are looking for new ways to measure web 2.0. *Computerworld*, *42*(45), 14–15.

Lin, H. C., Tu, Y. F., Hwang, G. J., & Huang, H. (2021). From precision education to precision medicine. *Educational Technology & Society*, *24*(1), 123–137.

Luckin, R., Holmes, W., Griffiths, M., & Forcier, L. B. (2016). Intelligence unleashed - An argument for AI in education. http://discovery.ucl.ac.uk/1475756/

Luo, X., Tong, S., Fang, Z., & Qu, Z. (2019). Frontiers: Machines vs. humans: The impact of artificial intelligence chatbot disclosure on customer purchases. *Marketing Science*, *38*(6), 937–947. https://doi.org/10.1287/mksc.2019.1192

Mcroy, S., & Freedman, R. (2000). What is an intelligent tutoring system. *Intelligence*, *11*(3), 15–16.

Mohamed, H., & Lamia, M. (2018). Implementing flipped classroom that used an intelligent tutoring system into learning process. *Computers & Education*, *124*, 62–76. https://doi.org/10.1109/TLT.2021.3072143

Montebello, M. (2018). *AI injected e-learning: The future of online education*. Springer. https://doi.org/10.1007/978-3-319-67928-0

Niemi, H., & Liu, J. (2021). AI in learning: Intelligent digital tools and environments for education. *Journal of Pacific Rim Psychology, 15*, 18344909211038110.

Nye, B. D., Graesser, A. C., & Hu, X. (2014). AutoTutor and family: A review of 17 years of natural language tutoring. *International Journal of Artificial Intelligence in Education, 24*, 427–469.

Ørnes, H., Gaard, H., Refsnes, S. I., Kristiansen, T., & Wilhelmsen, J. (2015). Digital Tilstand i Høyere Utdanning 2014 (Digital State in Higher Education). Norgesuniversitets monitor, Oslo.

Perez, S., Massey-Allard, J., Butler, D., Ives, J., Bonn, D., Yee, N., & Roll, I. (2017). Identifying productive inquiry in virtual labs using sequence mining. In E. André, R. Baker, X. Hu, M. M. T. Rodrigo, & B. du Boulay (Eds.), *Artificial intelligence in education* (Vol. 10,331, pp. 287–298). https://doi.org/10.1007/978-3-319-61425-0_24

Ritter, S., Anderson, J. R., Koedinger, K. R., & Corbett, A. (2007). Cognitive tutor: Applied researchin mathematics education. *Psychonomic Bulletin and Review, 14*, 249–255. https://doi.org/10.3758/BF03194060

Rus, V., & Stefanescu, D. (2016). Toward non-intrusive assessment in dialogue-based intelligenttutoring systems. In Y. Li, M. Chang, M. Kravcik, E. Popescu, R. Huang, Kinshuk, & N. S. Chen (Eds.), *State-of-the-art and future directions of smart learning* (pp. 231–241). Lecture Notes in Educational Technology. Singapore: Springer.

Russel, S., & Norvig, P. (2010). *Artificial intelligence – A modern approach.* New Jersey: Pearson Education.

Saghiri, M. A., Vakhnovetsky, J., & Nadershahi, N. (2022). Scoping review of artificial intelligence and immersive digital tools in dental education. *Journal of Dental Education, 86*(6), 736–750.

Singh, R. (2018). AI and chatbots in education: What does the future hold? https://chatbotsmagazine.com/ai-and-chatbots-in-education-what-does-the-futurehold-9772f5c13960

Wang, Y., & Zhao, P. (2020). A probe into spoken English recognition in English education based on computer-aided comprehensive analysis. *International Journal of Emerging Technologies in Learning (iJET), 15*(3), 223–233.

Zawacki-Richter, O., Marín, V. I., Bond, M., & Gouverneur, F. (2019). Systematic review of research on artificial intelligence applications in higher education–where are the educators?. *International Journal of Educational Technology in Higher Education, 16*(1), 1–27.

Zhang, Z. (2021, April). The impact of digital technologies on entrepreneurship education. In *2021 6th International Conference on Social Sciences and Economic Development (ICSSED 2021)* (pp. 448–452). Atlantis Press.

12 The AI Application for an Automated Education System

Alessio Faccia, Manjeet Ridon and Luigi Pio Leonardo Cavaliere

12.1 INTRODUCTION

In our constantly transforming world, combining technology with multiple domains revolutionizes our operations. Education is one sector profoundly impacted by this wave of change. There is an escalating interest in leveraging artificial intelligence (AI) to automate various facets of the educational landscape, igniting intriguing conversations. This chapter takes you on an exploratory journey into AI-enriched educational architectures, shedding light on their benefits (see Table 12.1 and Table 12.2), challenges, and potential to reshape how we dispense and assimilate knowledge (Cox, A.M., 2021).

AI's vast expanse within education enables the automation of assignments and pedagogical procedures, providing personalized assistance and smoothing the cumbersome assessment process. As we set sail on this transformative voyage, it is imperative to understand the multifaceted dynamics that AI introduces into the education sphere (Zawacki-Richter, O. et al., 2019).

This chapter invites you on an exciting expedition of AI's diverse applications in education. We will unpack the potential of intelligent tutoring systems, automated writing evaluation tools, and adaptive learning platforms, highlighting their attributes, functions, and impact on instructional and learning outcomes.

Deeper exploration reveals that AI possesses the potential to revamp education by boosting learner engagement, lifting academic performance, and enhancing institutional efficiency. By customizing learning experiences and offering prompt feedback, AI can morph conventional education paradigms into responsive, adaptable processes that serve individual needs and learning styles.

Nonetheless, like all technological progressions, infusing AI into education brings challenges and considerations (Zeide, E., 2017). Concerns around data privacy, biases, and the possibility of AI usurping human educators must be critically inspected (Da'u, A. and Salim, N., 2020). This chapter tackles these issues, analyzing AI's educational constraints and prospects.

Understanding that the triumphant integration of AI in education requires a coalition of multiple stakeholders is critical. Educators, IT experts, policymakers,

 DOI: 10.1201/9781003425809-12

TABLE 12.1
Summary

	Benefits of AI-driven learning environments	Challenges of AI-driven learning environments
Personalization	Allows individualized instruction based on learners' performance, learning styles, and preferences, enhancing engagement and motivation.	Striking a balance between data collection for personalization and protecting individuals' privacy.
Critical thinking and problem-solving skills	Fosters these skills through interactive simulations and virtual scenarios that require applying knowledge and decision-making. Provides immediate feedback to refine problem-solving approaches.	There may be concerns about the reliability and accuracy of AI algorithms in providing meaningful scenarios and accurate feedback.
Collaboration	Facilitates collaboration and communication between learners from diverse backgrounds and locations, enhancing teamwork, communication, and cultural awareness skills.	Not explicitly mentioned, but could include issues of the digital divide and ensuring equitable access to technology.
Data privacy and security	Not explicitly mentioned as a benefit.	Raises concerns as AI systems gather and analyze sensitive learner data. Requires careful consideration and management.
Reliability and accuracy of AI algorithms	Not explicitly mentioned as a benefit.	There may be concerns about the reliability and accuracy of AI algorithms. Transparent evaluation and continuous monitoring are necessary.

and others must collaborate to architect, create, and deploy AI-empowered educational frameworks that resonate with our educational institution's mission and values. By cultivating a culture of innovation and collaboration, we can fully leverage AI to enrich teaching and learning experiences (Hussin, H. et al., 2019). With AI's steady advancement, the potential to revolutionize education grows more evident. Personalized learning is one field where AI has exhibited remarkable potential (Sharef, N.M. et al., 2020). Traditional education methods often follow a uniform model, ignoring students' strengths, weaknesses, and learning styles.

AI-driven adaptive learning platforms have the potential to counter this issue (Pantelimon, F.V. et al., 2021). By analyzing extensive data on student performance, preferences, and progress, these platforms can customize learning resources and activities to cater to each student's unique needs. This personalized approach enhances student engagement and understanding, as they can learn independently, focusing on areas requiring additional assistance (Wang, S. et al., 2023).

TABLE 12.2
Summary

Topic	Benefits of AI in education	Challenges and considerations in AI-driven education
Role of educators	The transformation from information providers to facilitators, mentors, and orchestrators of learning experiences. AI assists educators by providing personalized support, automating administrative tasks, and offering valuable insights.	Preserving the human touch in education is crucial. The human element is vital in fostering meaningful connections, empathetic understanding, and social–emotional development in learners.
Personalization	AI allows for creating personalized learning pathways and adaptive curricula tailored to each student's individual needs and pace of learning.	Data privacy and security concerns as AI systems gather and analyze sensitive learner data. A balance between data collection for personalization and privacy preservation is essential.
Critical thinking and problem-solving Skills	AI helps cultivate these skills among learners through engaging interactive simulations and immersive virtual scenarios.	Concerns regarding the reliability and accuracy of AI algorithms in providing meaningful scenarios and accurate feedback.
Collaboration	AI facilitates cooperative projects and fosters connections among peers from diverse backgrounds and locations.	Not explicitly mentioned, but could include issues of the digital divide and ensuring equitable access to technology.
Data privacy and security	Not explicitly mentioned as a benefit.	AI systems gather and analyze sensitive learner data, raising questions about the adequacy of data protection measures.
Reliability and accuracy of AI algorithms	Not explicitly mentioned as a benefit.	Concerns about the reliability and accuracy of AI algorithms. The systems must be transparent in their operation, and continuous monitoring is necessary.
Ethical considerations	Not explicitly mentioned as a benefit.	Principles of fairness, equity, transparency, and privacy must be firmly embedded within AI-powered educational systems.
Democratization of education	AI has the potential to make quality education accessible to all, regardless of geographical location, economic status, or learning abilities.	Not explicitly mentioned, but it could include the risk of increased digital divide if not properly managed.

Intelligent tutoring systems (ITS) represent another thrilling AI application in education (Steenbergen-Hu, S. and Cooper, H., 2014). These systems use natural language processing (NLP) and machine learning algorithms to engage with students, reminiscent of one-on-one tutoring, providing personalized feedback and guidance (Baker, RSD et al., 2006).

Moreover, AI can automate and streamline administrative tasks within the education system (Votto, A.M. et al., 2021). AI-infused tools can automate the grading of multiple-choice exams, enabling teachers to concentrate on more enriching activities such as providing feedback and engaging in student discussions (Kommey, B. et al., 2022).

However, while the merits of AI in education are abundant, addressing its implementation challenges and considerations is crucial. Privacy concerns (Prinsloo, P. et al., 2022) arise as AI systems gather and analyze important student data, necessitating robust data protection measures. Equally vital is addressing potential bias in AI algorithms and ensuring AI systems supplement, not substitute, human educators. As educators navigate the AI-powered education environment, their roles become even more pivotal, employing AI tools to augment teaching practices and nurture critical skills such as critical thinking, problem-solving, and social–emotional learning.

12.1.1 UNLEASHING THE POTENTIAL: AI-DRIVEN LEARNING ENVIRONMENTS

In the rapidly evolving landscape of education, integrating artificial intelligence (AI) can potentially transform learning environments into dynamic and immersive spaces (Smuts, M. et al., 2019). AI-driven learning environments harness the power of technology to create personalized and engaging educational experiences for learners. By leveraging AI algorithms, virtual reality simulations, and natural language processing, these environments offer innovative pathways for acquiring knowledge and developing skills.

One of the most remarkable aspects of AI-driven learning environments is their ability to adapt to individual learners' needs and preferences (Premlatha, K.R. et al., 2016). Traditional classrooms often follow a one-size-fits-all approach, where instruction is delivered in a standardized manner. However, AI-powered systems can analyze vast data, including learners' performance, learning styles, and preferences, to provide tailored content and experiences. This level of personalization enhances learner engagement and motivation, ensuring that the educational material aligns with their unique interests and abilities.

Moreover, AI-driven learning environments have the potential to foster critical thinking and problem-solving skills. Through interactive simulations and virtual scenarios, learners can engage in authentic, real-world situations (Herrington, J. et al., 2004; Koivisto, J.M. et al., 2017) that require them to apply their knowledge and make decisions. AI algorithms can analyze learners' actions, provide immediate feedback, and offer guidance to help them refine their problem-solving approaches. This iterative learning and improvement process creates a rich and immersive educational experience that mirrors the complexities of the real world (Wu, C.H. et al., 2021).

Collaboration is another key component of AI-driven learning environments (Jones, P., 2010). By incorporating AI technologies, learners can engage in collaborative projects and connect with peers from diverse backgrounds and locations. Virtual platforms facilitate seamless communication and enable learners to collaborate on tasks, share ideas, and learn from each other's perspectives (Wong, L.H. et al., 2016). These collaborative experiences foster essential skills such as teamwork, communication, and cultural awareness, which are increasingly valuable in our interconnected global society.

While AI-driven learning environments offer exciting possibilities, it is essential to address the challenges that arise. Data privacy and security concerns must be carefully considered, as these systems gather and analyze sensitive learner data (Xu, L. et al., 2014). Striking a balance between data collection for personalization purposes and ensuring the protection of individuals' privacy is of utmost importance. Additionally, there may be concerns about the reliability and accuracy of AI algorithms (Shin, D., 2022). Transparent evaluation and continuous monitoring are necessary to ensure that the AI systems function effectively and provide reliable educational experiences.

AI-driven learning environments hold immense potential to revolutionize the educational landscape. By leveraging AI algorithms, virtual reality simulations, and natural language processing, these environments can provide personalized, engaging, and adaptive educational experiences (Kem, D., 2022). Learners benefit from tailored content, immersive simulations, and collaborative opportunities that enhance their engagement, critical thinking, and problem-solving skills. However, careful consideration must be given to data privacy and security, as well as the reliability and accuracy of AI algorithms. Through thoughtful implementation and ongoing evaluation, AI-driven learning environments can shape the future of education, empowering learners and educators alike.

12.1.2 FROM ASSISTIVE TO AUGMENTATIVE: REDEFINING THE ROLE OF EDUCATORS

In the realm of AI-powered education, the role of educators is undergoing a significant transformation. Rather than solely being information providers, educators become facilitators, mentors, and orchestrators of learning experiences (Laurillard D. et al., 2009). AI technologies offer unprecedented opportunities to assist and augment educators in their instructional practices, ultimately enhancing the quality and effectiveness of education (Hernandez-de-Menendez, M. et al., 2020).

One of the key aspects of AI's impact on educators is its ability to provide personalized support and guidance to individual learners (Alam, A., 2021). Through AI-powered adaptive learning systems, educators can gain insights into students' learning styles, preferences, and areas of strength or challenge. By leveraging this information, educators can tailor their instructional approaches, adapt content delivery, and provide targeted interventions to meet the specific needs of each learner.

Furthermore, AI technologies can automate routine administrative tasks, allowing educators to focus more on instructional design and individualized instruction (Alam, A. and Mohanty, A., 2023). Grading and assessment processes can be streamlined with the help of automated evaluation tools, freeing up valuable time for educators to engage in more meaningful interactions with their students. This shift in focus from administrative burdens to instructional excellence enables educators to provide the necessary support and guidance to foster students' intellectual growth and development.

In addition to assisting educators, AI technologies augment their instructional practices by offering valuable insights and resources (Dwivedi, YK et al., 2021). AI-powered analytics can provide educators with real-time data on students' progress, highlighting areas where additional support may be needed or identifying patterns that can inform instructional decisions. This data-driven approach empowers educators to make evidence-based interventions, allowing them to address learning gaps promptly and effectively.

Moreover, AI can facilitate the creation of personalized learning pathways and adaptive curricula (Xie, H. et al., 2019). By analyzing vast amounts of data on learner performance, AI algorithms can generate tailored learning plans that cater to each student's individual needs and pace of learning. This personalized approach maximizes the potential for academic growth and nurtures students' motivation and engagement, as they feel a sense of ownership and relevance in their learning journey.

However, as we embrace the augmentation provided by AI, it is crucial to maintain a human-centered approach to education (Bacciu, D. et al., 2021). While AI can offer valuable insights and automate certain tasks, the role of human educators remains irreplaceable. The human touch is essential in fostering meaningful connections, empathetic understanding, and social–emotional development in learners. Educators bring their expertise, intuition, and passion for creating nurturing and inclusive learning environments beyond what AI can offer alone (Ainscow, M. and Sandill, A., 2010).

Integrating AI in education redefines the role of educators from being solely instructors to facilitators, mentors, and designers of personalized learning experiences (Guilherme, A., 2019). AI technologies assist educators by providing personalized support, automating administrative tasks, and offering valuable insights. Additionally, AI augments educators' instructional practices by enabling data-driven decision-making, facilitating personalized learning pathways, and promoting student engagement. As we harness the power of AI, it is essential to strike a balance between technological advancements and the invaluable human qualities that educators bring to the table, ultimately creating a harmonious synergy that empowers learners and enhances the educational experience (Goulart, V.G. et al., 2022).

As we stride confidently into the dynamic world of AI-integrated education, we find ourselves standing at the precipice of a new era of learning. Environments sculpted with the chisel of AI showcase the marvels of technology, offering personalized, immersive educational experiences that carry the promise of revolutionizing the way we learn. By leveraging the power of AI algorithms, natural language processing, and the spellbinding allure of virtual reality simulations, we see the birth of novel methods for knowledge acquisition and skill development.

Arguably, the most compelling facet of these AI-driven learning environments is their innate ability to adapt and mold themselves to cater to learners' needs and preferences. A paradigm shift from the traditional 'one-size-fits-all' approach of classical classrooms (Haniya, S., 2023), these environments harness the immense processing power of AI to analyze enormous volumes of data about learners, from their academic performance and learning styles to their preferences and inclinations. The resultant content and experiences are finely tuned to enhance learner engagement and motivation, offering personalization that ensures alignment between the educational material and each student's unique interests and abilities (Kamruzzaman, M.M., 2023).

Beyond mere personalization, AI-driven learning environments harbor the potential to cultivate critical thinking and problem-solving skills among learners. Through engaging interactive simulations and immersive virtual scenarios, learners are placed within authentic, real-world situations that mandate the application of their acquired knowledge and decision-making skills (Calandra, D. et al., 2022). AI algorithms dissect learners' actions (Ochoa, X. et al., 2022), providing immediate feedback and offering guidance to refine their problem-solving approaches. The resulting iterative process of learning and self-improvement constructs a rich educational experience that faithfully mirrors the complexities and challenges of the real world.

Collaboration is another cornerstone of AI-driven learning environments. These environments employ AI technologies to facilitate cooperative projects (Yang, W., 2022) and foster connections among peers from diverse backgrounds and locations. Virtual platforms act as a conduit for seamless communication, empowering learners to work together on tasks, exchange ideas, and glean insights from each other's perspectives (Guache, M. et al., 2023). Such collaborative experiences engender crucial skills, including teamwork, communication, and cultural awareness, which hold immense value in our increasingly interconnected global society (Markauskaite, L. et al., 2022).

While the promise of AI-driven learning environments is captivating, we must address this nascent revolution's formidable challenges. Primary among these concerns are issues related to data privacy and security. AI systems gather and analyze sensitive learner data, raising questions about the adequacy of data protection measures (Meszaros, J., 2022). A delicate balance must be struck between the collection of data for personalization and the paramount necessity of preserving individual privacy. As mentioned before, the potential concerns regarding the reliability and accuracy of AI algorithms cannot be overlooked. The systems must be transparent in their operation, and continuous monitoring is crucial to ensure that the AI functions effectively and delivers reliable, beneficial educational experiences (Mhlanga, D., 2023). It includes periodically reviewing the systems to rectify inherent or emergent biases and ensuring fairness and equity in educational opportunities. AI-driven learning environments, therefore, embody an exciting paradox of immense potential coupled with significant challenges (Khogali, H.O. and Mekid, S., 2023). By leveraging AI algorithms, virtual reality simulations, and natural language processing, these environments can offer tailored, engaging, and adaptive educational experiences. They open doors to personalized content, immerse learners in compelling simulations, and provide platforms for collaborative efforts that nurture critical thinking, problem-solving skills, and the spirit of teamwork. However, these environments also demand meticulous attention to data privacy and security and the reliability and accuracy of the AI algorithms driving them. Through thoughtful implementation, ongoing evaluation, and proactive addressing of potential issues, AI-driven learning environments can shape the future of education (Schiff, D. et al., 2021). They stand as a testament to the prowess of AI in empowering learners and educators alike, redefining the contours of knowledge acquisition and skill development, and, ultimately, driving us toward a more enlightened world.

While opening doors to unprecedented opportunities for personalized and immersive learning, AI-powered education also calls for a deeper understanding of its underlying technologies (Dai, C. P. and Ke, F., 2022). This knowledge empowers stakeholders to make informed decisions, design effective strategies, and ensure that AI is a robust and reliable tool for enhancing educational experiences. Furthermore, ethical considerations must always be at the forefront of AI discussions in education. As we forge a future where AI plays an increasingly significant role, we must also ensure that principles of fairness, equity, transparency, and privacy are firmly embedded within the fabric of our AI-powered educational systems. In an era where data is an invaluable asset, maintaining the privacy and security of learner data must be a nonnegotiable priority. Ultimately, the integration of AI into education must be seen not as a replacement for human teachers but rather as a powerful tool that complements and enhances the skills of educators. AI has the potential to relieve educators of administrative burdens, freeing up time for more practical pedagogical activities. Teachers can then focus on fostering creativity, critical thinking, emotional intelligence, and other skills that are challenging to automate but vital for the holistic development of learners. The true power of AI in education lies in its ability to democratize learning. With AI, quality education can be accessible to all, regardless of geographical location, economic status, or learning abilities. With AI at its helm, the future of education promises to be one where every learner is empowered, every teacher is equipped, and every barrier to quality education is surmountable.

As we continue our journey into the landscape of AI-driven education, we must keep these considerations in mind. By balancing the promise of AI with the responsibilities that come with it, we can ensure that AI serves to enhance and enrich our educational experiences rather than overshadow them. Therefore, AI's influence on education presents an exciting opportunity and considerable responsibility. It necessitates a delicate balancing act that acknowledges and harnesses the potential of AI and recognizes and addresses the challenges that come along. By doing so, we will not only shape the educational landscape of the future but also ensure that it upholds our values and serves the needs of all learners.

12.2 PROBLEM STATEMENT

In the realm of education, the integration of artificial intelligence (AI) brings forth a range of opportunities and challenges. This chapter explores the challenges of incorporating AI into the automated education system. As educators and policymakers embrace AI technologies to enhance teaching and learning experiences, it is important to understand and address the potential drawbacks and concerns that arise. This problem statement examines the limitations, ethical considerations, and potential risks of AI implementation while emphasizing the need for a balanced approach that values the human element in education. By critically analyzing these challenges and providing insights into effective strategies and solutions, this chapter aims to guide educators and policymakers in harnessing the transformative potential of AI while navigating the complexities in the realm of education.

12.3   UNDERSTANDING THE AI TECHNOLOGIES IN EDUCATION

12.3.1   MACHINE LEARNING AND PREDICTIVE ANALYTICS

Artificial intelligence (AI) in education signifies a paradigm shift in teaching and learning (Rodney, B.D., 2020). A major driving force behind AI is the concept of neural networks and deep learning (Perrotta, C. and Selwyn, N., 2020). These powerful tools enable AI applications to deliver personalized, dynamic, and engaging learning experiences. To understand the role of these technologies in education, we must first comprehend the basics. Neural networks are AI systems modeled after the human brain, consisting of interconnected layers of nodes, or "neurons," that process information (Katal, A. and Singh, N., 2022). These layers constitute an input layer, one or more hidden layers, and an output layer. Each node processes the input it receives and passes on the result, simulating the process of human brain cells transmitting signals. Deep learning, a subset of machine learning, involves using neural networks with multiple hidden layers. These layers enable the system to learn from data inputs and adjust its internal parameters to make accurate predictions or decisions. The "depth" in deep learning denotes these multiple layers, and it is this depth that facilitates more complex, nuanced learning and prediction capabilities. In the context of education, these technologies present immense possibilities. Personalized learning is one of the most compelling applications of neural networks and deep learning in education (Wu, J.Y. et al., 2020). These technologies can analyze vast data on student performance and learning styles. By processing this data, AI systems can adapt teaching materials and instructional strategies to cater to the unique needs of each learner, thereby enhancing the efficacy of teaching and learning. AI can identify patterns in a student's learning behavior, detect areas of weakness or strength, and then modify the content delivery accordingly. It could mean presenting concepts in different formats, adjusting the difficulty level of questions, or suggesting additional resources for further learning. The system evolves and learns over time, continually refining its strategies to ensure optimal learner engagement and understanding. Another significant application is intelligent tutoring systems (Taub, M. et al., 2021). These systems, driven by neural networks and deep learning, can provide one-on-one tutoring to students, adapting to their learning pace and offering instant feedback. These systems can detect when a student struggles with a concept and provide additional explanations or examples, just as a human tutor would. Furthermore, these technologies can facilitate the automated evaluation of assignments and exams, relieving teachers of time-consuming grading tasks (Alam,

A., 2022). Deep learning algorithms can even evaluate more complex responses, like essays, by analyzing structure, grammar, and relevance to the topic (Salloum, S.A. et al., 2020). It provides students with instant feedback, helping them to improve faster. However, while neural networks and deep learning can revolutionize education, it is essential to consider potential challenges. Understanding how these systems arrive at a decision—also known as "explainability"—can be complex due to the multiple layers of computation (Ali, S. et al., 2023). Ensuring transparency and fairness in their operations is critical. Furthermore, educators must be mindful not to let technology replace the vital human element in education. While AI can adapt to individual learning styles and offer personalized feedback, it cannot replicate the social interactions and emotional support that teachers provide. Balancing the use of AI with the invaluable human touch will be vital to integrate these technologies into education successfully.

12.3.2 NEURAL NETWORKS AND DEEP LEARNING

Neural networks (NNs) and deep learning represent two of the most fascinating and significant advancements in artificial intelligence. Through these technologies, machines can learn, adapt, and even make decisions in a manner previously thought to be the exclusive domain of the human brain (Naim, A., 2022). Neural networks (NNs) draw inspiration from the human brain (Brabazon, A. and O'Neill, M., 2006). They constitute an interconnected web of artificial neurons or nodes modelled after biological neurons. Each node in this network processes the information it receives, and if the information is significant, the node passes it on to other nodes. This interconnected web creates a system capable of learning and adapting, much like our brains. Each neuron in a neural network takes several inputs, applies a function to them, and then passes the output to the next layer. These functions are typically nonlinear, allowing the network to learn complex patterns. Importantly, each input has an associated weight, which adjusts as the model learns. The weight indicates the importance of that particular input in the calculation performed by the neuron. Conversely, deep learning is a subset of machine learning that uses neural networks with three or more layers. These deep neural networks enable the model to learn and represent the world through a hierarchy of concepts, each defined through its relation to simpler ones. By assembling these simple concepts, a deep neural network can comprehend intricate structures flexibly and efficiently. One of the most striking examples of deep learning applications is image recognition. Convolutional neural networks (CNNs), a class of deep learning models (Jogin, M. et al., 2018), have significantly improved image recognition. They can identify faces, diagnose diseases from medical images, and even generate startlingly real images. In addition to image recognition, deep learning has revolutionized natural language processing (NLP). Recurrent neural networks (RNNs) (Sherstinsky, A., 2020) and more recent models like transformers have been used to develop language translation tools, sentiment analysis models, and even AI language models capable of generating human-like text. As we delve deeper into the potential of deep learning, one emerging area of interest is generative adversarial networks (GANs) (Pan, Z. et al., 2019). GANs pit two neural networks against each other, with one trying to generate real data (the generator) and the other (the discriminator) trying to distinguish the generated data from the real thing. This dynamic creates a feedback loop that allows both networks to improve over time, resulting in a powerful model that can generate highly realistic outputs.

However, while the implications of neural networks and deep learning are profound, they are not without challenges (Kumar, P.R. and Manash, E.B.K., 2019). One key issue is interpretability, often called the "black box" problem. Deep learning models, due to their complexity, often lack transparency, making it hard to understand why they have made a certain decision. Another challenge is the requirement for large amounts of data. Deep learning models typically need vast quantities of data to learn effectively. This requirement can present practical difficulties and ethical concerns, particularly around data privacy.

12.3.3 ROBOTIC PROCESS AUTOMATION

Artificial intelligence (AI) is transforming the landscape of education, and one of the standout technologies contributing to this change is robotic process automation (RPA) (Lasso-Rodríguez, G. and Gil-Herrera, R., 2019). RPA, at its core, involves automating repetitive tasks through software robots or "bots." These bots are programmed to follow rule-based procedures, performing tasks much quicker and more accurately than humans, freeing up time for more complex, creative tasks. RPA is unique in its ability to interact with computer systems at the user interface level, just like a human user. It follows preset rules and can handle structured data to perform repetitive tasks. RPA differs from traditional automation because it can adapt to different situations and handle exceptions, allowing for a higher degree of automation without requiring significant changes to existing systems (Syed, R. et al., 2020). RPA has enormous potential in education to streamline operations and enhance efficiency. Many administrative tasks in educational institutions are repetitive and time-consuming. Automating these tasks through RPA can save time and resources, allowing staff to focus on more strategic activities, such as improving the quality of education. For instance, one of the most labor-intensive tasks in any educational institution is the admissions process (Ahmad, S.F. et al., 2022). With hundreds, if not thousands, of applications to review, each consisting of multiple documents and data points, the process is highly time-consuming. With RPA, data extraction from application forms can be automated, ensuring quicker turnaround times and removing the possibility of human error.

Another example is the grading process. Teachers spend significant amounts of time grading student work. RPA, in conjunction with AI technologies like machine learning and natural language processing, can be used to automate certain aspects of this process. It saves teachers' time and provides students with quick and consistent feedback (Darvishi, A. et al., 2022).

Furthermore, RPA can also streamline routine communications (Turcu, C. and Turcu, C., 2020). Many educational institutions send out regular notifications to students and parents about class schedules, assignments, grades, and more.

Automating these communications with RPA can ensure timely and error-free notifications.

RPA can also play a role in data management and reporting. Educational institutions often must generate regular reports on student performance, attendance, and curriculum effectiveness (Issac, R. et al., 2018). Automating this process ensures that the reports are generated quickly and accurately, allowing institutions to analyze these reports more frequently and make data-driven decisions. However, while the potential of RPA is immense, it does not come without challenges. Implementation can be costly and requires careful planning to ensure compatibility with existing systems.

Furthermore, there are concerns about job displacement as tasks become automated, necessitating a careful approach to balance efficiency gains with workforce implications (Bursley, M., 2021). Moreover, as with any technology handling sensitive data, security and privacy issues must be considered. The bots used in RPA must adhere to strict data privacy rules to protect the sensitive information of students and staff.

12.4 THE ARCHITECTURE OF AN AI-DRIVEN AUTOMATED EDUCATION SYSTEM

12.4.1 DATA INFRASTRUCTURE AND MANAGEMENT

At the heart of any AI-driven system, including an automated education system, lies a robust data infrastructure and efficient data management practices. As the saying goes, "data is the new oil," and this could not be truer for AI technologies.

The architecture of an AI-driven automated education system starts with establishing a well-structured data infrastructure (Cao, L., 2022). This infrastructure is the backbone that enables data collection, storage, and processing. It encompasses databases, data warehouses, cloud storage systems, and data processing tools. A well-designed data infrastructure supports the efficient management and utilization of data, ensuring it can be easily accessed and used for AI applications. When building the data infrastructure for an AI-driven education system, the first consideration is the type and volume of data that will be handled. Education systems generate diverse data, including student demographics, academic performance data, administrative data, and more. The data infrastructure must handle this variety and volume of data. The infrastructure must also be scalable (Buitrago, P.A. et al., 2020). As the education system evolves and grows, the data infrastructure should be able to scale accordingly to accommodate more data and more complex data processing tasks. It is where cloud-based infrastructure becomes valuable as it allows for easy scaling and access to advanced data processing tools.

Data management is another critical component of an AI-driven automated education system (Ciolacu, M. et al., 2017). Effective data management involves governance, quality control, and security. These elements ensure data is accurate, reliable, and secure, making it a solid foundation for AI applications. Data governance involves defining who within an organization has authority and control over data assets and how those data assets may be used. It includes creating rules and policies for data management and usage. Good data governance ensures that data is used and managed ethically and that data-related practices align with organizational objectives and regulations. Data quality control is about ensuring the accuracy and consistency of data. Data quality is paramount in AI because AI models' performance heavily depends on the data quality they are trained on. Techniques such as data cleaning, data validation, and data integration are used to improve data quality.

Lastly, data security is vital in protecting sensitive information (Puthal, D. et al. 2021). It includes student personal data, academic records, and staff information in an educational context. Effective data security practices, including encryption, access control, and regular security audits, help prevent unauthorized access and data breaches. Implementing effective data infrastructure and management is no small task. It requires significant planning, investment, and ongoing maintenance. However, the effort is worth it. With robust data infrastructure and management, an AI-driven automated education system can deliver personalized learning experiences, efficient administrative processes, and valuable insights that improve education outcomes.

12.4.2 AI ALGORITHMS AND MODEL TRAINING

Artificial intelligence (AI) is reshaping the education sector, and a critical part of this transformation is the use of AI algorithms and the training of AI models. In an AI-driven automated education system, the "intelligence" results from these algorithms trained on data to make decisions, offer predictions, and perform tasks.

AI algorithms can range from relatively simple decision trees to complex deep learning models, depending on the specific application within the education system. These algorithms are mathematical formulas or statistical processes used to find patterns in data. They are the core of any AI system and directly influence its ability to perform tasks and make decisions. In the context of an AI-driven automated education system, AI algorithms play various roles. For instance, machine learning algorithms can personalize learning by adapting content to individual student's needs based on their learning styles and progress. They can also assist in administrative tasks, such as scheduling and grading, and provide predictive analytics for student performance and attrition rates.

Once the appropriate algorithms have been selected, training the AI models is the next step. Model training involves feeding the algorithm with data and allowing it to adjust its parameters to predict better or classify the output. This process involves splitting the available data into training and validation sets. The algorithm learns from the training data and then fine-tunes its parameters based on the validation data to avoid overfitting (where the model learns too well and performs poorly on unseen data) (Lucchese, C. et al., 2016). Model training might involve feeding the algorithm data about students' past performance, engagement levels, learning preferences, and other relevant factors in an educational setting. The model then learns from this data to predict future performance or recommend personalized learning resources.

It is worth noting that the training process often requires significant computational resources, especially for complex models like deep neural networks. Cloud computing platforms and specialized hardware like graphics processing units (GPUs) are commonly used. Furthermore, the choice of training data is crucial. The data needs to be representative of the problem at hand. The resulting AI model will also be biased if the training data is biased. For instance, if an AI model designed to predict student success is only trained on data from a specific demographic, its predictions for other demographics might not be accurate. Model training is iterative (Wang, X. and Cao, W., 2018). After the initial training, the model's performance needs to be evaluated, and if necessary, the model needs to be retrained or fine-tuned. The evaluation process often involves using a separate test data set to check the model's performance on unseen data. The training and implementation of AI models also involve ethical considerations. Data privacy is paramount, particularly when dealing with sensitive student data. Appropriate measures should be taken to anonymize data and protect student identities.

12.4.3 SYSTEM INTEGRATION AND TESTING

Implementing an AI-driven automated education system is not just about the data infrastructure or AI algorithms. System integration and testing are equally important parts of this process (Savadjiev, P. et al., 2019). These process stages ensure the AI system functions well within the existing education infrastructure and performs as expected. System integration is the process of combining the different components of the AI system and ensuring they function together seamlessly. In an AI-driven automated education system, this involves integrating the AI algorithms and models with the existing educational software and databases. This integration must be executed so that the AI system can interact with the existing components efficiently and effectively. The integration process often involves application programming interfaces (APIs) that allow different software components to communicate with each other (Perrotta, C. et al., 2021). For example, an AI algorithm designed to personalize learning content may need to interact with a learning management system (LMS) to access course content and student performance data. A well-designed API can facilitate this interaction.

The next step is system testing once the AI system has been integrated into the broader education system. Testing is crucial to ensure the system functions as expected and to identify and address any issues or bugs.

Testing an AI system is somewhat different from testing traditional software. Because AI systems learn and adapt over time, their behavior can be less predictable, and the output for a given input might change as the system learns. As such, testing an AI system often involves checking if the system is working correctly and evaluating the quality of its predictions or decisions. In an educational context, testing an AI system might involve verifying that it can correctly access and process data from the LMS, make accurate predictions about student performance and that its recommendations for personalized learning are appropriate and effective. Importantly, testing should not be a one-time activity. Given the dynamic nature of AI systems, regular testing and monitoring are necessary to ensure that the system continues to perform well as it interacts with new data and as the educational environment evolves. Beyond functional testing, it is also crucial to test the system from a user perspective. It means evaluating the system's usability and effectiveness in achieving its educational objectives. User testing can provide valuable feedback and help identify areas for improvement.

Lastly, integrating an AI system into education is not just a technical challenge. It also involves considering how the system will affect the users—the educators and students. Data privacy, fairness, and transparency must be addressed to ensure that the AI system is ethical and beneficial.

12.4.4   USER INTERFACE AND EXPERIENCE DESIGN

Implementing an AI-driven automated education system is incomplete without a robust user interface and a thoughtfully designed user experience (Grigera, J. et al., 2023). After all, it is through this interface that students, educators, and administrators will interact with the AI system. A well-designed interface and user experience can make the difference between a system that frustrates users and enhances the educational process.

The user interface (UI) is the point of human–computer interaction and communication in a device. In an AI-driven automated education system, this could be a web portal, a mobile app, or a voice-based interface. The interface's design directly affects the user's perception of and ability to use the system effectively. Designing the UI for an AI-driven system presents unique challenges and opportunities. Unlike traditional software, AI systems often can learn and adapt to individual users. The interface may need to change and evolve based on the user's interactions and preferences. This adaptability can provide a more personalized and engaging user experience, but it also requires careful design to ensure that changes in the interface do not confuse or frustrate users. The user experience (UX) goes beyond the UI (Rajeshkumar S. et al., 2013). It encompasses all aspects of the user's interaction with the system, including how easy it is to use, how it makes the user feel, and how well it meets their needs and expectations. In an AI-driven automated education system, the UX design should focus on enhancing the learning process, supporting educators, and streamlining administrative tasks. For students, a well-designed user experience could mean a system that adapts to their learning style, provides personalized feedback and helps them stay engaged and motivated. For educators, it could mean a system that reduces administrative workload, offers insights into student performance, and supports differentiated instruction. For administrators, it could mean a system that automates routine tasks, provides data-driven insights and helps improve the efficiency and effectiveness of the educational institution. A key aspect of UX design is user testing (Kuniavsky, M., 2010). It involves testing the system with actual users to get feedback and identify areas for improvement. In the context of an AI-driven automated education system, user testing could involve students, teachers, and administrators using the system and providing feedback on its usability, usefulness, and overall experience.

Another important consideration in UX design for AI systems is transparency and control. Users should clearly understand what the AI system is doing, why it is doing it, and how it is making its decisions. They should also have some level of control over the system's actions. For example, if the system is making recommendations for personalized learning, students and teachers should understand the basis for these recommendations and have the ability to override them if necessary.

12.5 ETHICAL CONSIDERATIONS IN AI-POWERED EDUCATION

12.5.1 DATA PRIVACY AND SECURITY

As we embrace the transformative power of AI in education, it is equally important to address the ethical considerations that come with it. Among these, data privacy and security emerge as paramount concerns. These issues cannot be overlooked, given the sensitive nature of information in an educational setting. AI-driven automated education systems rely heavily on data. From personal details of students to their learning patterns and academic performance, an array of information is used to personalize learning experiences, predict performance, and manage administrative tasks. This heavy reliance on data raises critical questions about how this information is collected, used, and protected. Data privacy revolves around the right to control personal information (Nair, M.M. and Tyagi, AK, 2021). In an AI-driven education system, this means ensuring that students, parents, and educators are fully aware of the data being collected and its use. Transparency is a key principle here. Users should be provided with clear, understandable information about the system's data practices and be able to opt-in or out of data collection and use.

Another key aspect of data privacy is the concept of data minimization (Antignac, T. et al., 2017). This principle suggests that only the data necessary to achieve a specific purpose should be collected and used. Applying this principle in an AI-driven education system could mean, for instance, only collecting student performance data relevant to personalizing a learning experience and avoiding unnecessary personal information. Data security, on the other hand, is about protecting data from unauthorized access and breaches. As AI-driven education systems store and process vast amounts of sensitive data, they can become cyberattack targets. It makes robust security measures indispensable. Effective data security involves a range of practices, such as encryption, access control, and regular security audits. Encryption involves transforming data into a format that can only be read with a decryption key, providing a robust defense against unauthorized access. Access control means ensuring that only authorized individuals can access certain data, and regular security audits involve systematically checking the system's security measures and addressing any vulnerabilities. Furthermore, any data breaches should be promptly addressed, with affected parties notified as data protection regulations require. In addition, organizations should have contingency plans to respond to and recover from security incidents.

Balancing the benefits of AI with these ethical considerations is a challenge. Striking the right balance requires ongoing dialogue among educators, administrators, technologists, and policymakers. Legal frameworks, such as the EU's General Data Protection Regulation (GDPR), can provide useful guidelines, but given the rapid pace of AI technology, ongoing vigilance and proactive ethical considerations are necessary.

12.5.2   AI BIAS AND FAIRNESS

Implementing AI in education is a powerful tool that can revolutionize learning but also brings forth important ethical considerations. Among these, the issues of AI bias and fairness are particularly significant. AI bias refers to the tendencies of AI systems to make unjust, prejudiced, or inequitable decisions. It typically happens when the data used to train the AI system reflects societal or historical biases or when the AI algorithms unintentionally favor certain groups over others. In AI-powered education, bias can manifest in numerous ways, including skewed performance predictions, unfair personalization of learning content, or discriminatory administrative decisions.

One common form of bias is selection bias, which can occur if the data used to train the AI system does not represent all student groups. For instance, if an AI model intended to predict student success is trained predominantly on data from urban students, its predictions may be less accurate for rural students (Simpson, O., 2006). Another form of bias is confirmation bias, which happens when an AI system reinforces existing prejudices. For example, if an AI tutoring system consistently recommends advanced math topics to boys more than to girls based on partial historical data, it could perpetuate gender stereotypes.

Addressing AI bias requires a combination of technical and nontechnical strategies (Glauner, P. et al., 2016). On the technical side, efforts should be made to ensure that the data used to train the AI system is diverse and representative. Techniques like bias detection and mitigation can also be employed during the AI model development process. These techniques aim to identify and reduce bias in the AI model's predictions. On the nontechnical side, involving a diverse group in the AI development process can help bring multiple perspectives and identify potential biases that might not be obvious to a more homogenous group. In addition, transparency about the AI system's decision-making process can help users understand and question its predictions or decisions. Closely related to the issue of bias is fairness. In AI-powered education, fairness can mean that the system provides equitable learning opportunities for all students, regardless of their background or characteristics. It can also mean that the system's predictions or decisions do not unfairly disadvantage any student group.

In AI-powered education, achieving fairness is challenging because fairness can mean different things in different contexts (Hakami, Eyad, and Davinia Hernández Leo, 2020). However, some general strategies can help promote fairness. These include involving stakeholders in decision-making about the AI system, regularly reviewing and updating the AI system to address any emerging fairness issues, and prioritizing transparency so that users can understand and challenge the system's decisions.

12.5.3 THE DIGITAL DIVIDE AND ACCESSIBILITY

Incorporating AI in education holds immense promise for enhancing learning experiences and outcomes. However, it also comes with ethical considerations that we must address: the digital divide and accessibility. The "digital divide" refers to the gap between those with ready access to computers and the internet and those without access (Luttrell, R. et al., 2020). In an AI-powered education system, the digital divide can be exacerbated if some students lack the necessary technology or internet connectivity to engage with AI tools fully. For instance, AI-driven personalized learning tools can provide rich, customized educational experiences. Still, these benefits can only be realized if students can access a device and a reliable internet connection. Without these, students can be left behind, widening educational disparities. Addressing the digital divide requires multifaceted solutions involving technological, policy, and community initiatives. Efforts to provide affordable devices and internet access are critical on the technology front. On the policy side, legislation can help ensure equitable access to technology through grants or public Wi-Fi initiatives. Community programs can also help by providing technology resources and training for students and families who lack them. Even when students have access to technology, there is another crucial consideration: accessibility. AI-driven education systems should be designed so that all students, including those with disabilities, can engage with them fully and effectively.

Accessibility (Bozkurt, A., 2023) in this context goes beyond compliance with regulations such as the Americans with Disabilities Act in the United States or the Web Content Accessibility Guidelines internationally. It ensures that all students benefit from the AI-driven education system, regardless of their abilities or disabilities. Designing for accessibility can involve a range of practices. For instance, an AI-driven tutoring system might include text-to-speech functionality to support students with visual impairments or speech-to-text functionality to assist students with hearing impairments. AI systems can also be designed to be compatible with assistive technologies like screen readers.

Nevertheless, accessibility is not just about technical features. It is also about designing the user experience to be intuitive and inclusive. It might involve user testing with a diverse group of students, including those with disabilities, to ensure the system is easy to use and meets the needs of all learners.

Beyond these considerations, ethical AI design in education should also be mindful of students' varying learning needs and preferences. AI systems should strive to offer a customizable user experience, accommodating the diverse ways students engage with educational content.

12.6 CONCLUSION

Integrating AI in education is a transformative venture with opportunities and challenges. The benefits of AI-powered education are numerous, from personalized learning experiences to efficient administrative processes and insightful data analytics. However, these benefits come with significant ethical considerations, including data privacy, AI bias, the digital divide, and accessibility. As we strive toward an era of AI-powered education, it becomes crucial to strike a balance between harnessing the potential of AI and addressing these ethical considerations.

As discussed earlier, machine learning and predictive analytics provide remarkable tools for understanding and shaping students' learning journeys. They enable adaptive learning paths, informed predictions on student performance, and efficient administrative functions. However, the proper handling and interpretation of data, in adherence to ethical standards, will determine the effectiveness and acceptability of these technologies.

Neural networks and deep learning, the core of many advanced AI systems, offer unprecedented capabilities for understanding complex patterns in student data and crafting personalized educational experiences. However, the same power that makes these technologies exciting makes them susceptible to bias and fairness concerns.

Robotic process automation (RPA) also brings an immense potential for improving efficiency in educational processes, allowing educators to focus more on their core teaching responsibilities. Nevertheless, it, too, like other AI technologies, must be implemented thoughtfully to respect privacy and maintain security.

From a systems perspective, we dove into the data infrastructure, AI algorithms, system integration, and user interface and experience. Each element forms a crucial part of an AI-driven automated education system. However, as we construct these systems, we must ensure they are designed to be technically robust, ethically sound, accessible, and equitable.

Finally, we delved into critical ethical considerations of AI-powered education. Data privacy and security, AI bias and fairness, the digital divide, and accessibility are issues that demand our attention as we design and implement these systems. Addressing these ethical considerations is not just a legal obligation or a nice-to-have feature. It is a critical prerequisite for building trust among students, educators, and parents, which, in turn, is key for successfully adopting AI in education.

A few key conclusions emerge as we reflect on our journey through this chapter. First, AI offers immense potential for enhancing education, but this potential can only be fully realized if we address the ethical considerations it brings. Second, while each AI technology offers unique benefits and challenges, common themes of data privacy, bias, fairness, the digital divide, and accessibility run across them all. Third, the success of AI in education hinges not just on the technologies themselves but on how they are implemented—from the data infrastructure and AI algorithms to the user interface, user experience, and system integration.

REFERENCES

Ahmad, S.F., Alam, M.M., Rahmat, M.K., Mubarik, M.S. and Hyder, S.I., 2022. Academic and administrative role of artificial intelligence in education. *Sustainability*, 14(3), p.1101.

Ainscow, M. and Sandill, A., 2010. Developing inclusive education systems: The role of organisational cultures and leadership. *International Journal of Inclusive Education*, 14(4), pp.401–416.

Alam, A., 2021, December. Should robots replace teachers? Mobilisation of AI and learning analytics in education. In *2021 International Conference on Advances in Computing, Communication, and Control (ICAC3)* (pp. 1–12). IEEE.

Alam, A., 2022. Employing adaptive learning and intelligent tutoring robots for virtual classrooms and smart campuses: Reforming education in the age of artificial intelligence. In *Advanced Computing and Intelligent Technologies: Proceedings of ICACIT 2022* (pp. 395–406). Singapore: Springer Nature Singapore.

Alam, A. and Mohanty, A., 2023, January. Foundation for the future of higher education or 'misplaced optimism'? Being human in the age of artificial intelligence. In *Innovations in Intelligent Computing and Communication: First International Conference, ICIICC 2022, Bhubaneswar, Odisha, December 16–17, 2022, Proceedings* (pp. 17–29). Cham: Springer International Publishing.

Ali, S., Abuhmed, T., El-Sappagh, S., Muhammad, K., Alonso-Moral, J.M., Confalonieri, R., Guidotti, R., Del Ser, J., Díaz-Rodríguez, N. and Herrera, F., 2023. Explainable Artificial Intelligence (XAI): What we know and what is left to attain Trustworthy Artificial Intelligence. *Information Fusion*, 99 p.101805.

Antignac, T., Sands, D. and Schneider, G., 2017. Data minimisation: A language-based approach. In *ICT Systems Security and Privacy Protection: 32nd IFIP TC 11 International Conference, SEC 2017, Rome, May 29–31, 2017* (pp. 442–456). Springer International Publishing.

Bacciu, D., Akarmazyan, S., Armengaud, E., Bacco, M., Bravos, G., Calandra, C., Carlini, E., Carta, A., Cassarà, P., Coppola, M. and Davalas, C., 2021, August. Teaching-trustworthy autonomous cyber-physical applications through human-centred intelligence. In *2021 IEEE International Conference on Omni-Layer Intelligent Systems (COINS)* (pp. 1–6). IEEE.

Baker, R.S.D., Corbett, A.T., Koedinger, K.R., Evenson, S., Roll, I., Wagner, A.Z., Naim, M., Raspat, J., Baker, D.J. and Beck, J.E., 2006, June 26–30. Adapting to when students game an intelligent tutoring system. In *Intelligent Tutoring Systems: 8th International Conference, ITS 2006. Proceedings 8*, Jhongli (pp. 392–401). Berlin: Springer.

Bozkurt, A., 2023. Generative artificial intelligence (AI) powered conversational educational agents: The inevitable paradigm shift. *Asian Journal of Distance Education*. 18(1), (pp 198–204).

Brabazon, A. and O'Neill, M., 2006. Neural network methodologies. In *Biologically Inspired Algorithms for Financial Modelling* (pp. 15–36). https://link.springer.com/chapter/10 .1007/3-540-31307-9_2

Buitrago, P.A., Nystrom, N.A., Gupta, R. and Saltz, J., 2020. Delivering scalable deep learning to research with bridges-AI. In *High Performance Computing: 6th Latin American Conference, CARLA 2019*, Turrialba, September 25–27, 2019, Revised Selected Papers 6 (pp. 200–214). Springer International Publishing.

Bursley, M., 2021. Job impact on automation in accounting: What will happen to job availability?. *Journal for Global Business and Community*, 12(1), pp.10–10.

Calandra, D., De Lorenzis, F., Cannavò, A. and Lamberti, F., 2022. Immersive virtual reality and passive haptic interfaces to improve procedural learning in a formal training course for first responders. *Virtual Reality*, 27, pp.985–1012.

Cao, L., 2022. A new age of AI: Features and futures. *IEEE Intelligent Systems*, 37(1), pp.25–37.

Ciolacu, M., Svasta, P.M., Berg, W. and Popp, H., 2017, October. Education 4.0 for tall thin engineer in a data driven society. In *2017 IEEE 23rd International Symposium for Design and Technology in Electronic Packaging (SIITME)* (pp. 432–437). IEEE.

Cox, A.M., 2021. Exploring the impact of Artificial Intelligence and robots on higher education through literature-based design fictions. *International Journal of Educational Technology in Higher Education*, 18(1), p.3.

Dai, C.P. and Ke, F., 2022. Educational applications of artificial intelligence in simulation-based learning: A systematic mapping review. *Computers and Education: Artificial Intelligence*, 3, p.100087.

Da'u, A. and Salim, N., 2020. Recommendation system based on deep learning methods: A systematic review and new directions. *Artificial Intelligence Review*, 53(4), pp.2709–2748.

Darvishi, A., Khosravi, H., Abdi, S., Sadiq, S. and Gašević, D., 2022, June. Incorporating training, self-monitoring and AI-assistance to improve peer feedback quality. In *Proceedings of the Ninth ACM Conference on Learning@ Scale* (pp. 35–47).

Da'u, A. and Salim, N., 2020. Recommendation system based on deep learning methods: A systematic review and new directions. *Artificial Intelligence Review*, 53(4), pp.2709–2748.

Dwivedi, Y.K., Hughes, L., Ismagilova, E., Aarts, G., Coombs, C., Crick, T., Duan, Y., Dwivedi, R., Edwards, J., Eirug, A. and Galanos, V., 2021. Artificial Intelligence (AI): Multidisciplinary perspectives on emerging challenges, opportunities, and agenda for research, practice and policy. *International Journal of Information Management*, 57, p.101994.

Glauner, P., Meira, J.A., Valtchev, P., State, R. and Bettinger, F., 2016. *The Challenge of Non-Technical Loss Detection using Artificial Intelligence: A Survey*. arXiv preprint arXiv:1606.00626.

Goulart, V.G., Liboni, L.B. and Cezarino, L.O., 2022. Balancing skills in the digital transformation era: The future of jobs and the role of higher education. *Industry and Higher Education*, 36(2), pp.118–127.

Grigera, J., Espada, J.P. and Rossi, G., 2023. AI in user interface design and evaluation. *IT Professional*, 25(2), pp.20–22.

Guache, M., Manaig, K., Tesoro, J.F., Yazon, A. and Sapin, S., 2023. Beyond words: Uncovering the untold stories of multilingual students' lived experiences in online distance learning. *Journal of Elementary and Secondary School* 1 (1), pp.1–15.

Guilherme, A., 2019. AI and education: The importance of teacher and student relations. *AI & Society*, 34, pp.47–54.

Hakami, E. and Leo, D.H. (2020). How are learning analytics considering the societal values of fairness, accountability, transparency and human well-being?: A literature review. In A. Martínez-Monés, A. Álvarez, M. Caeiro-Rodríguez, and Y. Dimitriadis (Eds.), *LASI-SPAIN 2020: Learning Analytics Summer Institute Spain 2020: Learning Analytics. Time for Adoption?* (pp. 121–41); 2020 Jun 15–16; Valladolid. Aachen: CEUR.

Haniya, S., 2023, March. Transcending the spacial boundaries in large lecture settings via e-learning: Strategies for a change. In *Society for Information Technology & Teacher Education International Conference* (pp. 501–504). Association for the Advancement of Computing in Education (AACE).

Hernandez-de-Menendez, M., Escobar Díaz, C. and Morales-Menendez, R., 2020. Technologies for the future of learning: State of the art. *International Journal on Interactive Design and Manufacturing (IJIDeM)*, 14, pp.683–695.

Herrington, J., Reeves, T.C., Oliver, R. and Woo, Y., 2004. Designing authentic activities in web-based courses. *Journal of Computing in Higher Education*, 16, pp.3–29.

Hussin, H., Jiea, P.Y., Rosly, R.N.R. and Omar, S.R., 2019. Integrated 21st century Science, Technology, Engineering, Mathematics (STEM) education through robotics project-based learning. *Humanities & Social Sciences Reviews*, 7(2), pp.204–211.

Issac, R., Muni, R. and Desai, K., 2018, February. Delineated analysis of robotic process automation tools. In *2018 Second International Conference on Advances in Electronics, Computers and Communications (ICAECC)* (pp. 1–5). IEEE.

Jogin, M., Madhulika, M.S., Divya, G.D., Meghana, R.K. and Apoorva, S., 2018, May. Feature extraction using convolution neural networks (CNN) and deep learning. In *2018 3rd IEEE International Conference on Recent Trends in Electronics, Information & Communication Technology (RTEICT)* (pp. 2319–2323). IEEE.

Jones, P., 2010. Collaboration at a distance: Using a wiki to create a collaborative learning environment for distance education and on-campus students in a social work course. *Journal of Teaching in Social Work*, 30(2), pp.225–236.

Kamruzzaman, M.M., Alanazi, S., Alruwaili, M., Alshammari, N., Elaiwat, S., Abu-Zanona, M., Innab, N., Mohammad Elzaghmouri, B. and Ahmed Alanazi, B., 2023. AI-and IoT-assisted sustainable education systems during pandemics, such as COVID-19, for smart cities. *Sustainability*, 15(10), p.8354.

Katal, A. and Singh, N., 2022. Artificial neural network: Models, applications, and challenges. In *Innovative Trends in Computational Intelligence* (pp. 235–257). https://link.springer.com/chapter/10.1007/978-3-030-78284-9_11

Kem, D., 2022. Personalised and adaptive learning: Emerging learning platforms in the era of digital and smart learning. *International Journal of Social Science and Human Research*, 5(2), pp.385–391.

Khogali, H.O. and Mekid, S., 2023. The blended future of automation and AI: Examining some long-term societal and ethical impact features. *Technology in Society*, 73, p.102232.

Koivisto, J.M., Niemi, H., Multisilta, J. and Eriksson, E., 2017. Nursing students' experiential learning processes using an online 3D simulation game. *Education and Information Technologies*, 22, pp.383–398.

Kommey, B., Keelson, E., Samuel, F., Twum-Asare, S. and Akuffo, K.K., 2022. Automatic multiple choice examination questions marking and grade generator software. *IPTEK The Journal for Technology and Science*, 33(3), pp.175–189.

Kommey, B., Gyimah, F., Kponyo, J.J. and Andam-Akorful, S.A., 2022. A web based system for easy and secured managing process of University Accreditation Information. *Indonesian Journal of Computing, Engineering and Design (IJoCED)*, 4(1), pp.17–29.

Kumar, P.R. and Manash, E.B.K., 2019, May. Deep learning: A branch of machine learning. In *Journal of Physics: Conference Series* (Vol. 1228, No. 1, p. 012045). IOP Publishing.

Kuniavsky, M., 2010. *Smart Things: Ubiquitous Computing User Experience Design*. Morgan Kaufmann Publishers: Elsevier.

Lasso-Rodríguez, G. and Gil-Herrera, R., 2019. Robotic process automation applied to education: A new kind of robot teacher?. In *ICERI2019 Proceedings* (pp. 2531–2540). IATED.

Laurillard, D., Oliver, M., Wasson, B. and Hoppe, U., 2009. Implementing technology-enhanced learning. In *Technology-Enhanced Learning: Principles and Products* (pp. 289–306). https://link.springer.com/chapter/10.1007/978-1-4020-9827-7_17

Lucchese, C., Nardini, F.M., Orlando, S., Perego, R., Silvestri, F. and Trani, S., 2016, July. Post-learning optimisation of tree ensembles for efficient ranking. In *Proceedings of the 39th International ACM SIGIR Conference on Research and Development in Information Retrieval* (pp. 949–952).

Luttrell, R., Wallace, A., McCollough, C. and Lee, J., 2020. The digital divide: Addressing artificial intelligence in communication education. *Journalism & Mass Communication Educator*, 75(4), pp.470–482.

Markauskaite, L., Marrone, R., Poquet, O., Knight, S., Martinez-Maldonado, R., Howard, S., Tondeur, J., De Laat, M., Shum, S.B., Gašević, D. and Siemens, G., 2022. Rethinking the entwinement between artificial intelligence and human learning: What capabilities do learners need for a world with AI?. *Computers and Education: Artificial Intelligence*, 3, p.100056.

Meszaros, J., 2022. The next challenge for data protection law: AI revolution in automated scientific research. Available at SSRN: https://ssrn.com/abstract=4030901

Mhlanga, D., 2023, February 11. Open AI in education, the responsible and ethical use of ChatGPT towards lifelong learning. (February 11, 2023). Available at SSRN: https://ssrn.com/abstract=4354422 or http://dx.doi.org/10.2139/ssrn.4354422

Naim, A., 2022. E-learning engagement through convolution neural networks in business education. *European Journal of Innovation in Nonformal Education*, 2(2), pp.497–501.

Nair, M.M. and Tyagi, A.K., 2021. Privacy: History, statistics, policy, laws, preservation and threat analysis. *Journal of Information Assurance & Security*, 16(1) pp. 024–034. © MIR Labs, www.mirlabs.net/jias/index.html

Ochoa, X., Lang, C., Siemens, G., Wise, A., Gasevic, D. and Merceron, A., 2022. Multimodal learning analytics-Rationale, process, examples, and direction. In *The Handbook of Learning Analytics* (pp. 54–65). Beaumont, Alberta: Soc. Learn. Analytics Res.

Pan, Z., Yu, W., Yi, X., Khan, A., Yuan, F. and Zheng, Y., 2019. Recent progress on generative adversarial networks (GANs): A survey. *IEEE Access*, 7, pp.36322–36333.

Pantelimon, F.V., Bologa, R., Toma, A. and Posedaru, B.S., 2021. The evolution of AI-driven educational systems during the COVID-19 pandemic. *Sustainability*, 13(23), p.13501.

Perrotta, C. and Selwyn, N., 2020. Deep learning goes to school: Toward a relational understanding of AI in education. *Learning, Media and Technology*, 45(3), pp.251–269.

Perrotta, C., Gulson, K.N., Williamson, B. and Witzenberger, K., 2021. Automation, APIs and the distributed labour of platform pedagogies in Google Classroom. *Critical Studies in Education*, 62(1), pp.97–113.

Premlatha, K.R., Dharani, B. and Geetha, T.V., 2016. Dynamic learner profiling and automatic learner classification for adaptive e-learning environment. *Interactive Learning Environments*, 24(6), pp.1054–1075.

Prinsloo, P., Slade, S. and Khalil, M., 2022. The answer is (not only) technological: Considering student data privacy in learning analytics. *British Journal of Educational Technology*, 53(4), pp.876–893.

Puthal, D., Mishra, A.K. and Sharma, S., 2021. AI-driven security solutions for the internet of everything. *IEEE Consumer Electronics Magazine*, 10(5), pp.70–71.

Rajeshkumar, S., Omar, R. and Mahmud, M., 2013, November. Taxonomies of user experience (UX) evaluation methods. In *2013 International Conference on Research and Innovation in Information Systems (ICRIIS)* (pp. 533–538). IEEE.

Rodney, B.D., 2020. Understanding the paradigm shift in education in the twenty-first century: The role of technology and the Internet of Things. *Worldwide Hospitality and Tourism Themes*. 12 (1), (pp.35–47). https://doi.org/10.1108/WHATT-10-2019-0068

Salloum, S.A., Khan, R. and Shaalan, K., 2020. A survey of semantic analysis approaches. In *Proceedings of the International Conference on Artificial Intelligence and Computer Vision (AICV2020)* (pp. 61–70). Springer International Publishing.

Savadjiev, P., Chong, J., Dohan, A., Vakalopoulou, M., Reinhold, C., Paragios, N. and Gallix, B., 2019. Demystification of AI-driven medical image interpretation: Past, present and future. *European Radiology*, 29, pp.1616–1624.

Schiff, D., Rakova, B., Ayesh, A., Fanti, A. and Lennon, M., 2021. Explaining the principles to practices gap in AI. *IEEE Technology and Society Magazine*, 40(2), pp.81–94.

Sharef, N.M., Murad, M.A.A., Mansor, E.I., Nasharuddin, N.A., Omar, M.K., Samian, N., Arshad, N.I., Ismail, W. and Shahbodin, F., 2020, October. Learning-analytics based intelligent simulator for personalised learning. In *2020 International Conference on Advancement in Data Science, E-learning and Information Systems (ICADEIS)* (pp. 1–6). IEEE.

Sherstinsky, A., 2020. Fundamentals of recurrent neural network (RNN) and long short-term memory (LSTM) network. *Physica D: Nonlinear Phenomena*, 404, p.132306.

Shin, D., 2022. How do people judge the credibility of algorithmic sources?. *Ai & Society*, 37, pp.81–96. Springer.

Simpson, O., 2006. Predicting student success in open and distance learning. *Open Learning: The Journal of Open, Distance and e-Learning*, 21(2), pp.125–138.

Smuts, M., Gardner, M., Callaghan, V. and Gutierrez, A.G., 2019, September. Towards dynamically adaptable immersive spaces for learning. In *2019 11th Computer Science and Electronic Engineering (CEEC)* (pp. 113–117). IEEE.

Steenbergen-Hu, S. and Cooper, H., 2014. A meta-analysis of the effectiveness of intelligent tutoring systems on college students' academic learning. *Journal of Educational Psychology*, 106(2), p.331.

Syed, R., Suriadi, S., Adams, M., Bandara, W., Leemans, S.J., Ouyang, C., ter Hofstede, A.H., van de Weerd, I., Wynn, M.T. and Reijers, H.A., 2020. Robotic process automation: Contemporary themes and challenges. *Computers in Industry*, 115, p.103162.

Taub, M., Azevedo, R., Rajendran, R., Cloude, E.B., Biswas, G. and Price, M.J., 2021. How are students' emotions related to the accuracy of cognitive and metacognitive processes during learning with an intelligent tutoring system?. *Learning and Instruction*, 72, p.101200.

Turcu, C. and Turcu, C., 2020, June. On robotic process automation and its integration in higher education. In *Conference Proceedings. The Future of Education*.

Votto, A.M., Valecha, R., Najafirad, P. and Rao, H.R., 2021. Artificial intelligence in tactical human resource management: A systematic literature review. *International Journal of Information Management Data Insights*, 1(2), p.100047.

Wang, X. and Cao, W., 2018. Non-iterative approaches in training feed-forward neural networks and their applications. *Soft Computing*, 22, pp.3473–3476.

Wang, S., Christensen, C., Cui, W., Tong, R., Yarnall, L., Shear, L. and Feng, M., 2023. When adaptive learning is effective learning: Comparison of an adaptive learning system to teacher-led instruction. *Interactive Learning Environments*, 31(2), pp.793–803.

Wong, L.H., King, R.B., Chai, C.S. and Liu, M., 2016. Seamlessly learning Chinese: Contextual meaning making and vocabulary growth in a seamless Chinese as a second language learning environment. *Instructional Science*, 44, pp.399–422.

Wu, J.Y., Hsiao, Y.C. and Nian, M.W., 2020. Using supervised machine learning on large-scale online forums to classify course-related Facebook messages in predicting learning achievement within the personal learning environment. *Interactive Learning Environments*, 28(1), pp.65–80.

Wu, C.H., Tang, Y.M., Tsang, Y.P. and Chau, K.Y., 2021. Immersive learning design for technology education: A soft systems methodology. *Frontiers in Psychology*, 12, p.6061.

Xie, H., Chu, H.C., Hwang, G.J. and Wang, C.C., 2019. Trends and development in technology-enhanced adaptive/personalised learning: A systematic review of journal publications from 2007 to 2017. *Computers & Education*, 140, p.103599.

Xu, L., Jiang, C., Wang, J., Yuan, J. and Ren, Y., 2014. Information security in big data: Privacy and data mining. *Ieee Access*, 2, pp.1149–1176.

Yang, W., 2022. Artificial Intelligence education for young children: Why, what, and how in curriculum design and implementation. *Computers and Education: Artificial Intelligence*, 3, p.100061.

Zawacki-Richter, O., Marín, V.I., Bond, M. and Gouverneur, F., 2019. Systematic review of research on artificial intelligence applications in higher education–where are the educators?. *International Journal of Educational Technology in Higher Education*, 16(1), pp.1–27.

Zeide, E., 2017. The structural consequences of big data-driven education. *Big Data*, 5(2), pp.164–172.

13 Impact of Information Technology on the Education System and Teaching Process

Sheeba Khalid

13.1 INTRODUCTION

Today, knowledge as well as information are the most important determinants of productivity, competition, prosperity, and comfort. Consequently, humans have focused on acquiring a higher education. In the 21st century, all changes and developments stem from education. Today, information technology can facilitate education and learning. Information technology refers to the knowledge process and its application of methods, as well as the processing, transfer, and development of information. IT encompasses the collection, organization, storage, publication, and utilization of information in the form of sound, image, text, and number through the use of computer and telecommunication technologies. Significant IT-related alterations have prompted fundamental class modifications. The most significant change is that technology has made it possible for students to focus on information outside of the classroom, which has increased their motivation to learn. The impact of information technology on teaching-related activities is evident. The learning process modified its methods, goals, and perceived potential. When necessary, information technology can provide educational resources

between students and information. Instead of being passive listeners, students now actively acquire, reorganize, and present information.

Learning and education are both lifelong pursuits with no definite beginning or end dates, hence the need for this study. Learning enables us to acquire new perspectives in daily life, thereby altering how we perceive the world and interpret the actions of others. Students are taught a variety of facts in school. Information technology can expedite the transmission of data, thereby enhancing the teaching–learning environment. Both teachers and pupils use technology to achieve specific instructional objectives. The cost of education has decreased as a result of technological advancements. For instance, the increasing prevalence of high-speed internet makes it easier for students to gain timely access to academic materials. Thanks to this high-speed

 DOI: 10.1201/9781003425809-13

internet, educators can now create and deliver teachings incorporating videos and visuals. It allows teachers and students to communicate via email. Information technology accelerates the dissemination and exchange of data. Students who pass online examinations are awarded degrees that qualify them for improved employment opportunities. Today, educational institutions publish their results online, enabling students to rapidly determine their performance. IT also facilitates group discussion. As a consequence of information technology, the emergence of audiovisual tools in the classroom has altered the way in which students learn.

It reaches privileged and underprivileged individuals, groups, and populations through its media and methods. Teachers, students, researchers, administrators, and educational planners can all benefit from information technology by having access to a plethora of knowledge, skills, and applications that will assist them in performing their respective responsibilities. Distance learning, virtual classrooms, m-learning, and e-learning are the newest ideas and trends on the horizon for education in our country.

13.2 SIGNIFICANCE OF INFORMATION TECHNOLOGY (IT) IN EDUCATION

The old methods of teaching and learning have been altered by new and developing technologies. Resources to improve teaching and learning techniques are made possible by information technology. IT can now be used to deliver audiovisual education with ease. The course materials have been expanded and widened. Learners are now encouraged to view computers as instruments to be used in many aspects of their studies and daily lives thanks to this colorful and extensive IT curriculum technique. They must employ the new multimedia technologies in particular to organize information in their work, describe their initiatives, and express novel ideas.

13.2.1 EMBRACING ADAPTABILITY

The way that students learn is drastically altered when they switch from receiving lectures face to face in traditional classrooms to receiving computer-based instruction through online platforms (i.e., virtual classrooms). Students are resistant to change as a result of this substantial change in the teaching methodology. They are unable to successfully adjust to the online learning environment due to this resistance (Pearcy, 2014).

Additionally, it takes a long time for students to become acclimated to the methods of computer-based education as well as the systems for managing their courses. In conventional classrooms, pupils are observed to passively listen to lectures while also being expected to take notes. To create a webpage or participate in an online debate, students must move quickly and be more proactive throughout the learning process in the context of online education (Boling et al., 2012).

As a result, it is challenging for students with traditional mindsets to adjust to this novel learning experience. If the students are able to accept the new conditions of learning with an open heart and mind, this problem can be resolved. Understanding the benefits of the e-Learning that gave students can adjust their mindset and be ready for the online sessions by learning about the computer science profession and talking about them with their peers. Teachers can help students with this element as well, which will help their learning process (Murphy, Walker, & Webb, 2013).

13.3   EFFECT OF MODERN TECHNOLOGIES ON EDUCATION

Education and training are lifetime processes; there are no restrictions on when to begin or end. In our daily lives, we gain new knowledge, which enables us to alter our lifestyles. Education equips us with knowledge, which we must then research and utilize. Education must be available to everyone at all times; this would help reduce illiteracy. The introduction of information technology has reduced the cost of accessing educational materials, allowing students to learn rapidly from anywhere in the world. New technologies are altering our perspective on learning, as well as the learning process itself. Teachers and students use these new educational technologies to document academic objectives. The only issue is the high cost of information technology; as a result, those who cannot afford it typically have difficulty utilizing the capabilities of information technology in education. For instance, the increased prevalence of broadband internet access facilitates students' prompt access to academic information. Teachers also use this high-speed internet to create and distribute academic data with the aid of videos and images.

13.3.1   Advantages for Students

- New technologies have had a profound effect on education, transforming how students learn and how instructors instruct. Here are several significant ways that new technologies have affected education:
- Internet access has revolutionized information accessibility. Students can now rapidly search for and gain access to an abundance of information on any subject. Online libraries, digital textbooks, and educational websites provide learning opportunities with resources.
- Technology has facilitated the rise of blended learning, which integrates traditional face-to-face instruction with online components. Online modules, interactive simulations, and virtual classrooms enable for personalized learning experiences for students.
- Online platforms and videoconferencing applications have made distance learning feasible. Participation in courses and degree programs offered by institutions worldwide is possible without the student's physical presence. This flexibility is advantageous for students who cannot attend conventional classes due to location, employment, or other obligations.
- Virtual reality (VR) and augmented reality (AR) technologies have introduced innovative ways to engage students in immersive learning environments. For instance, virtual reality can transport students to historical sites

or simulate scientific experiments, enhancing their comprehension and retention of complex ideas.

- Collaboration and communication: technology enables cross-geographic collaboration and communication between students and instructors. Tools such as online discussion forums, videoconferencing, and collaborative platforms facilitate group work, peer feedback, and the sharing of knowledge.

- Adaptive learning: educational software and platforms are capable of adapting to the specific requirements of each student, providing personalized learning paths and resources. Students' performance data is analyzed by machine learning algorithms to identify their strengths and deficiencies, allowing for individualized instruction and targeted interventions.

- Assessment and feedback: Technology provides new assessment and feedback methods. Online exams, automated grading systems, and data analytics allow for the efficient and timely assessment of student progress. Teachers are able to provide instantaneous feedback, monitor performance trends, and adapt their instructional strategies accordingly.

- Technology has increased the accessibility of education for pupils with disabilities. Assistive technologies, such as screen readers, captioning tools, and adaptive input devices, enable students with visual, auditory, or physical disabilities to participate in learning activities.

- Providing opportunities for continual learning, online courses, webinars, and massive open online courses (MOOCs) have contributed to the democratization of education. Individuals can acquire new skills, investigate new topics, and gain access to educational resources outside of traditional educational institutions.

- Technology facilitates teacher professional development by way of online courses, webinars, and virtual conferences. Teachers can gain access to resources, collaborate with peers, and remain current on the latest educational research and pedagogical practices.

- Group Learning: Information technology assisted both students and instructors in teaching students in groups. Earlier in the school year, we had group discussions in which every student participated. However, shy students avoided these groups for dread of speaking up. Now, with the assistance of information technology, academic forums have been established in institutions where students can freely discuss specific topics. They can also engage in text and video conversation. A further advantage of these online group discussions is that not all group members would have attended the same class or institution in the past. Students from institutions all over the world can participate in the same academic group and share academic information.

- The use of audiovisual media has altered the manner in which we acquire and interpret information. Using audiovisual education aids students in learning more quickly and efficiently. Unlike text and class notes, this method of instruction bores students. This is a human weakness, and since people do not want to peruse the text for too long, the introduction is audiovisual.

13.3.2 Advantages for Teachers

- Technology enables the transmission of resources, information, and ideas.
- It provides teachers with greater flexibility to perform various types of tasks at different times.
- Through a variety of instructional techniques, IT promotes the skills, confidence, and zeal of educators.
- It facilitates the planning, preparation, and design of educational materials for instructors.
- Through the use of illustrations, images, and PowerPoint, instructors can present the material in a more engaging and appealing manner.
- A teacher can direct and assist students in locating high-quality resources.
- Students gain knowledge through the use of interactive technologies, and the instructor facilitates their application and reflection on responses. He could be diagnosing learning problems and assisting students in locating solutions.
- By utilizing modern technological devices, instructors can expand their knowledge and hone their teaching abilities.

While new technologies have brought numerous benefits to education, it is essential to address issues such as the digital divide, guaranteeing equitable access to technology and closing the gap between those who have access and those who do not. In order to integrate technology into their teaching practices and maximize its potential, educators must also cultivate digital literacy skills.

13.4 THE ROLE OF INFORMATION TECHNOLOGY IN UNDERDEVELOPED COUNTRIES EDUCATION

Developing nations frequently contend with limited resources, infrastructure, and education access. Information technology offers the potential for overcoming these obstacles and improving educational outcomes. This section provides an overview of the research objectives and discusses the significance of information technology in addressing educational disparities in developing nations.

Based on the recommendation of the International Commission for the Study of Communications of the UNESCO. One of the roles of communication and information technology in education is to facilitate the transfer of information necessary for the growth, formation, and development of personality and skill training through the transmission of diverse and complex messages to help students recognize they understand and value one another and their unity in societal responsibilities. Education is one of the most effective means of acquiring mental activity, a sense of unity, the ability to argue, and self-confidence. Information technology plays a crucial role in this scenario. His development is developed, not developed. New educational opportunities are made available by nations, particularly in the field of corporate communication. On the other hand, it appears that less developed and developing nations are generally concerned about falling behind in the "information revolution," particularly in the field of education. This issue causes something significant. A portion of the state's financial resources are allocated to the procurement of cutting-edge technologies, without regard for the drug's absorption or utilization of its benefits. Countries in development should implement policies that shield them from the economic constraints that accompany political and cultural outcomes. Simultaneously, these nations should work toward establishing the essential infrastructure and controlling existing sources.

13.5 INFORMATION TECHNOLOGY AND THE REQUIREMENT FOR EDUCATION EVOLVE

The proliferation of PCs (personal computers) and internet access has created a globalized environment. Education systems must alter their structure in the major areas. The obligation of educational systems in light of the evident changes. Its primary objective should be to increase a person's resistance to change, i.e., by observing the economy, one can rapidly adapt to constant change. More attention is paid the more rapid the change. A focus should be placed on recognizing patterns in future events. To assist individuals in avoiding future disruptions, we must develop a meta-industrial educational system. Instead of searching in the past, we must discover our objectives and methods in the future in order to accomplish this. Education systems would be unable to adapt to the 21st century's accelerated technological, scientific, economic, cultural, and political changes. Islands are isolated from other social and national organizations in the global village. Because education, both in terms of historical empiricism and specific conditions comprising the 21st century, would unquestionably become the 21st century's steed of transformation, evolution, and multiplication. Clearly, society views him not only as an economic variable and political tool but also as an opportunity to transform education through the use of information technology. In light of this, what can be said about the proposed IT models in education in terms of the nature of knowledge, functional methodologies, and social control criteria.

13.6 E-LEARNING ALL OVER THE WORLD

Utilizing a multitude of technologies in the educational process is now standard practice. In the recent past, professors only had access to blackboards and chalk. Currently, they have blackboards and markers, if not whiteboards with multimedia capabilities, projectors, laser pointers, etc. This predominantly depends on the financial support of universities. However, whether educators are prepared to use the most advanced technologies and alter the traditional educational process depends on the educators themselves. For example, creating online courses, responding to student communications, moderating a forum created for their course, etc.

Regarding education, we should be receptive to the technologies that encircle us. Therefore, we must be receptive to the internet revolution of recent years, go online, and increase the number of instruments we employ. Sadly, this is not consistent everywhere. The country's current economic and social conditions have a significant impact on progress. During the Soviet era, cybernetics was a productive field of study. We are now experiencing the consequences of this, which include not only a lack of professors but also a lack of technological advancement in our universities. In Russia, information technology (IT) is just now beginning to expand. In addition, we must monitor what our European and American colleges have already accomplished. This also explains the differences within the educational system. Education in the Soviet Union was among the finest in the world, but when the Soviet Union collapsed, so did its legacy. We are currently attempting to return to the top universities in the globe, like a phoenix. However, all things require time. This is the primary explanation why we cannot utilize products utilized by universities around the globe. The system is completely unique. We converted to the Bologna system of education in Russia only a few years ago, and now we have our first bachelor's and master's degree holders. There are numerous examples of e-learning's successful implementation in mobile learning technologies. In addition, the systems that utilize foreign (Russian) universities encompass more than just coursework and assignments. They are modular and comprise a variety of modules that cater to the specific requirements of individuals with various roles on campus, including students, teachers, financiers, etc. All of this is integrated into a single system that depicts university life as a whole. We can also locate numerous solutions here. The diversity of products available on the market permits selection. Every platform has benefits and drawbacks. Therefore, each university can select the option that best meets its requirements. Typically, the initial thought is, "Let's try some popular frameworks!" So many individuals use it! This will likely result in either financial issues that render the problem unsolvable or a protracted procedure for establishing a solution-in-a-box for a specific university. Also, open source is not always the best option. This is customizable, but it is always difficult for a programmer to enter into someone else's code. In this instance, the deferred expense theory is applicable. We believe that creating something original is the greatest option. In addition, one of the benefits of this strategy is that you can always add something new and very company specific to this endeavor. And you are not required to wait until third parties declare that they will attempt to accommodate your request for the next product release. In the end, we believe that we can utilize all of the knowledge acquired from our European and American colleges, but we must now develop our own ideas. We cannot initially plan the development of a comprehensive system that will integrate all university resources, including finance, administration, library, etc. But we can begin with basic needs that will enable students and teachers to consistently participate in the process: to be informed, in touch, etc. We believe that this will increase the level of understanding between instructors and students and provide them with the opportunity to experience the latest technologies in education.

13.7 TECHNICAL DIFFICULTIES

The learning process of students in computer science is dependent not only on the quality of the lecture but also on the mediums used to convey the lecture. However, it is frequently observed that students enrolled in online courses are not provided with reliable internet connections and sufficient bandwidth. This causes them to fall behind their virtual classmates in online courses (Bennett et al., 2012). Students have a difficult time adhering to course administration systems due to the ineffectiveness of their monitors, which makes learning more difficult.

Similarly, since the majority of students reside outside of their campuses, they have difficulty meeting the technical requirements or demands of their chosen courses. Moreover, it has been observed that some students do not even own computers, compelling them to seek technical assistance from their learning resource centers. Before enrolling pupils in a particular online course, it is necessary to determine the precise technological support they will require. This also includes providing students with the necessary equipment or financial assistance so they can purchase the equipment themselves in order to successfully complete their online courses.

Technology has had a significant impact on the modern workplace, including the shift toward instruction delivered via technology. De Rouin, Fritzsche, and Salas (2004) note that organizations are drawn to online training in an effort to reduce costs and produce material that can be delivered anytime, anywhere, and customized to meet individual requirements. Despite the numerous advantages of online training (see Sitzmann, Kraiger, Stewart, & Wisher, 2006; Welsh, Wanberg, Brown, & Simmering, 2003), researchers have suggested that technical difficulties, which inevitably arise during online training, have the potential to disrupt the learning process (Webster & Hackley, 1997).

People encounter technical issues when interacting with technology, such as error messages caused by inappropriate configurations. (i.e., browser or computer settings; Munzer, 2002). Throughout the early years of classroom-based distance education, technological concerns remained a constant source of concern. Technology was frequently unreliable, resulting in interrupted connections and degraded media, which caused usability issues for instructors and students (Cavanaugh, Milkovich, & Tang, 2000; Webster & Hackley, 1997). As organizations adopt new delivery media (e.g., the Web) and technology-delivered instruction moves out of the classroom, additional technological challenges have emerged.

13.7.1 The Most Significant Drawbacks of Information Technology (IT)

- As everything is now available online or on mobile devices, it encourages students to cultivate poor study habits and a sluggish disposition through education. Nowadays pupils are more dependent on the internet as opposed to literature and teacher input.
- Discover unusual things on the computer: Internet does not always aid students in their quest for useful information. There are numerous items on the internet that are detrimental to students. Consequently, the student may take the incorrect path.
- Instead of using their laptops and devices for their studies and online tests, students are increasingly visiting social networking sites, which may hinder their academic performance.

- Expensive: The institutions lack IT facilities because they are too expensive. The majority of institutions cannot afford the purchase, maintenance, and other costs associated with its use. The cost of laptops and wireless broadband projectors, for instance, accounts for a significant portion of the school's budget.
- There is widespread ignorance about the use, applications, and benefits of IT among teachers, the head of the institution, and educational authorities tasked with enhancing the school's operation, particularly in relation to teaching–learning and the organization of cocurricular activities using such technologies.
- Teachers today are not well-equipped to use modern technology. There is a severe shortage of competent and skilled teachers who can use and integrate the appropriate technology for the effective integration of IT in addressing the school curriculum and bringing about the desired change in the behavior of the learners.
- The prescribed curriculum in schools, colleges, and universities, the examination and evaluation system, the available instructional materials, and the infrastructure do not adequately support the use and application of information technology in the teaching–learning process and other student-beneficial activities.
- Lessons delivered online or through digital resources reduce the face-to-face interaction that provides a more personal experience between teacher and student.

13.8   CONCLUSION

Information technology enables instructors and students to collaborate on the teaching and learning process. It broadens their thinking and knowledge and enables them to engage in a variety of educational activities. Diverse hardware and software technologies make the instructing and learning process more engaging. The use of sophisticated technologies has enormous potential for enhancing the products and procedures of education. Individualization of instruction, utilization of multisensory and multimedia aid material, and efficient and effective administration of various educational institutions are just a few of the current needs and demands in the field of instruction and education that are met by this technology. Information technologies facilitate a more productive instruction and learning process. Now, the instructor serves as a coach or mentor to the students in their academic endeavors. In conventional classrooms, the function of the teacher has shifted from being the focal point of instruction to that of a facilitator. He determines the contents, experiences, and activities; locates the resources; and instructs students on how to access and use the information to achieve the desired outcomes. As information technology advanced, teaching and learning procedures became simple, quick, unconventional, and interesting. In this context, distance learning is quite significant. Utilizing the capabilities of information technology, one can communicate virtually with students to interact with them, teach them, and exchange knowledge. In developing nations like India, distance learning supports the inclusive model of knowledge transfer and serves as a social catalyst. Utilizing multimedia, providing mass education at a distance, and industrializing the teaching process are the three characteristics of remote learning. Distance learning must be technically adaptable to the unique student in accordance with the Indian setting, as well as being affordable, participatory, and innovative. Distance learning has advanced significantly in India over the past 20 years in terms of educational quality and quantity. Modern information technology does not predetermine the future of education; rather, the future of education will largely depend on how we construct the role of technology. It was discovered that faculty still require assistance to utilize technology effectively for the advantage of their students. Institutions should provide this assistance. Today, the internet provides global information to millions of students, educators, and administrators. Therefore, introducing the internet into classrooms as well as administrative areas significantly improves modern education and enables individuals to utilize online database resources.

Modern education necessitates the introduction and proper use of advanced, moderate, and fundamental technologies. Education must implement policies, the most important of which are:

- Expanding human sources of IT through educational programs and promoting skills to boost the efficiency of work in education.
- The use of information technology to enhance the efficiency of an educational institution in order to provide a better education that fosters creativity.
- Support for IT, such as funding for research and the expansion of education.
- Using IT to foster an appropriate environment and participation spirit in education.
- Establishing cooperation and coordination among the various parties involved in the utilization of the aforementioned instruments.
- Expanding the use of IT in education by facilitating and encouraging its adoption.

When evaluating the various types of information technologies, education should consider issues such as necessity, scientific efficacy, cost savings, and the opportunities and potential skills available in this instance.

BIBLIOGRAPHY

Aggarwal, A. (2000). *Web-Based Learning and Teaching Technologies: Opportunities and Challenges.* London: Idea Group Publishing.

Ally, M. (2004). "Foundations of Educational Theory for Online Learning." In *Theory and Practice of Online Learning*, Edited by Anderson, T. and Elloumi, F., Athabasca University, Athabasca, pp. 3–31.

Bennett, S., Bishop, A., Dalgarno, B., Waycott, J., and Kennedy, G. (2012). "Implementing Web 2.0 Technologies in Higher Education: A Collective Case Study." *Computers and Education*, 59: 524–534.

Boling, E. C., Hough, M., Krinsky, H., Saleem, H., and Stevens, M. (2012). "Cutting the Distance in Distance Education: Perspectives on What Promotes Positive, Online Learning Experiences." *The Internet and Higher Education*, 15(2): 118–126.

Cavanaugh, M. A., Milkovich, G. T., and Tang, J. (2000). The Effective Use of Multimedia Distance Learning Technology: The Role of Technology Self-Efficacy, Attitudes, Reliability, Use and Distance in a Global Multimedia Distance Learning Classroom.

Cho, M. H. and Shen, D. (2013). "Self-Regulation in Online Learning." *Distance Education*. doi: 10.1080/01587919.2013.835770.

DeRouin, R. E., Fritzsche, B. A., and Salas, E. (2004). "Optimizing E-Learning: Research-Based Guidelines for Learner-Controlled Training." *Human Resource Management*, 43(2–3): 147–162.

Hussain, I. (2005). A Study of Emerging Technologies and their Impact on Teaching Learning Process. Un-published PhD thesis, Islamabad, Allama Iqbal Open University, Pakistan.

INACOL/International Association for K-12 Online Learning. (2011). "National Standards for Quality Online Courses, Version 2."

Korhonen, A. and Multisilta, J. (2017). "Learning Analytics." In *New Ways to Teach and Learn in China and Finland: Crossing Boundaries with Technology*, pp. 301–310.

Kozak, S. (2005). "The Role of Information Technology in the Profit and Cost Efficiency Improvements of the Banking Sector." *Journal of Academy of Business and Economics*, 3: 321–330.

Learning, D. (2010). "Innovative Teacher Professional Development." *International Review of Research in Open and Distance Learning*. doi: 10.3102/0013189X033008003.

Le Cun, Y. and Bottou, L. (2004). "Large Scale Online Learning." In *Advances in Neural Information Processing Systems 16 (NIPS 2003)*, Edited by Sebastian Thrun, Lawrence Saul and Bernhard Schölkopf, MIT Press, Cambridge, MA, 2004.

Lucey, T. (2005). *Management Information Systems*. 9th Edition. London, pp. 9–13.

Mansouri, F. (2007). "Cultural Diversity as an Educational Advantage." *Ethos*, 15(3): 15–18.

Menon, B. (2000). *Preface In Emerging Communication Technologies and the Society*. New Delhi: Indian National Science Academy.

Milne, A. (2006). "What Is In It For Us? Network Effects and Bank Payment Innovation." *Journal of Banking & Finance*, 30(6): 1613–1630.

Munzer, E. (2002). Managing the e in e-learning. Retrieved June 18, 2008 from http://www.learningcircuits.org/2002/nov2002/elearn.htm.

Murphy, D., Walker, R., and Webb, G. (2013). *Online Learning and teaching with Technology: Case studies, Experience and Practice*. Routledge.

Neapolitan, R. E. and Jiang, X. (2018). *Artificial Intelligence: With an Introduction to Machine Learning, Second Edition*. Chapman and Hall/CRC.

Oliner, S. and Sichel, D. (2000). "The Resurgence of Growth in the Late 1990s: Is Information Technology the Story?" *Journal of Economic Perspectives*, 14: 3–22.

Pearcy, M. (2014). "Student, Teacher, Professor: Three Perspectives on Online Education." *History Teacher*, 47(2): 169–185.

Rashid, M. (1998). *Educational Technology*. Islamabad: National Book Foundation.

State of the Internet 2009. (2009). "US Internet Council." Retrieved from http://www.usic.org/

Sitzmann, T., Kraiger, K., Stewart, D., and Wisher, R. (2006). "The Comparative Effectiveness of Web-based and Classroom Instruction: A Meta-Analysis." *Personnel Psychology*, 59(3): 623–664.

Webster, J. and Hackley, P. (1997). "Teaching Effectiveness in Technology-Mediated Distance Learning." *Academy of Management Journal*, 40(6): 1282–1309.

Welsh, E. T., Wanberg, C. R., Brown, K. G., and Simmering, M. J. (2003). "E-Learning: Emerging Uses, Empirical Results and Future Directions." *International Journal of Training and Development*, 7: 245–258.

14 The Application of AI for Automated Education System

*Bhagwati Sharan, Sourav Ghosh
and Megha Chhabra*

14.1 INTRODUCTION

Artificial intelligence (AI) is the field of computer science that intends to develop and apply algorithms and systems that can reproduce human intelligence in tasks including perception, reasoning, learning, and decision-making (Soham Banerjee et al., 2017). Machine learning (ML), one of the many subfields of AI, involves developing algorithms that can draw inferences from data without being explicitly trained to do so (S. Larry Goldenberg et al., 2019). A subset of ML called deep learning (DL) uses neural networks (NN) to find complex patterns in data. Understanding, synthesizing, and generating human language are all parts of developing natural language processing (NLP) algorithms (Moe Elbadawi et al., 2021).

All students are often taught the same subject at the same pace in the traditional educational system, regardless of their learning preferences and needs. Personalized and adaptive education systems, on the other hand, aim to provide students with learning opportunities that are tailored to their needs, interests, and skills.

14.1.1 Machine Learning

Machine learning (ML) helps computers with learning and making predictions or decisions without being specifically programmed (Joeky T. Senders et al., 2018). ML algorithms improve over time because of learning from patterns and past experiences. Machine learning is composed of three fundamental components: input data, model representation, and optimization approach. These components work together to enable machine learning and accurate prediction (Wei Ma et al., 2020).

There are four phases involved in the flow of the prediction with machine learning, discussed in Figure 14.1:

(a) Data Preprocessing: Preprocessing the data is necessary before training the ML model. In this stage, the data are cleaned by eliminating noise, dealing with missing values, and scaling or normalizing the features. Preprocessing the data makes ensuring the model is fed high-quality data. It may have a

DOI: 10.1201/9781003425809-14

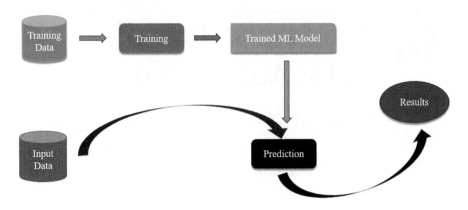

FIGURE 14.1   Machine learning processes

significant impact on the final output/performance of the model (Jianglin Huang et al., 2015).
(b) Training Phase: The ML model gains knowledge from the input data during the training phase. Based on the training examples, it modifies its internal settings to reduce mistakes or improve performance measures.
(c) Evaluation and Validation: The model must be reviewed after training to gauge its effectiveness, and to determine the model's accuracy, evaluation should include testing it on various data sets known as the validation set. Common metrics for evaluating ML models include accuracy, precision, recall, and F1 score (Megha Chhabra et al., 2022).
(d) Model Deployment: The ML model is prepared for deployment after successful training and validation. To make predictions in real-time, it may be implemented into a variety of systems or applications. Considerations such as scalability, robustness, and latency are often necessary for model implementation (Serkan Ayvaz et al., 2021).
    The term "ML" refers to a broad variety of methods and algorithms that support the learning process in Figure 14.2:
(e) Supervised Learning: In this class, ML models are trained using labeled data, where each occurrence of the data is linked to a predetermined desired result. Typical supervised learning methods include support vector machines (SVM), decision trees (DT), random forests (RF), logistic regression, and linear regression (Padraig Cunningham et al., 2008), in Figure 14.3.
(f) Unsupervised Learning: It is used to train models on unlabeled data without having specific desired outputs in mind. It includes dimensionality reduction methods like principal component analysis (PCA) and clustering algorithms like k-means and hierarchical clustering (H.B. Barlow et al., 1989), in Figure 14.4.
(g) Semi-Supervised Learning: It is an ML approach that combines labeled and unlabeled data to improve model performance by leveraging the additional

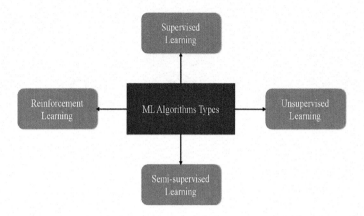

FIGURE 14.2   Classes of machine learning

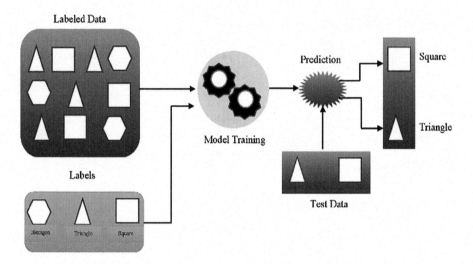

FIGURE 14.3   Supervised learning

information contained in the unlabeled data, allowing for more efficient and effective learning (Ani Vanyan et al., 2019), in Figure 14.5.

(h) Reinforcement Learning: It deals with the problems faced by an agent to make the best choices in changing situations through trial and error (Toru Miura et al., 1996) in Figure 14.6. Based on its behaviors, the agent gets feedback in the form of incentives or punishments.

(i) Deep Learning: A branch of ML called deep learning focuses on neural networks (NN) with many hidden layers (Shih-Hau Fang et al., 2017). Artificial neural networks (ANN), which are DL models, can recognize complex patterns because it can self-learn hierarchical data structures.

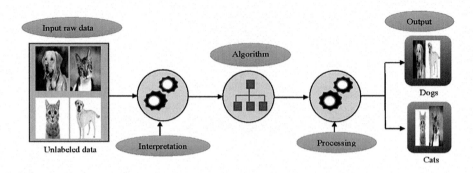

FIGURE 14.4   Unsupervised learning

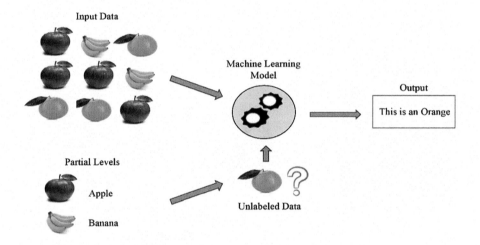

FIGURE 14.5   Semi-supervised learning

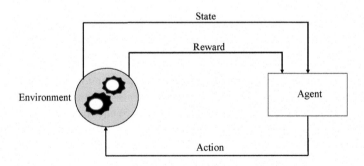

FIGURE 14.6   Reinforcement learning

RNNs are ideal for sequential data processing, whereas convolutional neural networks (CNNs) excel at picture analysis.

14.1.2 DIFFERENT AI ALGORITHMS IN EDUCATION

(a) Gaussian Naïve Bayes (GNB)

GNB is an ML-based classification approach that works on the probabilistic method and Gaussian distribution. Each parameter in the model called a feature or predictor can forecast the output variable. It is necessary to apply its probability density and refer to the method as Gaussian naive bayes if we assume that occurrences follow a Gaussian or normal distribution.

The following equation can be used for the naive Gaussian bayes:

$$P(x) = \frac{1}{\sqrt{2\pi\sigma^2}} e^{-\frac{(x-\mu)}{2\sigma^2}}$$

Since the conditional probabilities, P(x$_i$|y) also have a Gaussian distribution, it is required to calculate their respective means and variances using the largest likelihood method. This is rather simple, using a Gaussian characteristic, we get:

$$L\left((\mu;\sigma^2;x_i|y)\right) = log \prod_k p\left((x_i^{(k)}|y)\right) = \sum_k log\, p\left(x_i^{(k)}|y\right)$$

Here, the k index refers to the samples in our dataset and P(x$_i$|y) is a Gaussian itself (Bonaccorso, 2017).

(b) Logistic Regression (LR)

LR is an approach for approximating the probability of a discrete output given an input variable. This particular statistical method looks at the relationship between a large number of independent variables and the dependent binary variables. The most popular types of logistic regression imitate a binary result, like true or false. Regression models for events with more than two possible results may be constructed using multinomial logistic regression. When attempting to discover which category a new sample most closely resembles, classification issues are an appropriate application for using logistic regression as an analytical technique. Given that cyber security entails categorization difficulties, such as threat detection, logistic regression is a useful analytical technique (Thomas W. Edgar et al., 2017). In logistic regression, the logistic function, sometimes called the sigmoid function, can be implemented to conclude the association between independent variables or features, and the probability of the outcome.

(c) Random Forest (RF)

A machine learning approach to provide predictions for both the types of classification and regression problems. RF combines a variety of decision trees. It belongs to the ensemble learning approach. With this description, RF is a grouping of several classifiers and tree structures. A training sample set and a random variable, known as k in the model, are used to plant each tree in Breiman's RF model. The model generates a classifier (x, k), where x is the input vector. Since any two of these random variables may be independently distributed and have the same distribution. After k runs, the classifiers {$h_1(x)$, $h_2(x)$, $h_3(x)$,..., $h_k(x)$} are acquired. The system's final choice is made, and the decision function is

$$H(x) = \arg\max_{y} \sum_{i=1}^{k} I\left(h_i(x) = Y\right)$$

where Y represents the output variable, I(.) represents the indicator function, H(x) combines classification and decision tree models, and h_i is a single decision tree model. For a certain input variable, each tree can choose the valuable group result. the exact process is shown in Figure 14.7.

(d) Support Vector Classifier (SVC)

Support vector classifier (SVC), also known as support vector machine (SVM), is an ML approach used for classification tasks. The SVM model is a special kind of machine learning method dependent on a mathematical learning concept. It is supposed to make available the better separation that creates a complicated border between classes. Separate classes introduce genes on each edge of the available hyperplane, shown in Figure 14.8. By increasing the genes, we find the greater distance between the hyperplane available there and the samples present there. In subdivided sections, SVM classifies these classes by finding the correct hyper aircraft. As soon as the hyperplane is detected, we have to find the support vectors lying on their side (Dires Negash Fente et al., 2018). The objective of SVC is to maximize the margin between the support vectors of different classes while minimizing the classification error.

14.1.3 POTENTIAL APPLICATIONS OF AI IN TRADITIONAL EDUCATION SYSTEMS TO MAKE MORE PERSONALIZED AND ADAPTIVE EDUCATION SYSTEMS

Artificial intelligence (AI) has the potential to automate several traditional educational procedures, allowing for more personalized and effective learning possibilities for students. However, it's essential to guarantee that AI systems are developed responsibly and with the well-being of students in mind. A few automatic transitions from a traditional school system to one that is individualized and flexible have occurred. Here are a few instances: To assist instructors personalize their educational experience, AI may first analyze information about students, including exam and assignment results. The second is that intelligent education systems driven by AI can provide students with individualized feedback and direction based on their unique learning requirements and preferences. The third advantage of AI is that it may assist adaptive learning systems, which adjust courses and activities to each

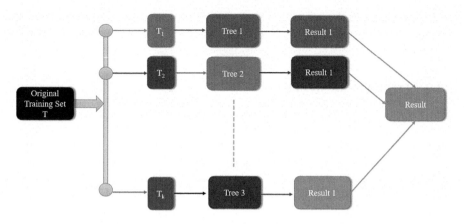

FIGURE 14.7   Random forest

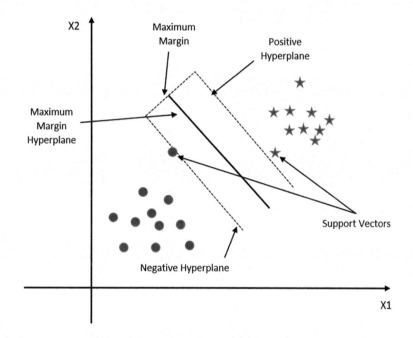

FIGURE 14.8   Hyperplane of support vector classifier

student's unique learning style and pace using machine learning algorithms. Fourth, chatbots and virtual assistants that can swiftly answer inquiries from students and aid in their understanding of the learning process may be created using AI-powered natural language processing. Teachers would be able to better assist and resource struggling pupils if AI was able to analyze student data and identify those who could be in danger of falling behind. Last but not least, AI can automate the marking of assignments and the delivery of feedback, freeing up instructors' time to concentrate on other crucial aspects of education, such as providing tailored help and feedback to students.

14.2 LITERATURE SURVEY

The market for AI in education is anticipated to increase from $537 million in 2018 to $3.68 billion by 2023 at a compound yearly growth rate (CAGR) of 47% throughout the forecast period, according to a study by MarketsandMarkets. The paper outlines several reasons that are promoting the development of AI in education, including the rise in demand for personalized learning opportunities, the expansion of educational platforms and tools driven by AI, and the need to lighten the burden on teachers and administrators.

In addition, according to a Pearson Education poll, 84% of education experts think that AI will improve education in the future. The poll also revealed that automating administrative processes and providing personalized learning experiences are where educators are most interested in using AI (Daniel Schiff, 2020).

The use of AI in education is expanding, along with investment in educational platforms and technologies that are AI-powered generally. However, there are also issues with the fair implications of using AI in education, such as the need to preserve student data secrecy and the probability of bias in decision-making.

The uses of machine learning models have been examined (Srujan Nalam et al., 2023) to predict the likelihood of a student being accepted into a master's program for providing a better understanding of the admission prospect.

A predictive model using Naïve Bayes classifiers—a machine learning algorithm has been built (Atul Rawal et al., 2023) to extract and analyze hidden patterns in students' academic records and their credentials. The major goal of the study is to lessen applicants' confusion about being admitted to institutions based on their prior qualifications and other crucial factors.

A recommender system has been proposed (Sibhi K. et al., 2022) to suggest the user a career in the IT field, this model suggests a career for that user based on his educational background, interest, and current education. The more information the user provides the more accurate the career will be predicted for that user.

Rahmtalla Yousif Yagoub et al. (2023) used the logistic regression model as one of the generalized linear models to determine some factors that influence academic tripping at the University of Tabuk. In this case, student status—whether they have tripped or not—is thought of as a binary variable. A survey based on a questionnaire was utilized to collect the data for this article. The results showed that the primary variables influencing kids' academic performance were familial and economic problems, as well as educational and academic challenges.

Employing computer-assisted instruction (CAI) created with natural language processing (NLP), machine learning, and information retrieval techniques (Lilly Ramesh et al., 2022) recommended an Educational Assistant for Software Testing (EAST) system to assist learners to enhance their abilities in software testing.

Hanh Thi-Hong Duong et al. (2022) developed a dataset using feature creation and feature selection approaches that are very helpful in forecasting students' academic warning status. As a two-stage performance warning system used in higher education, the F2-score indicates a score of more than 74% at the beginning of the term using the algorithm SVM and more than 92% before the final exam was suggested.

14.3   PROBLEM STATEMENT

Despite significant advancements in educational technology, traditional educational institutions often fall short of providing students with effective and customized learning experiences. Teachers sometimes neglect to give each student the attention they need in favor of administrative tasks like grading and documentation. Traditional educational institutions often are unable to adjust to the preferences and needs of every student, which leads to disengagement and a lack of interest in learning.

To address these difficulties, an automated education system powered by AI that can provide students with customized and flexible learning experiences is required. This system would use machine learning methods to examine student data and provide each student with tailored feedback and support. Additionally, it would simplify administrative procedures like grading and free up teachers' time to focus on providing tailored instruction to students. But before such a system could be implemented, it would be important to carefully evaluate moral considerations, such as ensuring student data privacy and removing any biases from AI decision-making.

14.4   METHODOLOGY

In this framework, we are using ML algorithms to get the best accuracy to predict students' dropout and academic success. So, beginning with the dataset we are taking it online from Kaggle and we will implement the existing ML algorithms on it to understand the implementation of ML in an automated education system.

The dataset used for this analysis is taken from Kaggle titled "Predict students' dropout and academic success" It is a comprehensive collection of data aimed at predicting students' likelihood of dropping out and their academic success., shown in Figure 14.9. The dataset includes both categorical and numerical variables, providing a diverse range of information about each student. The variables cover aspects such as demographic information (age, gender, marital status), academic performance (grades, test scores, previous scores), socioeconomic background (parents' qualification, family income, parental education), and student engagement (attendance, participation in extracurricular activities). We are splitting the dataset in ratio of 80% for training and 20% for testing.

After gathering the data, we will clean the data and do the preprocessing, that is we will try to remove errors and redundancies from it. Then we will go for feature encoding which is using an encoder to label the data. After that, we will start the model-building process which is taking the classifiers one by one and comparing the results to them, in Figure 14.10.

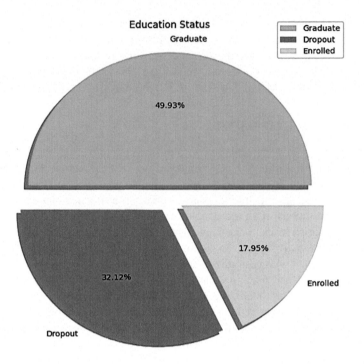

FIGURE 14.9   Data description

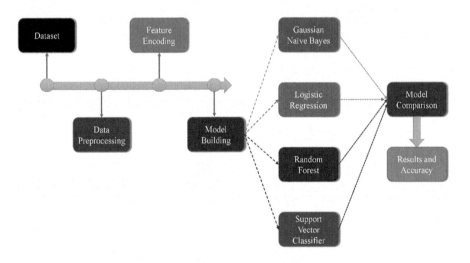

FIGURE 14.10   Implementation flow of the ML algorithms

14.5   RESULTS

The accuracy of an ML model is a very popular performance metric that refers to the ability to correctly classify or predict the target variable or outcomes. It is commonly used as a performance metric to evaluate the effectiveness of a model. Accuracy is obtained by taking a ratio of the correctly predicted instances to the total instances in the dataset. We have presented the accuracy of the ML models in the below Table 14.1 and Figure 14.11.

The other two crucial metrics for evaluating the effectiveness of a model used for classification are precision and recall, especially in cases where the class distribution is unbalanced or if the effects of false positives and false negatives vary. These measurements aid in analyzing the model's capacity to correctly categorize positive

TABLE 14.1
Accuracy of the Models

Model	Accuracy (%)
GNB	85.39
LR	92.01
RF	91.73
SVC	91.04

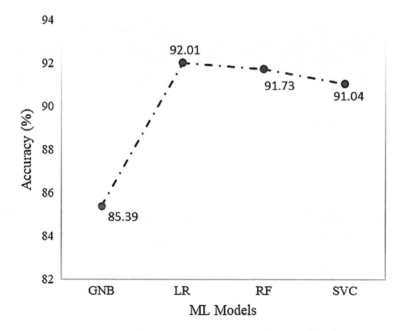

FIGURE 14.11   Accuracy of the ML models

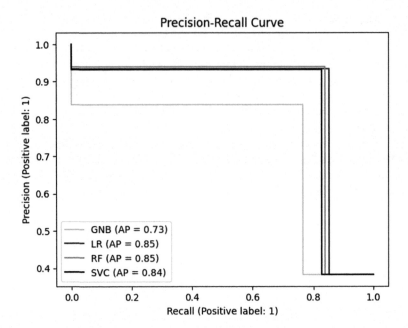

FIGURE 14.12   Precision vs recall

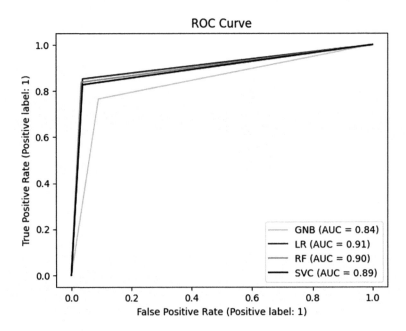

FIGURE 14.13   True positive rate vs. false-positive rate

cases and record every positive instance in the dataset. As can be seen in the output below, a confusion matrix was used to summarize the classification result as shown in Figure 14.12.

The true-positive rate (TPR) vs. false-positive rate (FPR) curve, also known as the receiver operating characteristic (ROC) curve, is a graphical representation of how well a binary classification model works at different classification thresholds as shown in Figure 14.13. It shows how the model must choose between accurately classifying positive occurrences and its propensity to misclassify negative examples as positive.

14.6 CONCLUSION

In conclusion, the incorporation of artificial intelligence (AI) into computerized and automated educational systems has enormous potential to change how we teach and learn. The main advantages and possibilities of AI in education have been addressed in this study, from personalized learning opportunities to intelligent tutoring systems and automated grading.

Some of the enduring issues in conventional educational environments may be resolved with the use of AI in education. Educational systems may provide personalized learning experiences that consider each student's requirements, preferences, and learning preferences by using AI algorithms and machine learning approaches. This tailored approach improves motivation, engagement, and eventually learning results.

Additionally, AI-driven tutoring systems may provide students with quick feedback and direction, encouraging self-paced learning and enabling teachers to concentrate on more individualized and significant interactions with students. Automated grading systems enable objective and consistent evaluation, avoiding biases and assuring fairness in the assessment process. They also save instructors time and effort.

REFERENCES

Ani Vanyan and Hrant Khachatrian, "A Survey on Semi-Supervised Learning," *Machine Learning*, vol. 109, no. 2, Springer Science and Business Media LLC, pp. 373–440, Nov. 15, 2019. doi: 10.1007/s10994-019-05855-6.

Atul Rawal and Bechoo Lal, "Predictive Model for Admission Uncertainty in High Education using Naïve Bayes Classifier," *Journal of Indian Business Research*, vol. 15, no. 2, Emerald, pp. 262–277, Jan. 10, 2023. doi: 10.1108/jibr-08-2022-0209.

Bonaccorso G. *Machine Learning Algorithms: A Reference Guide to Popular Algorithms for Data Science and Machine Learning*. Birmingham: Packt Publishing, UK, 2017. ISBN: 9781785889622.

Daniel Schiff, "Out of the Laboratory and into the Classroom: The Future of Artificial Intelligence in Education," *AI & Society*, vol. 36, no. 1, Springer Science and Business Media LLC, pp. 331–348, Aug. 9, 2020. doi: 10.1007/s00146-020-01033-8.

Dires Negash Fente and Dheeraj Kumar Singh, "Weather Forecasting Using Artificial Neural Network," 2018 Second International Conference on Inventive Communication and Computational Technologies (ICICCT). IEEE, Apr. 2018. doi: 10.1109/icicct.2018.8473167.

H. B. Barlow, "Unsupervised Learning," *Neural Computation*, vol. 1, no. 3, MIT Press - Journals, pp. 295–311, Sep. 1989. doi: 10.1162/neco.1989.1.3.295.

Hanh Thi-Hong Duong, Linh Thi-My Tran, Huy Quoc To, and Kiet Van Nguyen, "Academic Performance Warning System based on Data Driven for Higher Education," *Neural Computing and Applications*, vol. 35, no. 8, Springer Science and Business Media LLC, pp. 5819–5837, Nov. 07, 2022. doi: 10.1007/s00521-022-07997-6.

Jianglin Huang, Yan-Fu Li, and Min Xie, "An Empirical Analysis of Data Preprocessing for Machine Learning-Based Software Cost Estimation," *Information and Software Technology*, vol. 67, Elsevier BV, pp. 108–127, Nov. 2015. doi: 10.1016/j.infsof.2015.07.004.

Joeky T. Senders, Patrick C. Staples, Aditya V. Karhade, Mark M. Zaki, William B. Gormley, Marike L. D. Broekman, Timothy R. Smith, and Omar Arnaout, "Machine Learning and Neurosurgical Outcome Prediction: A Systematic Review," *World Neurosurgery*, vol. 109, Elsevier BV, pp. 476–486.e1, Jan. 2018. doi: 10.1016/j.wneu.2017.09.149.

K. Sibhi, S. Thanvir Ibrahim, Akil Malik, and I. R. Praveen Joe, "Career Prediction Using Naive Bayes," 2022 Third International Conference on Intelligent Computing Instrumentation and Control Technologies (ICICICT), Kannur, 2022, pp. 695–699. doi: 10.1109/ICICICT54557.2022.9917745.

Lilly Ramesh, S. Radhika, and S. Jothi, "Hybrid Support Vector Machine and K-nearest Neighbor-Based Software Testing for Educational Assistant," *Concurrency and Computation: Practice and Experience*, vol. 35, no. 1, Wiley, Nov. 21, 2022. doi: 10.1002/cpe.7433.

Megha Chhabra, Bhagwati Sharan, Keshav Gupta, and Rani Astya, "Waste Classification Using Improved CNN Architecture," *SSRN Electronic Journal*, Elsevier BV, 2022. doi: 10.2139/ssrn.4157549.

Moe Elbadawi, Simon Gaisford, and Abdul W. Basit, "Advanced Machine-Learning Techniques in Drug Discovery," *Drug Discovery Today*, vol. 26, no. 3, Elsevier BV, pp. 769–777, Mar. 2021. doi: 10.1016/j.drudis.2020.12.003.

Padraig Cunningham, Matthieu Cord, and Sarah Jane Delany, "Supervised Learning," *Machine Learning Techniques for Multimedia*. Springer, Berlin Heidelberg, pp. 21–49, 2008. doi: 10.1007/978-3-540-75171-7_2.

Rahmtalla Yousif Yagoub, Hussein Yousif Eledum, and Atif Ali Yassin, "Factors Affecting the Academic Tripping at University of Tabuk Using Logistic Regression," *SAGE Open*, vol. 13, no. 1, 2023. doi: 10.1177/21582440221145118.

S. Larry Goldenberg, Guy Nir, and Septimiu E. Salcudean, "A New Era: Artificial Intelligence and Machine Learning in Prostate Cancer," *Nature Reviews Urology*, vol. 16, no. 7, Springer Science and Business Media LLC, pp. 391–403, May 15, 2019. doi: 10.1038/s41585-019-0193-3.

Serkan Ayvaz and Koray Alpay, "Predictive Maintenance System for Production Lines in Manufacturing: A Machine Learning Approach using IoT Data in Real-Time," *Expert Systems with Applications*, vol. 173, Elsevier BV, p. 114598, Jul. 2021. doi: 10.1016/j.eswa.2021.114598.

Shih-Hau Fang, Yu-Xaing Fei, Zhezhuang Xu, and Yu Tsao, "Learning Transportation Modes From Smartphone Sensors Based on Deep Neural Network," *IEEE Sensors Journal*, vol. 17, no. 18, Institute of Electrical and Electronics Engineers (IEEE), pp. 6111–6118, Sep. 15, 2017. doi: 10.1109/jsen.2017.2737825.

Soham Banerjee, Pradeep Kumar Singh, and Jaya Bajpai, "A Comparative Study on Decision-Making Capability Between Human and Artificial Intelligence," *Nature Inspired Computing*, Springer Singapore, pp. 203–210, Oct. 4, 2017. doi: 10.1007/978-981-10-6747-1_23.

Srujan Nalam, Mohd Aleemuddin, Yuva Teja Kadari, and M. Nanda Kumar, "Advanced Graduate Admission Prediction," 2023 IEEE 8th International Conference for Convergence in Technology (I2CT), Lonavla, 2023, pp. 1–6. doi: 10.1109/I2CT57861.2023.10126307.

Thomas W. Edgar and D. O. Manz, "Exploratory Study," *Research Methods for Cyber Security*. Elsevier, pp. 95–130, 2017. doi: 10.1016/b978-0-12-805349-2.00004-2.

Toru Miura, Christian Braendle, Alexander Shingleton, Geoffroy Sisk, Srinivas Kambhampati, and David L. Stern, "Reinforcement Learning: A Survey," *Journal of Artificial Intelligence Research*, vol. 4, AI Access Foundation, pp. 237–285, May 1, 1996. doi: 10.1613/jair.301.

Wei Ma, Zhaocheng Liu, Zhaxylyk A. Kudyshev, Alexandra Boltasseva, Wenshan Cai, and Yongmin Liu, "Deep Learning for the Design of Photonic Structures," *Nature Photonics*, vol. 15, no. 2, Springer Science and Business Media LLC, pp. 77–90, Oct. 5, 2020. doi: 10.1038/s41566-020-0685-y.

Yanli Liu, Yourong Wang, and Jian Zhang, "New Machine Learning Algorithm: Random Forest," *Information Computing and Applications*. Springer, Berlin, pp. 246–252, 2012. doi: 10.1007/978-3-642-34062-8_32.

Index

3-dimension (3-D) technology, 67
3D models, 116–117, 126, 129, 131, 133–134, 136–137, 139–140

Accuracy, 11–12, 14–15, 17, 20, 105, 107, 130, 172, 178, 180, 182–183, 188, 212, 219, 221
Adaptability, 68, 190, 201
Adaptive learning systems, 1, 180, 216
Administrative, 20, 28, 31, 66–68, 83, 154, 169–170, 178, 179–181, 183, 186–188, 190–194, 208, 218–219
AI-Based Gamified Robotic Model Architecture (AIBGRM), 32
Algorithm, 3–4, 6–10, 13, 20, 56, 64–65, 105–106, 108, 129–132, 141, 172, 188–189, 218–219
Analysis, 3–4, 6, 14, 19–20, 34, 40, 44–49, 51, 56–57, 62–66, 69–70, 81, 85, 92, 96–98, 103, 111, 141, 145–147, 149–151, 153–157, 160–161, 169–170, 185, 212, 215, 219
Analytics, 1–2, 55, 62, 64–65, 69, 101–103, 105, 107, 109, 111, 113, 165, 180, 184, 188, 193–194, 203
Animations, 126, 128, 133, 136–137, 139
Approach, 2, 4–6, 13–14, 17, 23, 27, 36, 39–40, 44–45, 55, 62, 74, 89, 92, 98, 103–104, 131, 136, 139, 146, 153, 158, 160, 164, 167, 169, 173,181, 184, 187, 211–212, 215–216, 223
Architecture, 11, 32, 74–75, 118, 187, 223
AR-Learn app, 135, 140–141
Artificial intelligence (AI), 27, 29, 54, 74, 173, 176, 179, 183, 184, 186, 188, 211, 216, 223
Artificial intelligence in education (AIED), 67, 165
Assessment, 2, 19, 26, 28, 33, 56, 60, 62–63, 65, 69, 95, 98, 140, 156, 160, 167, 169–170, 173, 176, 180, 203, 223
Augmented reality, 1, 37, 116–117, 119–123, 125, 127–129, 131, 133–137, 139–140, 170, 202
Automated assessment systems, 167, 170, 173
Automated education system, 176–177, 179, 181–183, 185, 187–191, 193, 211–213, 215, 217, 219, 221, 223

Bibliographic coupling, 157, 159, 161
Burst, 127–128

Challenges, 3, 7, 10, 20, 27, 36–37, 39–40, 54–55, 57, 74–77, 79–81, 90, 101–102, 104, 109, 114, 118, 121, 123, 139, 153–154, 176–179, 182–187, 190, 193–194, 207–208, 218
Chatbot, 74–80, 84, 86–87, 89–92, 169–170
Chatbot Dialogue System, 74
ChatGPT, 79, 169, 171–172
Citation analysis, 155
Classroom, 1, 23, 29, 32, 39–40, 43–44, 49–51, 54, 58, 60, 68, 70, 83, 125, 200–201, 207
Coauthorship analysis, 156
Cocitation analysis, 156
Code obfuscation, 127
Coding, 20, 45
Collaboration, 4, 30–31, 33–34, 41, 44, 68, 87, 121, 141, 158, 160–161, 177–178, 180, 182, 203
Communication, 4, 7, 30–31, 54, 60, 74, 76–77, 83, 87, 136, 177, 180, 182, 190, 203–204
Competencies, 1, 4, 7, 29, 65, 143–144, 147, 149–150, 161
Continuous Professional Development (CPD), 4
Convolutional neural networks (CNNs), 185, 215
Cooperation, 2, 23, 31, 208
Corporate, 27, 29, 37, 204
Curipod, 171
Cutting-edge, 1–3, 14–15, 20, 25, 27, 88, 116–117, 205

Data, 1–7, 9–11, 14–20, 26–27, 33–34, 36, 44–46, 55–56, 58, 60, 62–66, 68–69, 76, 79, 81, 104–109, 111, 119, 129, 144–147, 150, 161, 164–165, 169–170, 176–184, 186–194, 200–203, 211–213, 215, 217–220, 223
Data Collection, 4–5, 105, 108, 178, 180, 187, 191
Data-driven, 1–3, 7, 19, 68, 181, 187, 190
Data Mining, 56, 62–66, 69, 165
Data preprocessing, 4, 105, 107, 211
Data splitting, 105
Decision tree (DT), 3
Deep learning, 56, 65, 74, 105, 107, 111, 164, 167, 184–186, 188, 194, 211, 213
Digital Competence Scale (DCS), 4
Digital divide, 29, 36–37, 178, 193–194, 204
Discussion forums, 31, 50, 203

Early childhood education (ECE), 55
Education 4.0, 27–29, 147, 149, 153, 161